## Dedication

"The simplest questions are the most profound.
Where were you born? Where is your home?"
- Richard Bach

*I wish to preserve and share our precious history with current and future generations. I dedicate this work to the many people who have assisted me and especially to my sons, Mitchell and Drew, with much love.*

| | |
|---|---|
| *"Friends"* | *Members of a Christian sect that stress inner light, rejects sacraments and an ordained ministry, and opposes war. Commonly referred to as Quakers.* |

# *Preface*

**TO ENHANCE THE READER'S ENJOYMENT, THERE ARE SEVERAL FACTS THAT ONE NEEDS TO KNOW TO FULLY APPRECIATE AND UNDERSTAND THIS MANUSCRIPT: 1)** Anytime a direct quote is used, it is quoted in universal bold 10 point italicized font, like this (***10 point Bold Italicized Font***); **2)** Within a direct quote, the square brackets, like this [ ], represent what the author thinks may be omitted from the text (example: ... ***this meeting hath solidly weighted*** [that request] ***and gives him to this liberty,...***); **3)** Endnotes or references are at the end of each chapter, and the said references are italicized numbers inside italicized brackets, like this *[17]*; **4)** The explanatory Footnotes are listed at the bottom of each page (example: ***Horace Henry Gawthrop*** [a] ***, a genealogist at the turn of the 20th century, pondered long and ...*** where [a] contains pertinent information about Horace Henry).

***Life is not a brief candle. It is a splendid torch that I want to make burn as brightly as possible before handing it on to future generations.***
– George Bernard Shaw

Thomas Gawthrop (1709-1780) spent almost 70% of his life preaching the Quaker ministry. Based in Westmoreland, England, he travelled widely in his ministry, visiting America, Ireland, Scotland and the West Indias. In this, the first of a planned 3 volumes history in the male line of Thomas Gawthrop's family, I bring together information on his forebears and the first and second generations of his America descendants. To provide a fuller appreciation of Thomas Gawthrop life and times, I include information on the role of Quakerism and the origin of the Gawthrop name. The name Gawthrop may have originated long before the Vikings or Romans and may date back to the Celtic tribes and their Druid Priesthood in pre-Christian times (Chapters 1 and 2).

Horace Henry Gawthrop [a], a genealogist at the turn of the 20th century, pondered long and hard both in England and America and generated what he called *Gawthrop – The Skipton Families*. Through his research, he concluded the point of origin for his Gawthrop ancestry was Skipton, North Yorkshire County, England. Thomas Gawthrop (1709-1780) (Chapter 5), was the key to his and my ancestral linage. Thomas was born in Skipton and in 1735 made Gatebeck, England his home. Thomas Gawthrop appeared in numerous Quaker journals in England, in America, in Scotland and in Ireland. Many of these journals looked on him as a loved, respected, diligent, and, most of all, a humble man. On one trip to Ireland, he is reported to have coin-the-phase, ... ***it was one thing to begin well, and another thing to end well ...*** *[33]*, but no record of a journal kept by Thomas has ever been found.

Two of Thomas Gawthrop's four sons, James (Chapter 6) and George (Chapter 7), emigrated to America in 1770 and settled in Nottingham, Pennsylvania. James moved to

---

[a] Horace Henry Gawthrop and Evan Brown Gawthrop (my great grandfather) were first cousins. That makes Horace Henry my first cousin - 3 times removed (see Appendix B for how relationships intertwine).

## Preface (continued)

Hampshire County, Virginia and George stayed in London Grove, Pennsylvania. Thus, James became the ancestor of the Virginia/West Virginia Gawthrops, and George became the ancestor of the Pennsylvania/Delaware Gawthrops.

This manuscript is meant to be ***A LIVING DOCUMENT***. Because this is a living document, anyone wishing to supply further information to clarify or add any item in any chapter can write/telephone the author at 1538 Endsley Place, Crofton, MD 21114-1509/301-858-0093 or Heritage Books, Inc., 1540–E Pointer Ridge Place, Bowie, MD 20716-1859/301-390-7709. Anyone wishing to supply information on the unfinished volumes 2 or 3 can write/telephone the author at the above address/phone number.

## Acknowledgment

This genealogy could not have been completed without the efforts of many people. The people who assisted me with data for Volume 1 are shown in alphabetically order based on first name:

- •Anthony J. Camp/Director of Society of Genealogists, London, England
- •Brain Clayton/Ilkley, West Yorkshire, England
- •Charles (Chuck) D. Thornton Jr./Cape Coral, FL
- •Chester County Historical Society/West Chester, PA
- •David Carl Gawthrop/Charlottesville, VA
- •Dorothy L. Hipple (grand-daughter of Horace Henry Gawthrop)/Lewes, DE
- •Emma J. Lapsansky, Curator, Special Collections, Associate History Professor, The Quaker Collection at the Library in Haverford College, Haverford, PA
- •George Gawthrop Jr./Winchester, KY
- •Gladys Thompson/Dent Sedbergh, Cumbria, England
- •Helen J. Gawthrop/Athens, Ohio
- •John (Jack) H. Gawthrop/Lansdale, PA
- •Mary Virginia (Merrifield) Gawthrop wife of Wilbur E. Gawthrop/WV
- •Nancy P. Speers, The Friends Historical Library, Swarthmore College, Swarthmore, PA
- •Patricia C. O'Donnell, The Friends Historical Library, Swarthmore College, Swarthmore, PA
- •Paul (Pete) H. Gawthrop Jr./Clearwater, FL
- •Pemberton Papers containing letters by Thomas Gawthrop (1709-1780), obtained from the Historical Society of Pennsylvania, Philadelphia, PA
- •Rebecka (Gawthrop) Garrett/Summerville, WV
- •Richard Carr Gawthrop/Vienna, VA
- •The Religious Society of Friends/London, England
- •V. M. Gate, Cumbria Records Office, Historical Research Department, Cumbria, England
- •William A. A. Gawthrop/Crofton, MD

# A Genealogical Record of the Descendants in the Male Line of Thomas Gawthrop

## An Early Traveling Friend (Quaker)

### Volume 1
### (through the 8th Generation)

Philip Evan Gawthrop

HERITAGE BOOKS
2016

**HERITAGE BOOKS**
***AN IMPRINT OF HERITAGE BOOKS, INC.***

**Books, CDs, and more—Worldwide**

For our listing of thousands of titles see our website
at
www.HeritageBooks.com

Published 2016 by
HERITAGE BOOKS, INC.
Publishing Division
5810 Ruatan Street
Berwyn Heights, Md. 20740



Cover: The horned god and sailing ship drawings on the cover were reproduced from Ann Ross' *The Pagan Celts* and a *May '95 Tidewater Publishing* catalog, respectively. Permission to reproduce the horned god was granted by publisher Barnes and Noble Imports of Lanham, Maryland. Permission to reproduce the sailing ship was granted by publisher Cornell Maritime Press, Inc. (including Tidewater Publishers), Centerville, Maryland. The Quaker was hand-drawn by the author.



International Standard Book Numbers
Paperbound: 978-0-7884-0399-6
Clothbound: 978-0-7884-6478-2

Contents (Volume 1)

# Chapter 1

## The Name – Gawthrop

***O***n November 10th 1896, Charles L. Gawthrop called at the U.S. Embassy in London, and was informed that Ambassador Bayard, whom he wished to see, was being interviewed by a gentleman from Reuter's telegraphic bureau. When the interviewer was shown out into the ante room, an usher said, ***His excellency will now see Mr. Gawthrop,*** *[1]* upon which Charles started in, and so did the gentleman from Reuter's who had just come out. Charles said, ***Excuse me but he mentioned my name.*** *[1]* The other replied, ***I think you must be mistaken, he mentioned my name.*** *[1]* Charles asked, ***What is your name?*** *[1]* The gentleman from Reuter's replied, ***Arnold Gawthrop*** *[1]*. Charles had good reason to think the usher was speaking to him because Gawthrop is a unique last name. What's in a name? What does it mean?

***T***he name Gawthrop is an ancient name and the first part of the name may have arisen sometime between 7,000 to 1,000 B.C. According to *The Concise Oxford Dictionary Of English Place-Names* [a] the name Gawthrop has been associated with several villages in Great Britain. The earliest reference, from the latter part of the 13th century, is to a village in Yorkshire, England (see Map #1 for the general lay of the Yorkshire land). One of the villages of Gawthorpe united with the township of Osset in Dewsbury parish, lower division of the Wapentake of Agbrigg and is called Osset (see Map #2). It's location is about 1 ½ miles from Horbury railway station, west-north-west from Wakefield, and about 2½ east-south-east from Dewsbury. Another village of Gawthrop is in the township of Lepton, and the parish of Kirkheaton, upper division of the Wapentake of Agbrigg, 4 miles east of Huddersfield. *[2]* There is also another village of Gawthrop, near Dent, in the parish of Sedbergh, Cumbria County (see Map #3) that may pre-date all other locations in Great Britain. This modern village of Gawthrop is 3/4 of a mile from the village of Dent on the road to Barbon. *[3]* These name-places, under various spellings, date back to the 13th or 14th century *[4]* and may date back even further before the Roman era and maybe before the Celtic

---

a *The Concise Oxford Dictionary Of English Place-Names*, by Ekwall (1960) lists two Gawthrop references: 1) Gauxhole La [*Gawkeholme* 1521 DL]. '*Gauk's* holm or island.' *Gauk* is ON *Gauker*, OSw *Goker*, pers. n., really *gaukr* 'cuckoo' and 2) Gawthorpe YW nr Dewsbury [*Goukethorpe* 1274 ff.Wakef], G YW nr Huddersfield [*Goutthorp* 1297 Subs, *Gawkethorp* 1324 Goodall]. Cf. GAUKHOLME. Gawthorpe Hall La [*Gouthorp* 1256, *Gouketthorp* 1324 PNLa] was probably named from a family.

Map #1 of the North, West, and South Yorkshire, England

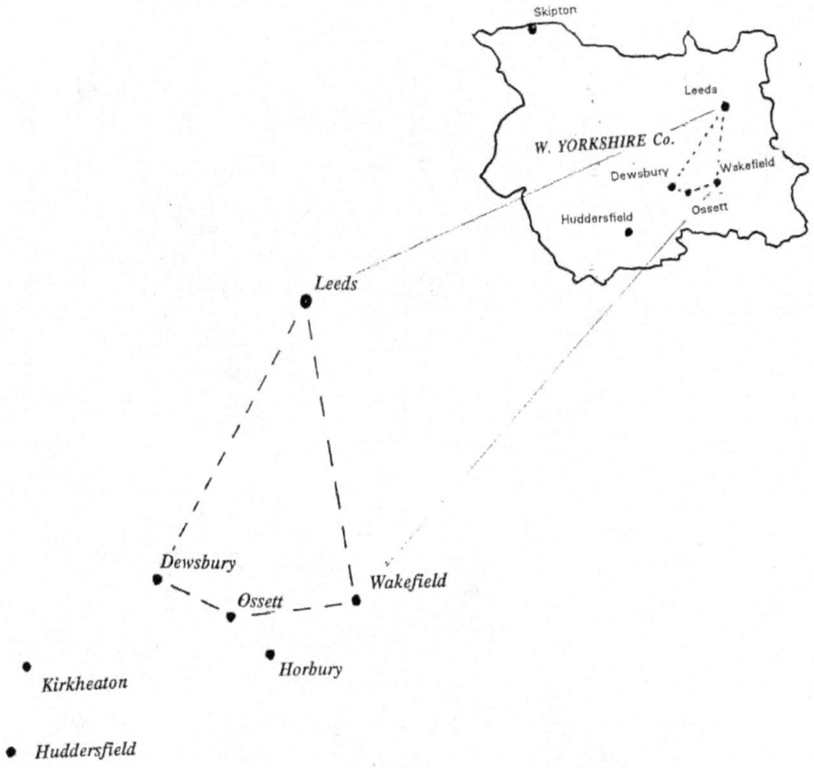


Map #2 of West Yorkshire, England

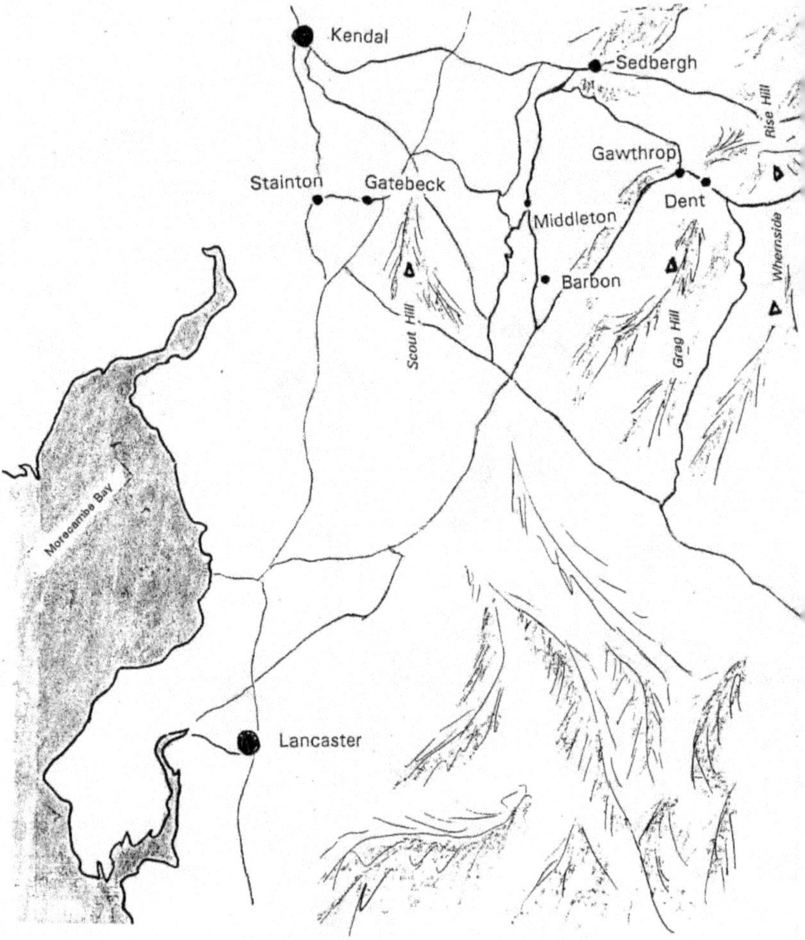


**Map #3 of Gatebeck, Gawthrop, Sedbergh, Kendal, and Lancaster, England**

tribe era.[b]

**O**ver three hundred names like *Althorp, Bishopsthorpe, Gawthorpe, Linthorpe, etc.,* contain the Danish/Scandinavian[c] word *thorpe* (for village).*[7]* The place-suffix, "thorpe", is handed down from the Latin and Greek and its origin evidently dates far back in the language of the race - meaning at first, a crowd or throng and than later, a small village or hamlet.*[2]* These place-suffixes are found in terminations of the names of many modern places. The Saxon place-suffix "thorp" and the Danes place-suffix "torp or thorp" are found in the Dutch as, "dorp" and in German as, "dorp or dorf." In the late nineteenth century, Mr. Tennyson writes, ***There is a pretty word which has been restored from an undeserved oblivion within the last few years .... as an idyll perhaps the distinctly finest thing of its kind in the English language. The word referred to is "thorpe," a village, pronounced "throp" or "trop" by our forefathers.****[2]*

**I**t is said that the Danish derivation of the name Gawthrop is that the word GAW meant "a God" and the place-suffix for a village is "throp." Hence, GAW-THROP is "a God like village." This derivation of the name Gawthrop seems to be confirmed by finding in the 13th century records a reference to "Thomas, Knight of Gawthorp or Godmanthorp."*[2]* The Scandinavian[d] people, specifically the Norwegian people, believed that their Gods took on human form but were "larger-than-life." These early Scandinavian people, in general, possessed the gift of telling many "tall" tales. These tales may just tie in with a much older version for "God" or maybe even the Celtic version of the "horned god" (as seen four paragraphs hence).

---

b England, which use to be connected to Northern Europe, was inhabited some 50,000 years ago. Around 8000-9000 years ago it was cut off from the continent by melting raising seas of the last ice age. The old stone age era inhabitants were similar to the Basque, who populated Spain and had their own language unrelated to any other European language. These stone age inhabitants populated England about 7000-4000 B.C. The Neolithic man immigrated to England about 4000 B.C. The Celtic tribes came to England about 3000 B.C. The late Bronze Age began about 1000 B.C. and lasted until about 400 B.C. The Iron Age overlapped the Bronze Age by about 100 years (the overlap occurred between 500 to 400 B.C.).*[5]* The Celtic tribes and the Bronze Age (at least in Northern Britain) were present until about 100 B.C.*[5]* The Roman invaded England in 55 A.D. In 449 A.D. the Jutes, Angles and the Saxons came from Scandinavia and northern Germany. The Vikings invaded England starting in 787 A.D. and the Norman French came about 1000 A.D.

c The Vikings sailed into England about 780 A.D. and settled widely in northeastern England.*[6]* The Danes/Vikings left a number of their words, mostly name-places; one source estimates about five hundred while another source finds more than six hundred places like *Grimsby, Whitby, Derby, Rugby,* and *Thoresby*. These words ending in *-by* are evidence that the Danes settled and flourished in northern England. The Danish word *-by* means "farm or town"; as is evidenced by the American word *bylaw* (town law).*[7]* The Danish/Scandinavian influence over the name-places is found in the largest numbers in Yorkshire and Lincolnshire, England.*[7]* The word *Thorpe* (Danish) and the word *thwaite* (Norwegian) are also very common Viking words and name-places.*[8]*

d The Skagerrak inlet (some 60 miles) separates Denmark and Norway and only about 260 miles of the North Sea separates these countries from Northern England.

**H**owever, if the original spelling of the name Gawthrop was really GAU-THORPE then another ***Celtic suggestion for the meaning of the name is provided. GAU = an unenclosed district with independent jurisdiction, like the Celtic TREF. Independence would suit the local spirit. ...and I expect it was a characteristic of those members of the family who sailed off to the West all those years ago.*** *[10]*[e] Again, the THORPE, pronounced "throp", meant village.

**A**nother source, that being a letter from the Director of Society of Genealogists in England, states that the definition of "Gauk's thorp" is that GAUK is derived from an Old Norse[f] personal name and a THORP (as defined above) seems to have been a farm or very small hamlet. So the place-name means Gauk's small hamlet or Gauk's farm *[9]*.

**T**he most interesting and most probable meaning of the name Gawthrop or at least the first part of the name, GAW, is much older than the Vikings or Romans. According to the now obsolete Welsh, the old Celtic tongue, there are two possibilities for the original meaning of *GAW* (GAW is a shorten version of GWAWR). The first meaning of *GWAWR* [now totally obsolete] is "lord, hero, and king" whereas the second meaning of *GWAWR* is "hue or dawn."*[11]*

**A**n explanation is now in order. The village of Gawthrop (see Chapter 2) is in a valley overlooked by an ancient Roman camp-site (fort) called Gawthrop. This fort is located such that the suns first light streams through this fort onto the valley floor below and some believe that the name Gawthrop means *first light*. However, the location of the Roman fort of Gawthrop is below and just West of the impressive cliff called Combe Scar. About 2/3 of the way down Combe Scar ... ***there stands a block of stone that would serve well as a possible ALTAR STONE.*** *[11]* Some distance below the Altar Stone there used to be a lake. When the lake was drained some years ago there were bones found in it. ***When I was told about the bones in the lake it was suggested they were the bones of wild ponies chased to their death over the "fell"*** [g] ***above by early hunters. I did not believe the hunters would leave their "kill" to rot in the water! The meat was food for their families. Bones from a sacrifice makes more sense.*** *[11]* The site across the valley on the top of the rise is called Fanny Hill ***(FANNY = TAN = FIRE = Fanny Hill)***.*[11]* This

---

e The "striving for independence" characteristic could be referring to Thomas Gawthrop (1709-1780), the Travelling Friend (Quaker) or his sons who emigrated to America. The Quaker religion is predicated on independent thought and independent worship.

f *The Random House Dictionary of the English Language* defines Norse as relating to Scandinavia or Norway.

g *The Random House Dictionary of the English Language* defines "fell" as *"Scot. and North Eng. an upland pasture, moor, or thicket; a highland plateau.* [ME ⟨ Scand; cf. Icel *fjall* mountain, akin to G *Fels(en)* rock, cliff] rise, like the altar stone, will see the morning sunrise*(3)* and recalls the Beltane[h] fires of Celtic years.*(10)* Another interesting fact, there is a town just West of Combe Scar*(10)* whose name is Cornclose. The name Cornclose might refer to the Horned God, because ***CORN = horn in Welsh**(10, 11)* or ***in Latin CORNU = horn**.(11)* Anne Ross' book, *The Pagan Celts*, reports the people of the area (see Chapter 2) worshipped a horned god*(12)* and held the kingdom of Dentdale (the current location of Gawthrop and Dent). If one likes conjecture, at least in Celtic days, the name Gaw(throp) was the place where sacrifices to the horned god were made perhaps by the first mornings light. Many worshippers could witness these sacrifices

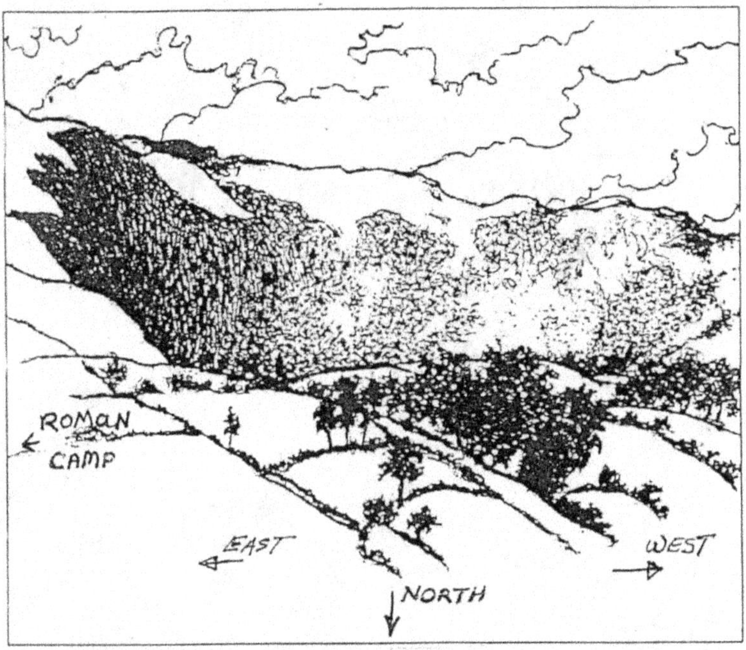


**COMBE SCAR dominates the Southern slopes of the valley of Dentdale. Further East the Romans had a military camp above the present village of Gawthrop.**

---

h *Wedster's New Collegiate Dictionary (principal copyright 1973)* defines "Beltane" as the Celtic May Day festival.

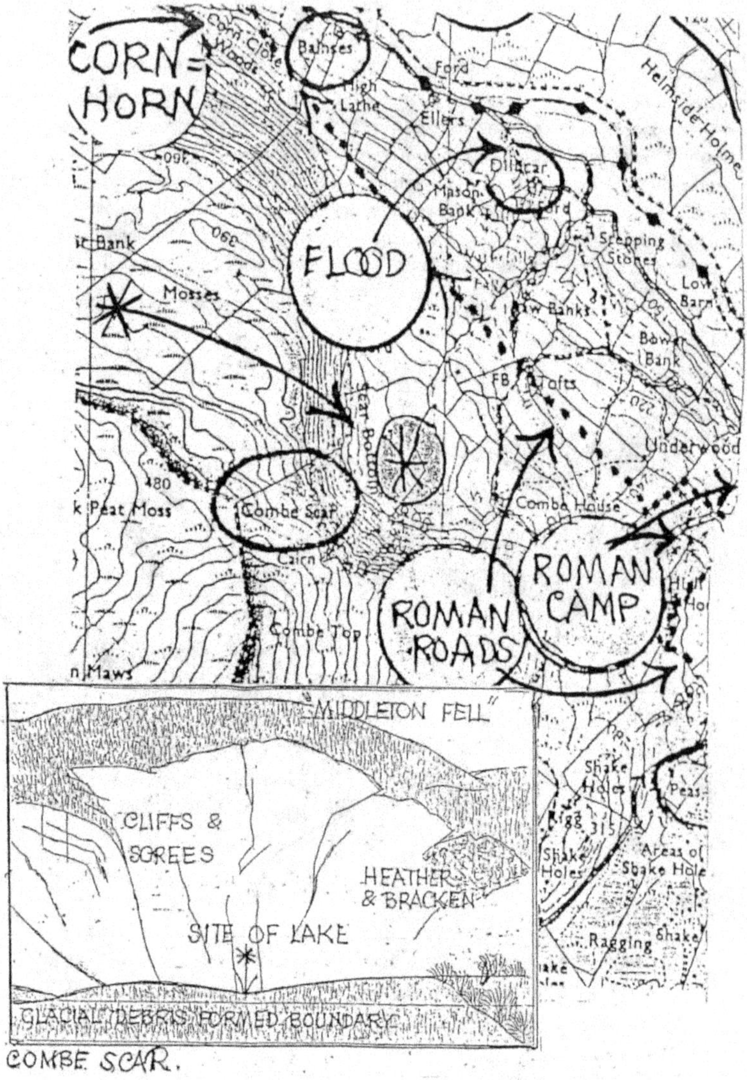


**The lake that was under the foot of Combe Scar.**

from the rise across the lake (Fanny Hill). Thus, in Celtic times or before, the name Gaw(throp) may have been the place for worshipping the *horned god* or the place where sacrifices to the *horned god* could be witnessed. The implication is that the current village of Gawthrop, England in Dentdale pre-dates all others of that same name.

**A**fter England became well established with tradition, the name creeps into English literature. In the *Life of Charlotte Bronte*, Chapter XIX, there is the following reference to the name Gawthorpe: ***Among this number were Sir James and Lady Kay Shuttleworth. Their house lies over the crest of the moors which rise above Haworth, at about a dozen miles distance as the crow flies, though much further by the road. - - - - Sir James and his wife drove over one morning, at the beginning of March, to call upon Miss Bronte and her father. Before taking leave, they pressed her to visit them at Gawthorpe Hall, their residence on the borders of East Lancashire.*** *[2]* She made the visit and took great pleasure in the ***... quiet drives to old ruins and old halls, situated among older hills and woods; the dialogues by the old fireside in the antique oak-panelled drawing-room, while they suited him, did not too much oppress and exhaust me. The house, too, is much to my taste; near three centuries old, gray stately and picturesque.*** *[2]*

**M**any people over the course of the last century have done research and attempted to document the Gawthrop family history. For instant, the preceding paragraph was found by Charles L. Gawthrop, son of Alfred and Hannah (Stroud) Gawthrop and grandson of Allen and Mary Ann (Newlin) Gawthrop. When Charles visited England in 1896 from Chester County, Pennsylvania Horace Henry Gawthrop, his uncle, asked him to check on the genealogy and archaeology of the Gawthrop name. He found the previous paragraph concerning Gawthorpe Hall. He proceeded by the most direct methods of modern American diplomacy and called on the owner, Sir Ughtred James Kay-Shuttleworth. *[2]*

**C**harles sent in his card and was received with much courtesy by Sir Ughtred. He was introduced to Sir Ughtred's wife and daughter. He was shown nearly every room in the large estate including the bedrooms. The house is Elizabethan built between 1601 through 1605 by a family ancestor of Sir Ughtred, (Sir Ughtred Shuttleworth). Charles noted that the estate house has not changed much over the years. *[2]*

**A**s Sir Ughtred tells it, in Yorkshire Folk-Talk (folk tales), the definition of ***Gawk or gowk = The cuckoo - - - and young cuckoo and its foster-mother are still called gowk.*** *[2]* Sir Ughtred had been curious to know the derivation of the name given to his house. Sir Ughtred explained what he has learned about the meaning of the name -- "Gaw" which means a cuckoo and "thorpe" which means a place; hence, "Gawthorpe," a place of cuckoos. Another definition in *A Dictionary Of Surnames* confirms the name Gawthorpe (note: "thorpe") comes from an Old Norse *gaukr* cuckoo. *[4]*

**A**s far as Sir Ughtred knows, the name Gawthrop, regardless of spelling, may come from one of the more ancient places and no person of the Gawthrop name has ever been connected with the Gawthrop Hall[i] at any time in history.*[2]* However, the early spelling with a "k" may indicate that the definition given above by Sir Ughtred may be somewhat true. There may be two separate yet distinct meanings. Gawthorpe Hall, because of its location, could very well be the place of cuckoo while the village of Gawthrop near Dent may have another meaning altogether; that being the place where sacrifices were made to the horned god.

**C**loser to home, an article in the Detroit News Tribune in 1905, says that many American families can claim lineal relationship with monarchs that trace their ancestry straight back to Kings Edward I and Edward III.*[13]* There may be some relationship between Dorothy Gascoique and the Gawthrop family.

**T**wo important steps mark the genealogic descent from the royal summit of the beginning of these families to the widely spread but more or less aristocratic plain of their present social status in America. If a romance were to be written the connecting link was undoubtedly the marriage in 1524 of Sir Robert Mauleverer and Alice Markenfield, daughter of Sir Ninian Markenfield both belonging to distinguished noble families in the English.. Sir Robert Mauleverer's ancestral line went back to the beginning of Anglican history, but those who trace their line up to that union are more interested in the family history of his wife, Alice Markenfield. Her mother, wife of Sir Ninian Markenfield, was in maiden life, Dorothy Gascoique, daughter of Sir William Gascoique, Knight of Gawthrop. Sir William Gascoique's great, great grandfather was Sir William Gascoique[j], Lord Chief Justice of England.*[13]*

**T**he wife of Sir William Gascoique and the mother of Dorothy (Gascoique) Markenfield was Margaret Percy, daughter of Henry, the third Earl of Northumderland. Margaret Percy's line of ancestry runs back to the De Burgh family, and through it to the Duke of Clarence, son of King Edward III. Also, the Percy family went back in another line to Gilbert de Claire, seventh Earl of Hertford ("Red" Hertford) whose wife was Princess Joane of Acres, daughter of Edward I and Queen Eleanor of Castile.*[13]* Back at the turn of the century the aristocratic lines may have been important to some people but now, in the 90's, the aristocratic link is not as important at least in the eyes of this author.

---

i Gawthorpe Hall [*Gouthorp* 1256, *Goukethorp* 1324] was probably named from a family. However, based on Sir Ughtred's narrative that no Gawthrop has ever lived at Gawthrop Hall, the house name was not associated with any Gawthrops. Another reference source talks about the Kay-Shuttleworth estate, Gawthorpe Hall, *The Literary Guide and Companion to Northern England*, by Robert M. Cooper, page 327, (to-be-published by Ohio University Press, Athens, Ohio, date entered into this record, Oct. 1994).

j Sir William Gascoique, Lord Chief Justice of England place his name on the rolls of the immortals for daring to commit to prison for contempt of court, Henry, Prince of Wales. Henry, Prince of Wales, later became King Henry V of England.

***S***everal definitions and references to the name Gawthrop have previously been discussed. The list below is a selection from the Yorkshire records (Name Indexed) and other sources. At that time Dent and Gawthrop were just inside North Yorkshire County*[10]*, (see Map #1). This list shows the various spellings and the evolution of the name since the 13th century.

| No. | Year | Name | Indexed |
|---|---|---|---|
| 1 | 1274 | Henry de Goukethorpe | Gawthorp |
| 2 | 1275 | Hanne de Goukethorp | Gawthorp |
| 3 | 1306 | Manor of Goulkthorp | Gawthorp |
| 4 | 1346 | Gerlethorp | Garthorpe |
| 5 | 1352 | Bridge of Gerlthorp | Garthorpe |
| 6 | 1379 | Willelmus De Gawkthorp[k] | |
| 7 | ≈1380 | Sir William Gaskon of Gawkthorpe | |
| | | *(probably Sir William Gascoique, Lord Chief Justice of England [14])* | |
| 8 | ≈1440 | Thomas, Knight of Gawthorp or Godmanthorp | |
| 9 | 1476 | Lands in Gawkethorp | Gawthorp |
| 10 | | Gaskon of Gelsthorp | |
| | | *(the last name of Gaskon was probably spelled Gascoique [14])* | |
| 11 | 1524 | Sir William Gascoique, Knight of Gawthrop | |
| 12 | | Christiana de Gelsthorp | Gawthorpe |
| 13 | 1541 | Robert Gawkthorp | |
| 14 | 1550 | Gawthorpe (the place or village) | |
| 15 | 1551 | Manor of Gawkethorpe | |
| 16 | 1553 | Property in Gawthorpp | |
| 17 | 1556 | Richard Gauthroppe | Gawthorp |
| 18 | 1585 | Robert Gawthorppe | |
| 19 | 1597 | William Gawthrope | |
| 20 | 1598 | Petrus (peter) Gawthorpe | |
| 21 | 1613 | Henry Gawthroppe | Gawthrop |
| 22 | 1621 | Thomas Gawthrop | Gawthrop |
| 23 | 1644 | Robert Gauthrop | Gawthrop |
| 24 | 1650 | Henrye Gathroppe | Gawthrop |
| 25 | 1655 | An Gawthropp | Gawthrop |
| 26 | 1670 | Hugh Gawthrop of Skipton | |

---

k Letter from Mrs. Gladys Thompson, Cumbria, England, in September 1994, ***As far as I know the oldest list of persons of local importance was made in 1379. On that lists there are some varied spelling! WILLELMUS DE GAWKTHORP will be your ancestor.*** *[10]*

| | | | |
|---|---|---|---|
| 27 | 1681 | John Gathrop | Gathrope |
| 28 | 1683 | William Gawthrop of Skipton | |
| 29 | 1683 | Thomas Gathrope of Skipton | |
| 30 | 1692 | John Gawthorp[1] | Gathrope |


REFERENCES:

SOURCE [1]: Information extracted from *"GAWTHROP," Chapter II, entitled "AN ANGLO-AMERICAN PROBLEM SOLVED,"* written at Christmas 1902 by Horace Henry Gawthrop (part of his unfinished manuscript). Obtained at a interview in 1990 with Dorothy L. Hipple, granddaughter of Horace Henry Gawthrop.

SOURCE [2]: Information extracted from *"GAWTHROP," Chapter I, entitled "GAWTHROP - Places and Persons"*, written at Christmas 1902 by Horace Henry Gawthrop (part of his unfinished manuscript).

SOURCE [3]: Draft manuscript from Mrs. Gladys Corbyn Thompson, Cumbria, England, *GAWTHROP, TODAY & YESTERDAY*, received from Major Wm. A. A. Gawthrop in January 1994.

SOURCE [4]: Two place in the West Riding of Yorkshire and one place in Lancashire, *Gawthorpe Hall,* appear in *The Concise Oxford Dictionary of English Place-Names*, By Eilert Ekwall (1960), page 194.

SOURCE [5]: Churchill, Winston S., *The Birth of Britain, A History of the England-Speaking Peoples*, (C)1956 by The Right Honourable Sir Winston Churchill, K.G.O.M.C.H.M.P., Originally published 1st ed., Dodd, Mead 1956-1958, First published as a Dodd, Mead Quality Paperback in 1983, Dodd, Mead & Company, Inc., NY.

SOURCE [6]: Letter sent to P.E. Gawthrop on 5 April 1994 from Helen J. Gawthrop, Athens, Ohio.

SOURCE [7]: Albert C. Baugh and Thomas Cable, *A History of the English Language*, 3rd ed., (C) 1978, 1957 Prentice Hall, Inc., Englewood Cliffs, NJ, page 97 in the chapter *"Foreign influences on old English"*, obtained from H.J. Gawthrop in a letter written on 7 March 1994.

SOURCE [8]: R. McCrum, W. Cran, and R. MacNeil, *The Story of English*, (C) 1986 Elizabeth Sifton Books - Viking Penguin, New York, NY, page 71 in the chapter *"The mother tongue"*, obtained from H.J. Gawthrop/'94.

SOURCE [9]: Letter from the Director of Genealogists in England, Anthony J. Camp, B.A., FSG (Hon), London.

SOURCE [10]: *Dentdale the Little Kingdom*, Written and Illustrated by Gladys Gorbyn (she used her maiden name to avoid confusion with another Gladys Thompson), Dentdale D.T.P. and Printing Services, Dent, Printed by Stramongate Press, Kendal, England, no date found, (date entered September 30, 1994).

SOURCE [11]: Letter to P.E. Gawthrop from Mrs. Gladys Corbyn Thompson, Cumbria, England, in September 1994.

SOURCE [12]: *The Pagan Celts*, Anne Ross, First published as *Everyday Life of the Pagan Celts*, 1970, This updated, expand and reillustrated edition, first published in the USA, 1986 by Barnes & Noble Books, Totowa, NJ, page 126, ***The Celts venerated animals to a great degree, as we shall see presently. For this reason it is not surprising that one of the best attested of their god-types throughout the pagan Celtic world is the horned god*** (some called that god a stag god).

SOURCE [13]: From a newspaper article entitled *American Families Whose Progenitors Were The Edwards of England*, in The Detroit News Tribune, October 22, 1905. Philip E. Gawthrop has said article (date entered Feb. 1992).

SOURCE [14]: Notes by Philip E. Gawthrop made in 1991/1992.


---

1 {Horace Henry Gawthrop has this note} ***This list is not complete and some have been omitted as doubtful. The several spellings like "Gerlethorp" should also be left out, perhaps, though the indexing comes near the name Gawthrop.*** There is special interest in this particular name for it appears in the Domesday Book {William the Conqueror [Wm I] in 1086 ordered a survey for fiscal purposes. This became known as the Domesday Book.}

# Chapter 2

## Gawthrop in Dentdale, Today & Yesterday

*T*he modern village of Gawthrop, England is some 3/4 of a mile from the village of Dent (see Map #3) on the road to Barbon. Gawthrop and Dent are located in a valley that has been given the name of DENTDALE. DENT is a Celtic name and, with the Norse[a] invasion influence, the scandinavian people added the ending, DALE.*[10]* Hence, the name Dentdale.

*T*he earliest known settlement in Dentdale was established on the slopes rising above the valley-floor. These slopes were thickly forested (...***COEDWIG** = **forest*** ...)*[11]* and overlooked by swamps (... ***DILYW** = **flood*** ...)*[11]* The firmer ground of these slopes made the first settlement location at and slightly above the current location of Gawthrop, England today.

***Here and there a few stones have remained to suggest they were placed for a propose, or a footpath retains a convenient route, but mostly the turf has covered the ruins. However, local memory is long, indicating a continuity of occupation, and the field names can tell a long story. Where the Barbon road begins to climb to the fell[b], there are fields called "Grusk"*** *[11]* (the word comes from the Danish and means "ruins"). The name of "Grusk" both locates and dates the use of the land slightly above the present village of Gawthrop (give or take a few hundred years).

*B*y the time the Roman invaders took over, there was enough left over litter on the slopes to be conspicuous. Who was there before the Romans? At this point in time the historians gave a name to the Celtic tribes that held the area, they were the Brigantines. Ann Ross' book, *The Pagan Celts*, reports that the Brigantines worshipped a *horned god* through their Druid priesthood in pre-Christian times.*[12]*[c] The Brigantines were a wild and quarrelsome people or at least they seem to have been. ***Certainly, they are known to have given the Romans trouble on their northern campaign to establish control up to, and including, the lowlands of Scotland.*** *[3]* It is very probable that the site that the Romans used for a camp site was part

---

a *The Random House Dictionary of the English Language* defines Norse as relating to Scandinavia or Norway.

b *The Random House Dictionary of the English Language* defines "fell" as *"Scot. and North Eng. an upland pasture, moor, or thicket; a highland plateau.* [ME ⟨ Scand; cf. Icel *fjall* mountain, akin to G *Fels(en)* rock, cliff]

c In Celtic days, the name Gaw(throp) may have been the place where animals and even humans were sacrificed to the *horned god* by first morning sunrise.

of a Celtic Settlement.*[3]*[d] The Gawthrop campsite is conspicuous from the valley road and when one is on the site its quality as a defensible military point is obvious. ***Did the Celtic Settlement occupy that conspicuous site or was it only on the fields now called Grusk?****[10]* The relationship between the campsite and the fields called Grusk can be seen on the next page. Perhaps the ruins were those of another or an auxiliary settlement that developed alongside the campsite. However, there is a farm just below the campsite named ***"Foulsyke" = stinking drain****[11]*, which suggests how the land was used. It is believed that the campsite was in continuous occupation long before the Romans.*[3]* On the old Roman road below the campsite there is a place known locally as "Branta Casa." Branta is a Danish word meaning "steep" and Casa is a Latin words meaning "a small building." An early Celtic Church in Scotland was called "Candida Casa." Looking at the two names, "Branta Casa" and "Candida Casa," this brings to mind a question - Did the site at Gawthrop have an early Celtic Church located on the hillside?*[3]* That question may never be answered but this site and the possibility of an early church should not to be confused with the current Dent Church in the valley of Dentdale built some 400 years later (discussed later in this chapter in footnote g).

**R**omans in Dentdale - ***The Gawthrop campsite was first identified by Mr. Whitehead, some years ago. Since then, the roads to and from the site have been sought.****[3]* Two connecting roads leading into the Dentdale valley are: ***one from Bainbridge and one from Ingleton. They meet quite conspicuously just behind Whernside Manor*** (see Map #4). ***The reported discovery of Roman lettering on a stone there suggests that site was of some importan. The roads are only narrow pathways but the nature of infill can still keep weeds at bay. They show as level grass paths on weedy or bracken infested slopes.****[3]* In Roman times ***wagons and pack ponies were using the roads. An un-mortared construction of stone takes the roads across the beck***[e].*[3]*

**R**oman – British – "Cat-Holes" – ***Within that period of time after the departure of the Romans, the British Isles were at the mercy of many invaders. It*** (England) ***was also being torn-apart from within itself. Legends abound, and modern careful research is discovering a few facts which begin to clarify those legends.****[3]*

***"Cat Holes" is the name of a farm on the outskirts of Sedbergh*** (see Map #3), ***close to the River Rawthey. Obviously, the name could be taken at face value, but to most farmers of the past***

---

d The Iron Age overlapped the Bronze Age (about 500 B.C. to 400 B.C.). The Iron Age immigrations brought with them a revival of hill-top camps, which had ceased to be constructed since the Neolithic Age, about 4000 B.C. These camps were not mere places of refuge but often they were settlements had private dwellings, and were permanently inhabited. They do not seem to have served the purpose of strongholds for invading enemy armies. On the contrary, they appear to have come into existence gradually as the Iron Age newcomers multiplied and developed a tribal system from which tribal wars eventually arose.*[5]*

e *Webster's New World Dictionary, Everyday Encyclopedia Edition*, General Editor - David B. Guralnik, copyright 1963, defines BECK as a little stream especially a stream with a rocky bottom.

Taken from the *Dentdale the Little Kingdom*, by Gladys Corbyn

Looking West, the field name is derived from the Danish language. It implies the presence of debris on the land.

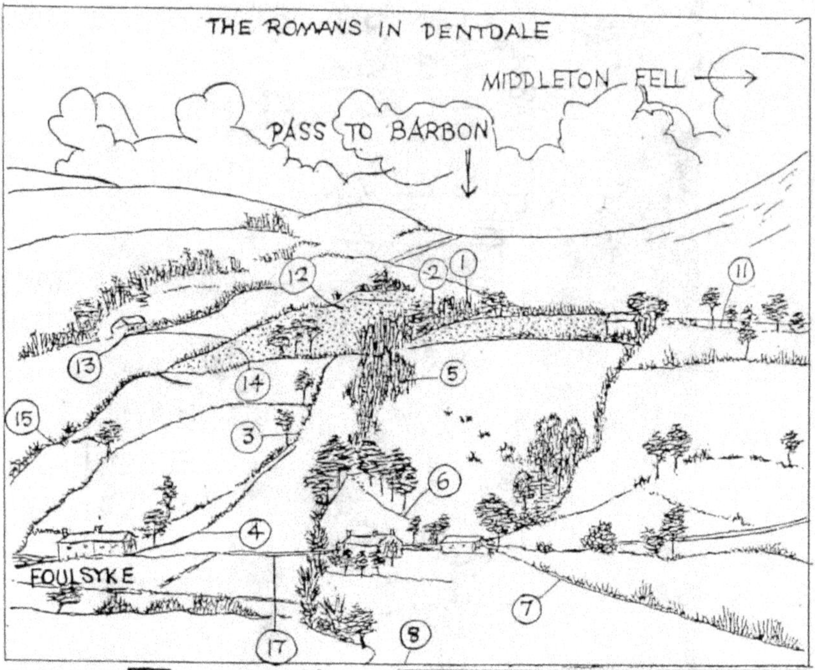


THE CAMPSITE [dotted area] AS SEEN FROM RISE HILL.

(1)(2) GATEWAY.
(3)(4)(5)(6) ROADS UP TO GATE.
(7)(8) ROUTES TO RIVER CROSSINGS.
(11) ROAD TO JOIN LUNE · NORTH.
(12) ROAD IN FROM SOUTH.
(13) BATH-HOUSE SITE ?
(14) LATRINES.
(15) OLD ROAD UP FROM GAWTHROP.
(17) MODERN ROAD

(3) & (4) KNOWN AS "JERKIN LANE."
(5) & (6) CLIMB UP "GRUBBINS."

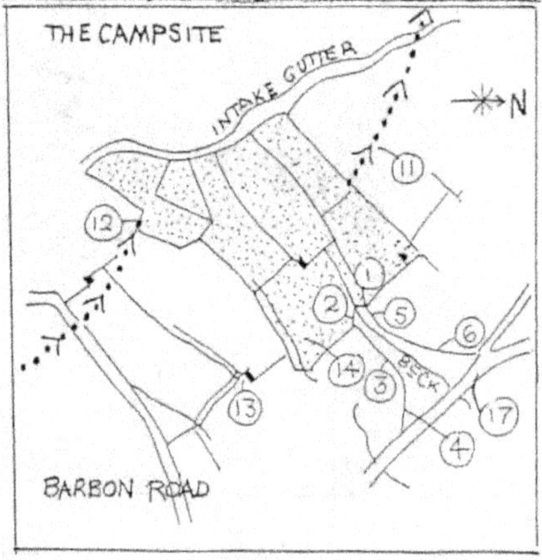


Taken from the *Dentdale the Little Kingdom*, by Gladys Corbyn

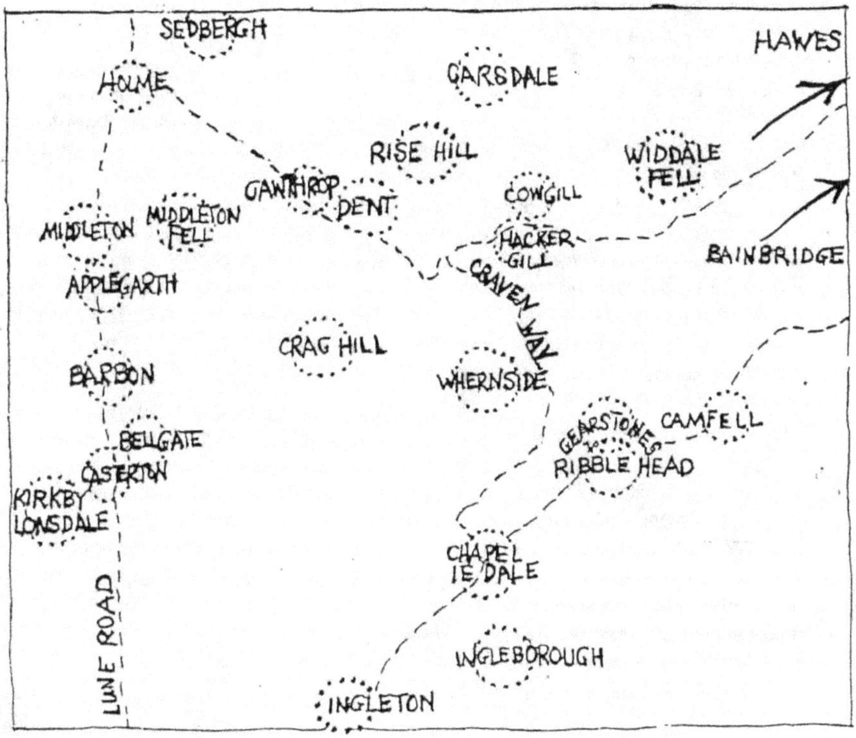


Map #4. The old roads passing through Gawthrop and Dent.

***wild cats would only be a pest, so why name your farm after them. Investigations in a Welsh dictionary suggested an origin for the name that made more sense, and keyed in with the fortifications nearby at the foot of Holme Fell. Cat Holes = the Warrior's road (CAD = warrior).*** *[3]* But the Warrior's road is not the route taken by the Roman Road. Cat Holes climbs the Homes Fell behind "Cornclose" (see page 8) and its sound foundation defies the weeds that have grown over these roads, leaving the road as a straight green lane.*[3]*

**So** who were the warriors whose road and fortifications follow the Rawthey River below Holme Fell? These warriors quite possibility could have been Celtic. ***There is a legend of a King in Dentdale. When the Romans departed there was a certain Coel, a member of a prominent Celtic family who had been in an important administrative post under the Romans.*** *[3]* ***When the Romans pulled out he took over and made himself KING on the WALL.*** *[10]* ***Coel Hen = the old, he became known as in folk lore. Yes, old King Coel.*** *[3]* He founded a dynasty that had a custom; the Celtic Princes, sons of the King, demand equal shares of the Kingdom when the King died. So it went down through the generations, reducing the Kingdom to little shreds within a few generations. ***By the time Young DONATUS inherited all he got was Dentdale.*** *[3]* His Kingdom was about 10.5 miles long with varied width. However, he did not rule long, his Kingdom of Dentdale was attacked and he was killed.*[10]* The Kingdoms came one after another and with this constant skirmishing for power, the situation became easier for invaders.[f] The Celtic culture has vanished but the Celtic place-names have survived even to today.

**The** Coming of the Monks - Christianity came to Britain during the Roman rule, but it is for the Pagan rites and the establishment of Pagan sites that we remember the earlier Celtic Kingdoms. Dentdale has "Fanny Hill" which is high on the rise, where it would be accessible from two valleys. Fanny Hill is derived from TAN = fire (FANNY = TAN = FIRE) and recalls perhaps the Beltane fires of long ages ago, a feature of the Celtic years.*[11]*

**With** the departure of the Romans there was a void that the Celtic missionaries fulfilled. A Celtic Monastery was established in Dentdale, but the site is long forgotten. The early Celtic Christian missionaries went to known Pagan sacred sites (like the natural spring of pure water in Dentdale) ***and there preached this new religion. There, as time went on, a Church was built***[g]. *[10]* ***Only the fact that a Saxon Monastery asked to take over the land because the Celtic Monastery was gone, records this fact for posterity. The actual site is not known.*** *[3]*

---

f The Roman invaded England in 55 AD. In 449 AD the Jutes, Angles and the Saxons came from Scandinavia and northern Germany. The Vikings sailed into English water and shores starting in 787 AD and settled widely in northeastern England. The Norman French came later some three hundred years after the Viking.

g The old pagan site of that precious spring water establishment one of the early Celtic settlement. The Church in Dentdale is nearer the modern day village of Dent and in the morning light the *Dent* Church on its mound dominates the valley.

*I*f one stands in the center of the village[h] of Dent directly in front of the Church and looks south to the top of the hill, there are piles of stone called the Meggerstones. ***The MEGGERSTONES get their name from the Welsh (MYGED = Praise, honour, respect; MYG = Holy, honoured; MEGYR = Fine, glorious). The stones themselves are not "fine," "glorious," but if the local Pagan leaders had traced the supply of that fresh water to that spot then the SOURCE OF LIFE should be honoured and worshipped. By SACRIFICES if need be!*** *[10]* These sacrifices might tie into the meaning the name Gaw(throp), that being the place where animals and maybe humans were sacrificed to the *horned god.*

***It was not until the time of the Normans that the Monastic movement really got under way, and it was one of the later "orders" that came to Dentdale.*** *[10]* In the 1200's the Monks from Coverham, the pre-monstratensians strict break-away branch of the Cistercian Order, established a Grange at Gawthrop. The Monks were ***keen business men, they encouraged the local industries. Wool was an international saleable product, woven and knitted goods were becoming profitable; they discovered and developed a Lead Mine and they built or encouraged the building of a water driven corn mill at Gawthrop.*** *[10]* There were Coal mines and Iron mines, but ***all these were in small quantities and have mostly been worked out now leaving the grassed-over sites for the walkers[i] to discover. SHEEP GRAZED THE HILLSIDE and their wool was put to good use. It took 8 spinners to keep ONE WEAVER busy. When the fabric was woven it had to be Fulled.[j] After Fulling the wet fabric was hung up to dry, stretched to the right measurements on Tenter Frames. The expression "on Tenterhooks" is used today to describe Tension.*** *[10]* This development of commerce required bridges, roads, housing, and part-time lodging at the Inns for travellers. The Tudor style of the few remaining secular buildings suggests that these houses were in existence at the time of the Monks. The style and proportions of the houses suggest that indeed these houses may have been built for the Monks.

*C*hildren began to learn their grammar skills at Dame Schools. The Dame Schools were in houses all over the Dentdale valley. Many young children travelled great distances to go

---

h In the center of *Dent* today there is a fountain dedicated to the memory of ADAM SEDGWICK (who began to develop the study of Geology and is said to be England's first Geologist). From the beginning of life in the valley there was a spring at that point. The source of that pure water was traced to a place high in the hills exactly south of the present church.

i In the past *Gawthrop* was a busy place. The noise of the Mill just beside the hill that leads up to the village was significant. Now-a-days it is a walkers village! All throughout the year the walkers arrive in droves and comb the hills, the valleys, the kilns, the fells, etc.

j Fulling, the thickening and cleaning of newly woven cloth, is an ancient craft (evidence of the Romans using fulling is found in many cemetery carving). The fuller stands in a tub of warm soft water and tramples underfoot cloth covered with a detergent such as fuller's earth. Friction causes wet woolen fibers to mat together, or felt, reducing the size of the piece of cloth by as much as third.

to grammar school. The Dent's Grammar school opened in 1613 and may have been one of the first public school system in existance.*[11]*

***At the dissolution of the Monastic Properties, William Parr,*** (the brother of the Queen, Catherine Parr, and brother-in-law to Henry the Eight) ***purchased both Coverham Monastery itself and the Grange's Mill on the Gawthrop hillside. He did not have control of the Monastery or the Mill for very long but the Mill has been known as PARKIN MILL ever since.****[10]* The Mill continued to serve the village well into the 1800's. Disaster struck, the dam collapsed and a new channel from another creek was built. Parkins Mill continued to operate long after it was really needed to do work for the village.*[3]*

**B**efore the "motoring age" Dentdale was not easily accessible except from the West, the Westmoreland side (see Map #1).[k] In the late 1800's, the Settle Carlisle Railway Line was built. Dentdale was one of the Stations on that line. The railway line flurished for better than 80 years. ***Today the "Settle-Carlisle Walk" has joined the ranks of the "Long-Distance Walk"... all 80 scenic miles of it! From the Roman Roads to Today's Transport Needs, well shod feet are walking the miles. One way or another, the*** [Dentdale] ***valley remembers.****[10]*


REFERENCES

SOURCE [3]: Draft manuscript from Mrs. Gladys Corbyn Thompson, Cumbria, England, entitled *GAWTHROP, TODAY & YESTERDAY*, received from Major Wm. A. A. Gawthrop in January 1994.

SOURCE [5]: Churchill, Winston S., *The Birth of Britain, A History of the England-Speaking Peoples*, Copyright 1956 by The Right Honourable Sir Winston Churchill, K.G.O.M.C.H.M.P., Originally published 1st ed., Dodd, Mead 1956-1958, First published as a Dodd, Mead Quality Paperback in 1983, Dodd, Mead & Company, Inc., New York, N.Y.

SOURCE [10]: *Dentdale the Little Kingdom*, Written and Illustrated by Gladys Corbyn (she used her maiden name to avoid confusion with another Gladys Thompson), Dentdale D.T.P. and Printing Services, Dent, Printed by Stramongate Press, Kendal, England, no date found, (date entered September 30, 1994).

SOURCE [11]: Letter to Philip E. Gawthrop from Mrs. Gladys Corbyn Thompson, Cumbria, England, in September 1994.

SOURCE [12]: *The Pagan Celts*, Anne Ross, First published as *Everyday Life of the Pagan Celts*, 1970, This updated, expand and reillustrated edition, first published in the USA, 1986 by Barnes & Noble Books, Totowa, New Jersey, page 126, ***The Celts venerated animals to a great degree, as we shall see presently. For this reason it is not surprising that one of the best attested of their god-types throughout the pagan Celtic world is the horned god.***


---

k In modern times, Westmoreland County was changed to Cumbria County. Sedbergh is about 4 miles in a North-West direction from Dent/Gawthrop; Gatebeck is about 10 miles in a West direction from Dent/Gawthrop; Kendal is about 11 miles in a West-North-West direction from Dent/Gawthrop; and (not on Map #1) Skipton is about 29 miles is South-East direction from Dentdale (Dent/Gawthrop).

# Chapter 3

## Gawthrop - The Skipton Families

Charles L. Gawthrop, an American businessman, and Arnold E. Gawthrop, a reporter and an Englishman, met under extreme chance circumstance at the U.S. Embassy, London in 1896 (see Chapter 1). They exchanged business cards and so began their acquaintance. The two Gawthrops soon learned that they were both of Quaker ancestry. With the aid of Friends (Quaker) records, they traced Arnold's line to **William Gawthrop of Skipton** and Charles' line to **Hugh Gawthrop of Skipton,** both of the latter part of the 17th century and believed to be brothers.*[1]*

***H***orace Henry Gawthrop had logistical problems with the relationship of these two contemporaries in mind when he visited Skipton, England in 1901 (see Map #5). On his request of the rector of the church in Skipton, showed him the old handwritten registers as well as the newer printed registers. Returning to America, Horace Henry thoroughly examined three volumes in the library of the Historical Society of Pennsylvania. He found several groups with the name Gawthrop. With the data found in Skipton and in the data found in Pennsylvania, he verified what Arnold and Charles had concluded; that Hugh and William were indeed brothers, both sons of Thomas Gawthrop. However, from one sect to another, inevitably, confusion in the records had occurred*[1]*. Horace Henry reconciled that both of these families ancestors were from Skipton and that his ancestors were also from Skipton.*[1]* In an unfinished manuscript, Horace Henry details his ancestry in the Skipton Families below.*[1]* Another source, a letter from Brian Clayton in 1993*[15]*, has verified much of this information:

SKIPTON FAMILIES

**1**, Thomas Gawthroppe *[1, 16]* (Gawthrop *[17]*) was born in the late 16th century (however, in pencil in Horace Henry's work, there is written ***born about 1587*** probably in Horace Henry's writing). In another source*[15]* Thomas' birthdate is shown as circa 1585/90 with the possibility that his father being William Gawthrop, who is also buried in Skipton on 19 April 1605.*[15]* Thomas died on the 16th day of October 1626*[17]* and was buried Oct. 17th 1626.*[15, 16]* Thomas married Janet Stott of Skipton*[15]* on 24 Oct. 1609. Other sources have different spellings of Janet; Gennett*[17]* and Jenet Stot.*[16]* Janet died on the 23rd Aug. 1623.*[17]* There is some discrepancy as to when she was buried; one source indicates that she was buried in Skipton on 23 Aug. 1633*[15]* whereas another source indicates that she was buried on Aug. 23rd, 1623.*[16]*

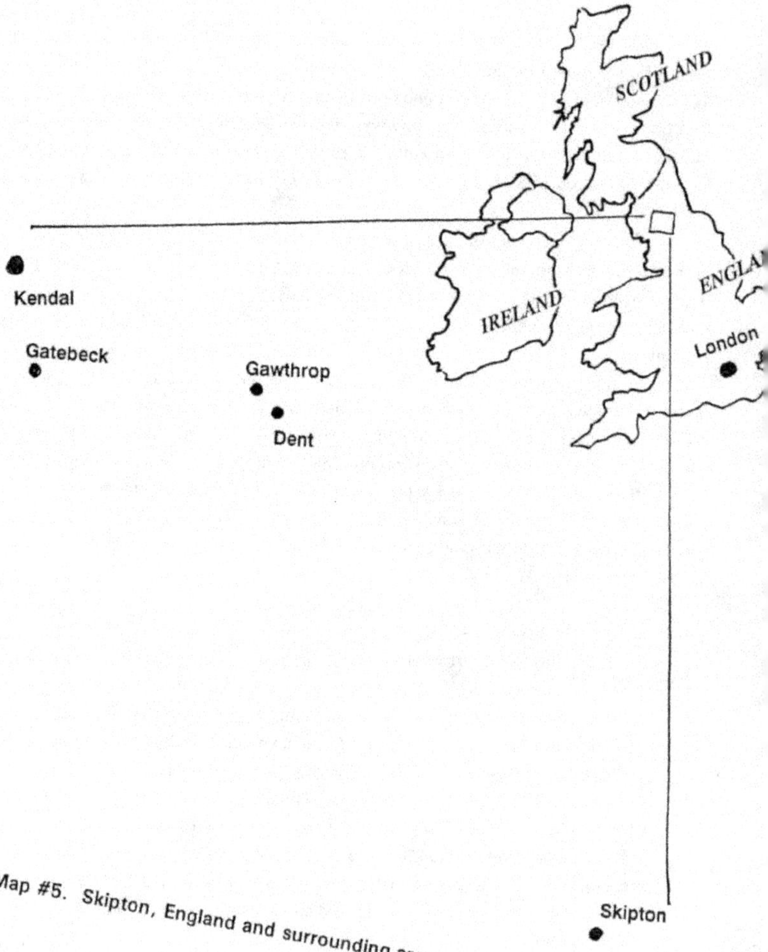


Map #5. Skipton, England and surrounding areas.

**11**, William Gawthrop*/15/* was baptized at Skipton on 20 Jan. 1609/10*/15/* and was buried on 11 March 1610/11.*/15/*

**12**, Dorothy Gawthrop*/15/* was baptized at Skipton on 11 March 1610/11.*/15/*

**13**, Elizabeth Gawthrop*/15/* was baptized at Skipton on 20 Dec. 1613.*/15/*

**14**, William Gawthrop*/15, 16, 17/* (Gauthrop*/1/*) was baptized at Skipton on 23 Sept. 1617*/15/* and was buried on 30 Sept. 1617.*/15/*

**15**, Thomas Gawthrop*/15, 16, 17/* (Gauthrop*/1/*) was baptized at Skipton on 31 Jan. 1618/19*/15/* and was buried at Skipton on 26 May 1657*/15/* (two other sources show the month as a number.*/16, 17/* Thomas married Margaret Winterbounre*/16/* (Winterburne*/17/*, Winterburn*/15/*) on the 24 Nov. 1640.*/15/* Margaret, a Widow, was buried at Skipton on 28 Nov. 1678*/15/* (two other sources show the month as a number*/16, 17/*).

**16**, Anne Gawthrop*/15, 16, 17/* was baptized at Skipton on 4 Nov. 1621*/15/* and is buried 1 July 1626.*/17/*

**151**, Thomas Gawthrop*/15, 16, 17/* (Gauthrop*/1/*) was baptized at Skipton on 29 Aug. 1641*/15/* and was buried at Skipton on 27 July 1704*/15/* (other sources show the month as a number*/16, 17/* and one source*/16/* shows a different day date). Thomas married an unknown woman.*/17/*

**152**, John Gawthrop*/15, 17/* was baptized at Skipton on 28 Aug. 1643.*/15/*

**153**, Anna*/15/* (Ann*/17/*) Gawthrop was baptized at Skipton on 7 Dec. 1652.*/15/*

**1511**, John Gawthrop*/15, 17/* was baptized at Skipton on 13 Sept. 1668.*/15/*

**1512**, Hugh Gawthrop*/1, 15, 16, 17/* of Skipton was baptized at Skipton on 9 Oct. 1670*/15/* (other sources*/1, 16, 17/* show the month as a number). Hugh married Ruth Stott of Skipton on 3 May 1698*/15, 16/* (another source*/17/* shows the month as a number).

**1513**, Margaret Gawthrop*/15, 17/* was baptized at Skipton on 3 Sept. 1677*/15/* (another source*/17/* shows the month as a number).

**1514**, Isabel Gawthrop*/15, 17/* was baptized at Skipton on 11 Oct. 1680.*/15/*

**1515**, William Gawthrop*/1, 15, 17/* of Skipton was baptized at Skipton on 17 April 1683*/15/* (other sources show the month as a number*/1, 17/*). William married Mary of Skipton.*/1/* Mary was born in the year 1679 and died 4th month 10th day 1771 at age 92 years.*/1/* She was buried at Skipton, England.*/1/*

**15121**, Mary Gawthrop was born on the 4th month [June] 13th day 1700.*/17/*

**15122**, Rebekkay Gawthrop was born on 3rd month [May] 3rd day 1702.*/15/*

**15123**, Ruth Gawthrop was baptized on 9th month [Nov.] 17th day 1703.*/15/*

**15124**, Thomas Gawthrop (q.v.) was born in the year 1709*/1, 15, 16, 17, 18, 19, 20/* and died 9th month 29th day 1780.*/16, 17, 18, 19/* Thomas became a Quaker minister in 1733. He married Isabel Crosfield on the 31 x. [Dec.] 1735.*[20]*

**15125**, Jane Gawthrop*[15, 17, 19]* was born circa 1715/16*[15]* and was christened 4th month [June] 24th day 1726.*[17]* She was buried at Skipton at age 10 years on 24 April 1726.*[15]*

**15151**, Grace Gawthrop was born 1709-1-23*[1]* (March 23rd) and died 1774-2-3*[1]* (April 3rd).

**15152**, Joseph Gawthrop was born 1718-2-18*[1]* (April 18th). Joseph married Mary Wilson daughter of Henry Wilson of Cononley.*[15]*

**15153**, Hugh Gawthrop was born 1723-2-9*[1]* (April 9th) and died 1724-12-14*[1]* (Feb. 14th).

**15152?**, Hugh Gawthrop*[1]*

**15152??**, William Gawthrop*[1]*

**15152???**, Hugh Gawthrop*[1]*

**15152????**, Arnold E. Gawthrop*[1]*

**15152?????**, John Trevelyen Gawthrop*[1]*

Thomas (15124), son of Hugh (1512), moved to Preston Patrick, England near Kendal.*[1]* Hugh (15152?), son of Joseph (15152) and grandson of William (1515), moved to Liverpool, England.*[1]*

The chart on the next page shows the relationship between Arnold and Charles and develops the two lines of descent. It was noted that our American emigrant ancestor was a second cousin of Arnold E. Gawthrop's great-grandfather and Charles L. was a 5th cousin once removed to Arnold E. (see Appendix B for how relationships are intertwined).


REFERENCES:

SOURCE [1]: Information extracted from *"GAWTHROP," Chapter II, entitled "AN ANGLO-AMERICAN PROBLEM SOLVED,"* written at Christmas 1902 by Horace Henry Gawthrop part of his unfinished manuscript and updated by P.E. Gawthrop in 1990. Obtained at a interview in 1990 with Dorothy L. Hipple, granddaughter of Horace Henry Gawthrop. Note by Horace Henry Gawthrop - ***The part underscored*** in this case highlighted ***are from the Friends' records, all other from church records.***

SOURCE [15]: Letter/Chart dated 11 Jan. 1993 from Brian Clayton, Ilkley, West Yorkshire, England to Philip E. Gawthrop. Follow-on letter from same source dated 5 Feb. 1993. (DE March 1993)

SOURCE [16]: *A handwritten family tree, "OUR CHILDREN'S ANCESTORS,"* compiled by Rev. Darward and Dorothy Brown for their children and grandchildren, no date was available; however, Rev Darward Belmont Brown was born on 12 January 1897. It is thought that the Brown Family Tree and the Everard C. Gawthrop Family Tree were commissioned approximately the same time. P.E.Gawthrop has the original work on Everard's family tree prepared by genealogist G. Cope in the early to mid 1920's.

SOURCE [17]: Genealogy work compiled by Thomas Carr Gawthrop. This manuscript was not published by a publisher; however, Thomas Carr Gawthrop was born Jan. 1938 and died Sept. 1966. This compiled work was obtained from Mary Virginia (Merrifield) Gawthrop wife of Wilbur Edmond Gawthrop (deceased) and her son, Richard Carr Gawthrop in early 1992. Thomas Carr Gawthrop was her nephew and Richard's cousin.

SOURCE [18]: A handwritten family tree prepared for Everard Conard Gawthrop by G. Cope (Jr. ??) of Pittsburgh, PA done in the mid 1920's. Philip Evan Gawthrop (Grandson of Everard) has the original work on this family tree.

SOURCE [19]: A handwritten family tree prepared by Allen Gawthrop in 1871. Allen was the son of Thomas and Elizabeth (Thompson) Gawthrop. The son of Allen and Mary Ann (Newlin) Gawthrop, Henry Gawthrop, collected data from Allen's work along with the assistance of several family members to generate another work entitled *GEORGE GAWTHROP, The Emigrate*, by H. Gawthrop, dated Christmas 1900. Henry's work (in typescript, not published by a publisher) is available from the Friends Historical Library, Swarthmore College, PA.

SOURCE [20]: A.M. Gummere (ed) *The Journal and Essays of John Woolman*, (Philadelphia & London 1922), pages 171 and 577.

## Chart

**1**, Thomas Gawthroppe

**15**, Thomas Gauthrop

**151**, Thomas GAUTHROP (Gawthrop) of Skipton - C: Aug 29, 1641, B: July 1704

| | | |
|---|---|---|
| **1512**, Hugh Gawthrop (C: 1670) (m: Ruth STOTT) | brothers | **1515**, William Gawthrop (C: 1683) (m: Mary of Skipton) |
| **15124**, Thomas Gawthrop (b: 1709, d: 1780) | 1st cousins | **15152**, Joseph Gawthrop (b: 1718) |
| **151246**, George Gawthrop (emigrant) (b: 1743, d: 1795) | 2nd cousins | **15152?**, Hugh Gawthrop |
| **1512461**, Thomas Gawthrop (b: 1774, d: 1851) | 3rd cousins | **15152??**, William Gawthrop |
| **15124615**, Allen Gawthrop (b: 1810, d: 1885) | 4th cousins | **15152???**, Hugh Gawthrop |
| **151246153**, Alfred Gawthrop (b: 1835, d: 1909) | 5th cousins | **15152????**, Arnold E. Gawthrop |
| **1512461532**, Charles L. Gawthrop (b: 1868) | 6th cousins | **15152?????**, John Trevelyen Gawthrop |

# Chapter 4

## Quakerism

The infinite wisdom of God is within reach of even the feeblest of human spirit; the Will of God is voiced in the soul of every man. The faith that God speaks directly to the human spirit and that true and genuine religion must be experienced first-hand is Quakerism. Quakerism arose in the British Isles in the east midland (York, Leeds, Skipton, Shelfield, etc.) in the late 1640's, spreading north (New Castle, Glasgow, Edinburgh, etc.) in 1650 and south (London, Dover, Southhampton, etc.) in 1654. From its inception, the Quaker religion (Society of Friends) and Quakers (Friends) themselves were subject to sporadic persecution (sometime quite severe) throughout the British Isles.

Quakers were persecuted for not attending the "English Church", for holding meeting under the pretense of worship, for refusal to swear an oath[a], for refusal to pay titles (voluntary tax) supporting the "English Church", for opening their shop on Sunday, for travelling on Sunday, for contempt of magistrates and courts (by refusing to remove their hats), for teaching without a bishop's license, etc. to name a few. The Quaker movement was a rebellion against the lack of humanity in the government, the conditions of the prisons, the appalling housing and the inhuman asylums. Everywhere, George Fox ( the founder of the Quakers) could find evidence of man's inhumanity to man, he tryed countering with man's humanity to man. The Quaker could be persecuted under common law, statute law or church law (Canon law). Around 1660 a series of enactments penalized all dissenters including Quakers. Many religious dissenters including Quakers complained about these Acts: the Quaker Act 1662, the Conventicle Acts 1664, 1670 (the later giving the common informer sweeping powers), and the recusancy acts of Elizabeth I and James I (which was originally passed against Roman Catholics), under which Quakers were liable for fines of up to £20 per month and possible loss of land.

The Toleration Act of 1689 passed early in the reign of William and Mary granted freedom of worship to dissenters under certain conditions; however, Quakers were still disdained and prosecuted for non-payment of the voluntary tax supporting the "English Church" and many Quakers incurred penalties under the 18th century militia acts for failure to serve in the fighting military.*/22/*

---

a A famous Quaker, John Archdale, famous for his prominent part in making of three American Colonies – Maine, North Carolina and South Carolina – was elected to the English Parliament in 1698. However, his refusal to take an oath cost him his seat in Parliament, and ended all attempts on the part of English Quakers to enter into public office.*/21/*

Between 1655 and 1662 records show that better than 60 Quakers missionaries arrived in America. These missionaries converted many Christians to their philosophy of inner light with their preaching style and soon established meetings in New England (mainly in the Rhode Island area), New Amsterdam and Long Island (later New York), Maryland, Virginia, and the West Indies. Quakers developed a financial base in West New Jersey and soon took possession of West New Jersey. Then five years later East New Jersey came into the Quaker possession (New Jersey stayed in control of Quakers until it became a royal Colony). In 1682 William Penn's constitution for the place he called Pennsylvania was adopted. Emigration to America had begun on a very large scale and by the end of the 17th century autonomous yearly meetings were in existence in Rhode Island, Maryland, Eastern Pennsylvania, New York, Virginia, North Carolina and a small contingent of Friends in the West Indies.

Between 1656 and 1780, Quakerism played a strong and expanding force in the American Colonies. There were times during that period when it seemed destined to become the religion of choice in America. Quakers leaders clearly expected, from their own writings, that the Society of Friends or the Quaker religion would be the dominate religious belief in America. In Great Britain Quakers were barred from public and political service to the state.[a] The majority of Quakers were forced into a life apart from the main stream. However, in the New World the Quaker ideals had much influence in the political life in America and eventually in the Colonies.

The Old World looked to the New World as the land of promise. No pains were spared to spread the "Quaker Seed" in this new region along the Atlantic coast. By the middle of the 18th century there were more Quakers in the Western hemisphere than in the British Isles.*/21/* By the middle of the 18th century, there were better than 50,000 Quakers in America; about 3,000 Quakers in southern Massachusetts (once the exclusive domain of the Pilgrim Fathers), inland Massachusetts and Rhode Island were predominantly Quakers, Quakers constituted an influential body in the Long Island, inland New York and New York City, about 25,000 Quakers in Pennsylvania, 6,000 Quakers in New Jersey, 3,000 Quakers in Maryland, 5,000 Quakers in Virginia, and 5,000 Quakers in both Carolinas.

These American Quakers believed, with white-hot intensity, the spiritual Principle (always spelled with a capital P) which they thought was destined to revolutionize life, society, civil government and religion. The Principle was the presence of a Divine Light in man, a radiance from the central Light of the spiritual universe, which if responded to, obeyed, and accepted as a guiding star, would lead to the truth. The Quaker belief was that the infinite wisdom of God is within reach of human spirit; the Will of God is voiced in every mans soul.

The great body of American Quakers were neither great saints nor great sinners, neither highly educated or grossly ignorant. In general, they were part of a farming community or county people. In the 17th and 18th centuries, the American Quakers tended to be the coarser element of the Quaker religion. The farming community is apt to be economical somewhat conservative and hence, slow to take a risk. With the Quaker religion so prominent in the colonies, the peripatetic ministers from abroad had great influence in strengthening and preserving Quakerism in the American colonists.[b] These English Quaker ministers were said to be the most spiritual and often the best educated men and women in the Society. These Friends (amoung them there were many British citizens) had originational skills which influenced the Society in many ways. One of the ways in which the British Friends influenced the Meetings was with the Preparative Meetings.

The Friends Preparative Meetings, in general, were set up in about 1700 to attend to the more personal work required to bring the business of the Monthly Meetings into good shape such that Meetings would flow better. The appointees (or overseers or elders) to these Preparative Meetings were generally more experienced and reliable Friends. In the case of an offense to the Quaker Religion, these overseers were expected to quietly reform the offender. If these overseers were successful, then no record was made of the case in the Monthly Meeting.

During the better than ninety years which intervened between the founding of the American colonies and the War of Independence with the English over a hundred Quakers from outside America engaged in this travelling ministry. Many British Friends first told their Preparative Meetings of their wish to travel to visit Friends in America. This is the spirit in which Thomas Gawthrop became a travelling Quaker minister and remained a travelling Friend for over forty seven years.*[23]*

REFERENCES

SOURCE [21]: R.M. Jones, et. al, *THE QUAKERS in the AMERICAN COLONIES*, W.W. Norton & Company, Inc., copyright 1966, Preface by a serior staff of Haverford College, Haverford, Pennsylvania, 1911.

SOURCE [22]: E.H. Milligan & M.J. Thomas, *My Ancestors were Quakers, How can I find out more about them?*, published by Society of Genealogists, London, England, copyright 1983, (Reprinted 1990).

SOURCE [23]: In an unfinished manuscript by Horace Henry Gawthrop called *GAWTHROP, Thomas Gawthrop - Life - Memorial, Chapter III*, page 19, written at Christmas 1902. It is believed, however, that he obtained much of the information about Thomas' death from the Testimony of Kendal Monthly Meeting in *Testimonies Concerning Ministers Deceased*, Vol 3.

Note: Patricia C. O'Donnell, Archivist for the Friends Historical Library of Swarthmore College Pennsylvania has given comments on this chapter in December 1994.

---

b In order to stop the spread of Quakerism, the early New England Puritans looked with disdain on travelling Quaker ministers and they even had a plan (although never enacted) of prohibiting their journeying in the eighteenth century.*[21]*

# Chapter 5

5th Generation

## 15124, THOMAS GAWTHROP (1709 - 1780), the Travelling Friend

Thomas Gawthrop*/15, 16, 17, 18, 19, 23/* was born in 1709 at Skipton, Yorkshire County, England*/15, 25/* the son of Hugh Gawthrop.*/15, 26/* ***His parents were Friends...*** */27/*[a] ***He was born of honest parents of our religious profession at Skipton.*** */28/* ***His father died when he was young and he was apprenticed to a man near Leeds, not a Friend, who did not treat him well. To free himself from this service, he was induced towards the end of his apprenticeship to enlist in the army***[b] ***in which he remained five years. While on leave, on a visit to his relations at Skipton, he attended*** [a] ***meeting, where he was "effectually reached" by the testimony of Mary Slater. From that time he attended meetings whenever opportunity offered, and though he was under great exercise of mind on account of his situation, he was not free to have his discharge purchased, "fearing how he might*** [not] ***stand his ground." An officer, however, offered him his discharge provided he repaid the money which he received upon enlisting, which he did as soon as he had earned enough. He returned to Skipton, where he did not stay long, but during his time there he came forth in public testimony.***[c] ***This was about 1733. He removed to Kendal, and soon after accompanied a Friend on a religious visit to Scotland.*** */29/*

On his return from Scotland, Thomas married a young woman, a Friend of Preston Patrick, Isabel Crosfield, daughter of Simon Crosfield of Lowpark, Preston Patrick, Westmoreland.*/30/* The date of the marriage was 31 x. 1735*/20, 29/* (x. = Dec.). Other sources show the same date in different forms (31 December 1735*/31/*) or the same date but the month shown as a number.*/16, 19, 23/* The site of the marriage was at Park End, near Preston Patrick. They settled within a few miles of Kendal*/29/* (under 5 miles) in the picturesque village of Gatebeck.*/20, 28/* The Gatebeck land plat shown is dated 1771*/32/* (see Map #6) and, although more than 30 years had elapsed since 1735, this plat of land is more than likely where they settled. They called Gatebeck their home for the rest of their lives.

Most of Thomas' life he was a minister for the Society of Friends (47 years). He travelled extensively in the ministry into England and Scotland, and visited Ireland in 1741*/33/*

---

a In a letter to P.E. Gawthrop from Brian Clayton written January 11th, 1993, there is verification, or at least conjecture, to suggest that it was Hugh Gawthrop who took up the Quaker faith. The reason for this conjecture is that some of Hugh's first born children, Bebekkay and Ruth to be exact, were baptized in the Skipton Parish Church but his remaining children, Thomas and Jane, are not recorded in this church. There is an exception; the burial of Jane age 10 years in 1726.

b He was about 17 years of age when he went into the Army.

c ***Coming forth in public testimony*** indicates that members of his monthly meeting (church), and Quakers in general, revered him as a minister.

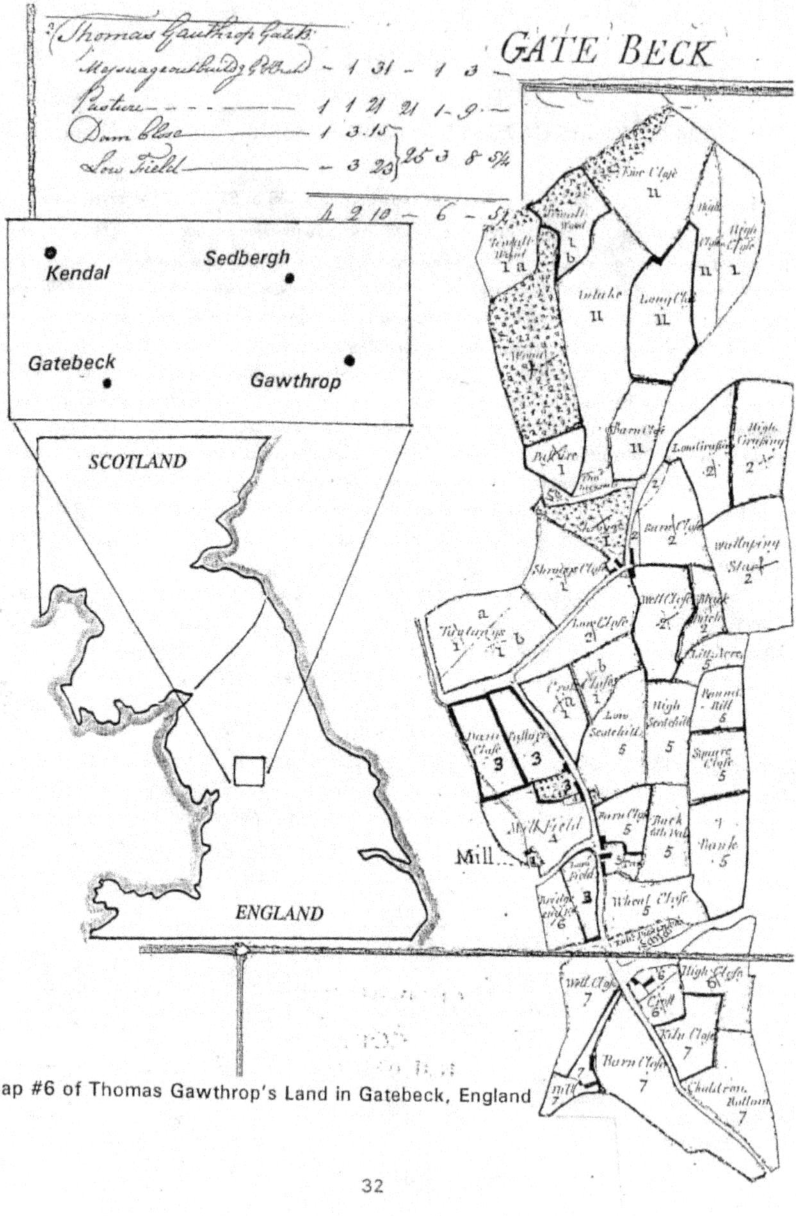


Map #6 of Thomas Gawthrop's Land in Gatebeck, England

and 1769[34]. When Thomas visited Ireland in 1741 he attended a six day meeting where ***...his concern was chiefly to the Elders being very strong and fervent, saying it was one thing to begin well, and another thing to end well, ...*** *[33]* On another day at this six day meeting, ***He had a meeting with the Young People, which was pretty well attended by them wherein he laboured plainly and fully with them, yet in great love and tenderness, Saying he sympathiz'd*** (sic) ***with poor tempted souls that the Enemy was likely to be too hard for, It seem'd to have good effect on some, and he was generally lik'd*** (sic). *[33]* Thomas also visited Friends in America five times, in 1739, 1747, 1756/7, 1766 and 1775.

Samuel Fothergill, who was himself a revered Quaker minister, recalls soon after Thomas came forth in the ministry, ***his mind being devoted to the service of his great Master, and obedient to the manifestations of Truth, he grew in the gift received, and became a deep and able minister of the gospel; diligently labouring, in the openings of life, for the exaltation of Truth in the hearts of the people.*** *[35]* Fothergill writes about the pertinent counsel Thomas delivered, ***... not in the wisdom of the man, nor in the eloquence of words, but in the simplicity of the gospel, and with the demonstration of Divine authority. He, nevertheless, often found it his place to repress a too eager desire after words, by setting an example of humble and awful worship in solemn silence.*** *[35]*

**1739**

Thomas Gawthrop's first appearance in America was reportedly at ***the Yearly Meeting in Philadelphia in 1739.*** *[21]*[d] ***There can be no doubt that the peripatetic ministers, both English and American, had a great influence in strengthening and preserving Quakerism among the colonists. They were the most spiritual and often the best educated men and women of the Society. They were listened to, especially those for England, with the greatest respect. Their journals nearly always speak of the great crowds which attended their ministry. ... the following ministers from abroad were engaged in religious visits in Philadelphia Yearly Meeting:- ... 1739 Thomas Gawthrop . . . Westmoreland.*** *[21]* Not much more is reported of this minister from England except that he was from Westmoreland. He became a publick Friend in 1733 and, in the six intervening years between 1733 to 1739, he would have had the time to developed many of his virtuous attitudes. It is believed he returned home in the fall of 1739.[e]

**1740/1741**

The Friends Preparative Meetings, in general, were set up in about 1700 to attend to the more personal work required to bring the business of the Monthly Meetings into good shape such that the Meetings would flow better. The appointees (or overseers) to these

---

d E. Michener in *A Retrospect of Early Quakerism*, (reference 36) states that the Yearly Meetings were alternated between Burlington, NJ and Philadelphia, PA. Burlington was the site of the Yearly Meeting in 1739. So ***the Yearly Meeting in Philadelphia in 1739*** probably meant the Burlington\Philadelphia.

e Thomas Gawthrop's daughter, Ruth, was born on November 1, 1739 and it was felt that he would have been home for this birth. There is also evidence that he stayed at home at least until late fall 1741; Hugh, his second son's birth-date was 15 May 1741. Thus, calculating backwards, it was late summer/early fall of 1740 that Hugh was conceived.

Preparative Meetings were generally the more experienced and reliable Friends. In the case of an offense to the Quaker Religion, these overseers were expected to quietly reform the offender. If these overseers were successful, then no record of the case was made at the Monthly Meeting. In the Preston Patrick Men's Preparative Meeting, Thomas' name appeared on the 27th day of the 12th month 1740 (27 Feb.*[37]* [f]). He was also appointed to the next Preparative Monthly Meeting.*[38]* Thomas, at the age of 31, was looked on in a different light, more like an elder. He had several children, a loving wife and was devoted to the service of The Master.

In the minutes of the Men's Preparative Meeting of the 1st day of the 9th month 1741 (1 Nov.), ***Tho Gawthrop lays before this meeting that he has had for some time ammed*** (aimed) ***to visit friends in Ireland and desires that he may acquaint the mo. meeting therewith to wch*** (which) ***this meeting agrees and desires Ric. Sill and Hen. Skyrin to provide a few lines by way of Certificate.****[38]* Another reference verifies that he visited Ireland in 1741.*[33]* Apparently, he travelled to Ireland very soon after the third son, James, was conceived.[g] He came back from Ireland early summer that next year (1742) for the birth of James. There is no record found of Thomas' travelling from mid-year 1742 to the spring of 1747. To add credence to this assertion that Thomas did not travel; George, his forth son, was conceived early in 1743.[h]

## 1746/1747

In the Preston Patrick Men's Preparative Meeting, Thomas requested a visit to America at the meeting of the 27th of the 5th month 1746 (27 July).*[38]* Apparently the Preston Patrick Preparative Meeting had passed on Thomas' request to visit America to the Hindsles Monthly Meeting and then on to the Grace Street Monthly Meeting because on the 11th day of the 2nd month 1747 (11 April), Thomas appeared in Virginia at the Cedar Creek Monthly Meeting. He showed that he had received certificates from Hindsles Monthly Meeting, Westmoreland Co., England, dated the 6th day of the 6th month 1746 (6 Aug.) and from Grace Street Monthly Meeting, London, England, dated the 1st day of the 7th month 1746 (1 Sept.).*[40]*

---

f The Julian Calendar was adopted by the Romans over 1600 years ago. In 1582, Pope Gregory XIII gave us what is known as the Gregorian Calendar. Because the Gregorian Calendar originated with the Catholic Church, it was not universal excepted by English Protestants. An Act by the English Parliament in 1751 set the date for the universal adoption of the Gregorian Calendar at January 1, 1752. The Julian Calendar had the 1st month being March, the 2nd month was April, 3rd month was May, and so on with the 12th month being February. The new style Gregorian Calendar had the 1st month being January, 2nd month was February, 3rd month was March, etc with the 12th month being December.

g James' birth-date was 4 July 1742. Thus, calculating backwards, it was late fall when James was conceived (after Nov. 1741). (Date of comment April 1994)

h George's birth-date was 17 Dec. 1743. Thus, calculating backwards, it was early spring of 1743 that George was conceived. (Date of comment April 1994)

**O**n the 3rd day of the 5th month 1747 (3 July), Thomas wrote from New York to Israel Pemberton Jr. in Philadelphia concerning his worries that life in America had affected some Friends in roguish ways. He writes, ... ***oft have had to say it was good for me that I was aflicted*** (sic), ***wounded and brused*** (sic) ***by ye foul friends.*** *[41, in Appendix-A]* This was Thomas' second trip to America[i] and he may not have been ready for the brash treatment that he received from many of his American Friends. Horse racing, fighting, open profaneness, immorality, disorderly conduct of going out of Meetings during the time of worship and excessive drinking were disturbing to many English Friends including Thomas. He was from the small English village of Gatebeck and many of these American Friends relied on the rough and ready nature of pioneer quakerism that was new and exciting in this land. Many American Quakers had very little education or the desire to obtain such education because practical education in the trades, especially in America, was considered very important.

**T**homas visited Nantucket Island (Mass) Meeting in 1747. *[42]* There is also a record of his visiting Newport (Rhode Island) Meeting in the 5th month 1747. *[43]* At this meeting it is said that Thomas was an exemplary Friend who exerted much influence wherever and whenever he spoke. *[43]* John Woolman's Journal mentions meeting Thomas in his travels in New England in the summer of 1747. Woolman's Journal says, ***We visited Friends in and about Newport and Dartmouth, and the meetings generaly*** (sic) ***in those parts, and then to Bostony, and proceeded Eastward as far as Dover*** [New Hampshire], ***and then returned to Newport, and not far from thence,*** [we] ***met our Friend Thomas Gawthrop from England, who was on a visit to these parts.*** *[20]*

**I**t is clear that Thomas made several stops in his pilgrimage of America in 1747. One might speculate that he landed in the early spring of 1747, travelled to Virginia in April, then travelled to New York and New England in June/July, and then came back to Philadelphia in October/November. Thomas may have stayed with some Friends who lived in the Philadelphia area but no record is found of his visiting any friends in Philadelphia.

**O**n the 30th day of the 9th month 1747 (30 Nov.), Thomas, John Griffith, Peter Davis, and a merchant, Isaac Greenleaf travelled from Philadelphia to Chester, Pennsylvania, a trip was about 25 miles, for a voyage to England (see Map #7). *The Widow*, a new ship, was their choice for the voyage. There were many well wishers (mainly Friends) at Chester. That evening, after arriving at Chester, the assembly met at an ancient Friends house, Grace Lloyd's house, for a solemn Meeting.

**J**ohn Griffith's Journal recounts these plans, ***Soon after my health was restored, an ancient friend, whose name was Peter Davis, from New-England, came to Philadelphia, in order to take a passage for England, and our friend Thomas Gawthrop, having performed a religious visit to friends***

---

i This is believed to be his first religious trip; he may have travelled in 1739, as is referenced in R.M. Jones, THE QUAKERS in the AMERICAN COLONIES, on his own using his own money.

Map #7 of the East Coast of America (Enlargement of Delaware Bay & River)

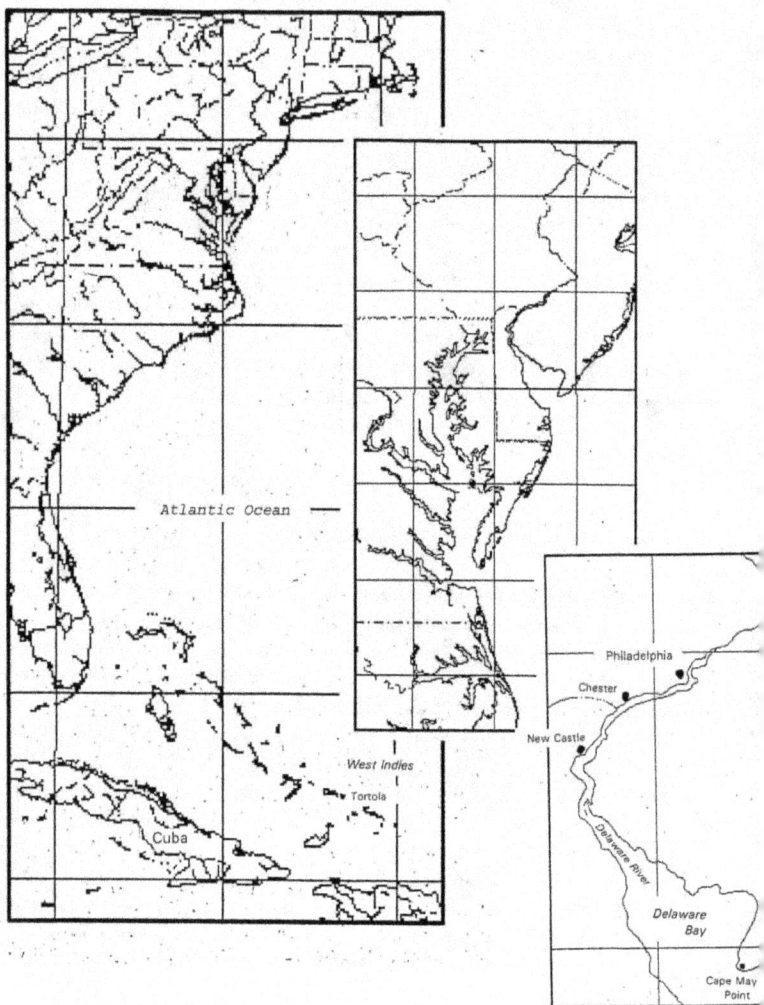

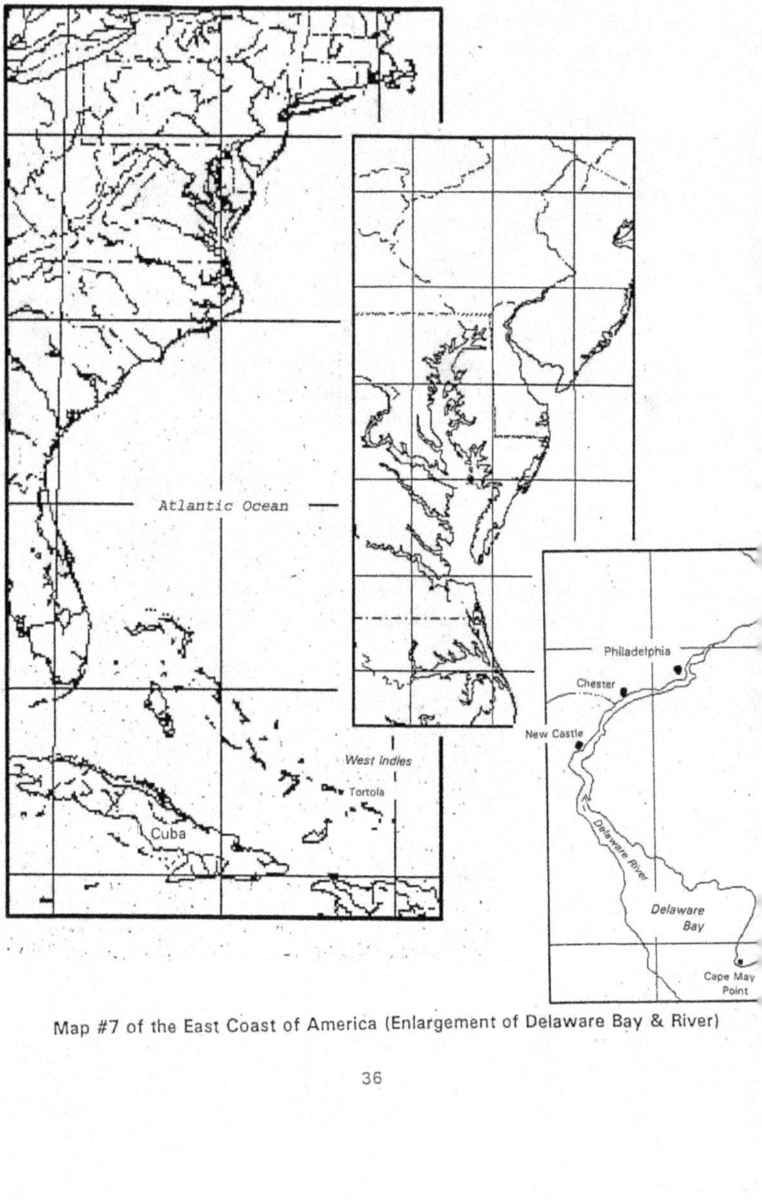

on the continent of America, intending to embark shortly for the same, with Isaac Greenleaf, a friend on trade, I joined, them; all agreeing to take our passage in a new ship bound for London. .... On the 30th of the 9th month 1747, the before-mentioned friends, who were to be my companions upon the mighty ocean, set out from Philadelphia, in order to embark at Chester, in company with many friends, and called for me at my house in Derby, being [on] the direct road./44/ Their probable route was from Philadelphia through Darby, Collingdale, Sharon Hill, Glen Olden, Norwood, Prospect Park, Ridley Park, Eddystone, to Chester (see Map #8).

On the 1st day of the 10th month 1747 (1 Dec.) at two o'clock in the afternoon this group boarded *The Widow* and began their voyage by setting sail down the Delaware River. Late that same evening *The Widow* anchored just below New Castle, Delaware. John Griffith's Journal recounts this, *Next day, being the 1st of the 10th month, about two o'clock in the afternoon, we took leave of friends, in great love and tenderness, and went on board the ship, which fell down the river that evening, a little lower than Newcastle./44/* From on-board ship at their first anchorage point, Thomas wrote a letter to Israel Pemberton Jr. This letter gives a brief account of how the ministers were cheerful and that he would write to Israel later in the voyage./46, in Appendix-A/ Thomas had spent a very productive pilgrimage in the colonies, travelling throughout most of the known new world. The pilgrimage was over and apparently, there was the natural inclination to be cheerful because he was going home to his family.

The next evening they anchored near Reedy Island where the ship and passengers experienced delay by an intense storm that lasted until the morning of the 5th day of the voyage. While the ship was waylaid at Reddy Island by the storm, Thomas wrote to Israel Pemberton Jr. about a piece of property, 1,728 acres of land in West New Jersey, which he had bought with Israel's money. This letter was written on the 4th day of the 10th month 1747 and has a promissory note (bill of sale) which is transcribed below./47, 48, in Appendix-A/

Promise to Make and Deliver to Thos. Gawthrop or order Twelve months after date hereof, a Good and Sufficent (sic) Deed or Conveyance for a Warrent (sic) Granted to Wm. Stub (which my Partner John Hunt bought of him) for One Thousand seven hundred & Twenty Eight Acres of Land to be taken Up's in the 3rd & 4th Dividend Right's in the Province of West New Jersey, which said Warrent (sic) I have left in the hands of Joseph Cooper in Glocester County in the said Province unts (sic) whom I have given order this day to Deliver to said Warrent (sic) to Thos. Gawthrop or his Order, In Consideration whereof I have this day Received the Sum of Fifty five pounds Pennsylvania (some word that is indistinguishable).

Ready Island, 2nd day of the x month 1747,

£55                              For   Jn.   Hunt   &   self,   (Isaac
                                 Greenleaf signature)

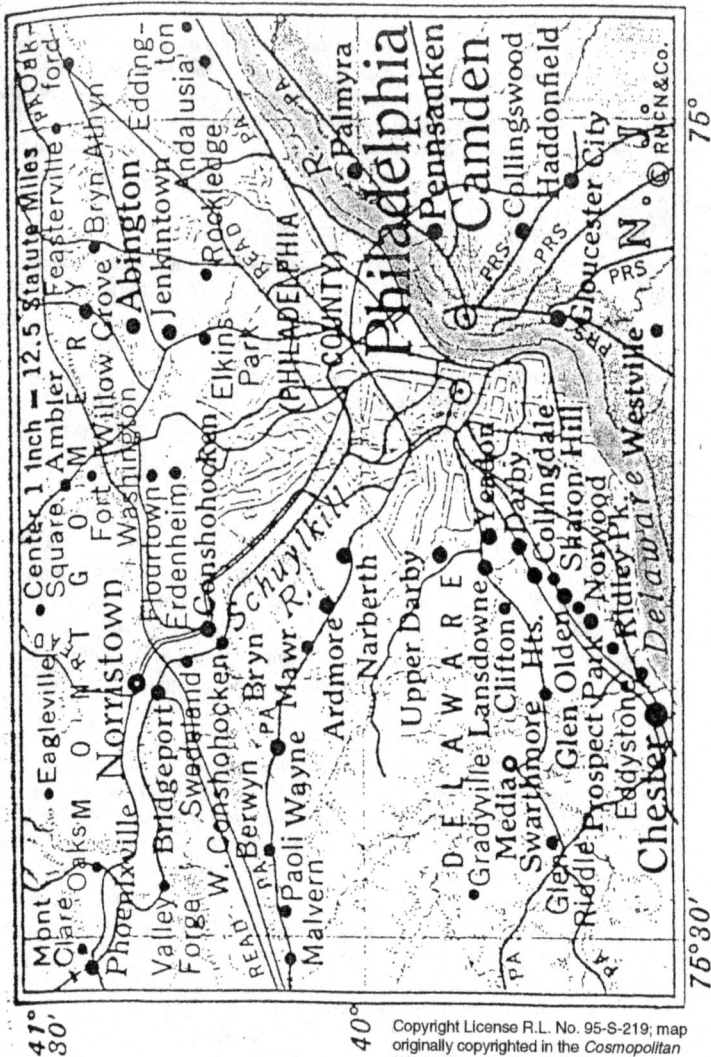

Copyright License R.L. No. 95-S-219; map originally copyrighted in the *Cosmopolitan World Atlas Centennial Edition 1956.*

Map #8 of the towns of Philadelphia, Chester and surrounding area

On the 5th day of the 10th month 1747 (5 Dec.) at 6 o'clock in the evening, the ship sailed out of the Delaware Bay into the Atlantic Ocean. The ship had good sailing with very strong wind until the 18th day out or by the Captain calculations about 2/3 of their passage. The ship experienced milder yet still favorable weather until the 23rd day out. For the next six days the ship experienced very stormy weather. The waves were so violent that the ship, although she was a new ship, almost sunk several time, or at least it appeared so to the passengers. However, the morning of the 29th, although beaten and battered, *The Widow*, her crew and her passengers were still afloat. This day proved to be the last time during *The Widow's* voyage that piece and harmony existed amoung its occupancy. Again John Griffith Journal recounts, *The 29th proved a fine day, so that they had a good observation, and judged we were then about a hundred and fifty leagues from the Land's-End of England.[44]*

Early in the morning on the 30th day out, Thomas stepped on deck and saw a sail off in the distance. Thomas had a troublesome night and dreamed of being taken captive and, therefore, he quickly brought the sighting of a sail to the attention of the captain. The captain soon perceived that his ship was being chased. He then almost appeared to give up because his crew was so poorly manned due, in part, to their London destination. The captain had stated many times that he was unable to get the best crew because of the unwillingness to serve in any ship bound for Great Britain. The ministers urged the captain to try and escape. *The Widow* soon was sailing through the gentle whitecap in an attempt to outdistance their pursuer. However, at five o'clock that evening, after a nine hour chase, the ship was overtaken and captured by a French Privateer.[44, 49]

The year was 1747, during the war between England, France and Spain, when this illustrious group of Thomas Gawthrop, John Griffith, Peter Davis and Isaac Greenleaf, set sail from Chester Pennsylvania bound for Great Britain. *... some friends, and, as I understood, some others also, taking notice how providentially publick (sic) friends had been preserved during the war, which was then with France and Spain, so that none of them had been taken by the enemy, did presume thereon; and would say There is no need to insure goods in that ship, as so many publick (sic) friends are going in her; she will doubtless go safe.[44]* In other words, that Friends are seen as providentially preserved { seen as lucky } during the war and that the ships carrying Quaker ministers would no doubt go safe.[49] However, the ship was captured by a French vessel[44] commanded by Captain Peter Garalon with the second in command, second Captain Andrew De St. Andrew. The privateer ship *... was a snow privateer belonging to Bayonne, mounting ten carriage guns, and about one hundred men...[44]* He (Captain De St. Andrew) *took notice, that we were of the people called Quakers; by which he gave us to understand, that he was not altogether a stranger to us as a people.[44]* Captain Andrew showed compassion for the non-fighting Quakers and he promised the ministers good passage to some port in either France or Spain because they were Quakers. He also allowed them to stay the seized ship because it was more comfortable then his privateer.[49]

***C**aptains Garalon and De St. Andrew decided to escort the seized ship into Spanish waters before looting its cargo. Looting the cargo may not have been the motive for the escort, the captains had designs on the ship itself. It was on this journey that it became clear that if the Widow's crew had been better manned, they could have out sailed the French privateer. It also became clear to the ministers during this voyage why the two captains valued this captured ship as a prize; it had speed.

***I**t was twenty five days after the ship was seized and fifty five days out of Chester that the ministers finally saw land again, the Spanish coastline (see Map #9). The two ships sailed into the Spanish coastal port of San Sebastian on the 24th day of the 11th month 1748 (24 Jan.). However, a severe storm drove both ships out to sea again and eventually into separate ports. On the 26th, the captives went ashore in the sea-port called St. Jean-de-Luz. The three ministers and the merchant were glad to have solid ground under their feet again.*[44]* Only the French privateer's doctor accompanied them on horseback some thirty miles to Bayonne, France where Captain De St. Andrew had told the ministers that they would be paroled (set free). The ministers were expecting to be set free and for that reason they did not try an escape; however, this freedom was not to be.*[49]*

***T**he ministers spent more than a month as prisoners of war. The first few days were spent at Bayonne and then they travelled to Darc (also called Dax*[44]*) for their remaining captivity. Darc, France is an ancient town arrived at by water some forty five miles up river from Bayonne.*[49]* These three ministers and the merchant were incarcerate in a plush castle in Bayonne. When transferred to Darc, however, they were in less plush quarters but allowed to keep their clothes, papers and money. The money, however, went quickly because they had to bribe guards for everything.

***O**n the 21st day of the 12th month 1747 (21 Feb.), a messenger from Bayonne brought news of a cartel-ship[j] from England that arrived in Port-Passage. This messenger also brought an order for the ministers to leave Darc and to embark for England from Port-Passage on the 24th. Leaving Port-Passage, the cartel-ship sailed to St. Jean-de-Luz and then on to San Sebastian. Thomas wrote to Israel Pemberton in Philadelphia via. Lisbon while in San Sebastian. He gave brief details of their incarceration and subsequent release, ***We arived*** (sic) ***at Beyon*** (Bayonne) ***was put in ye Chatto in nafty Louse beds and very poor provisions 24 of 11m. We got leave to go to Dax with 14 other prisoners where we stade*** (sic) ***till ye 24*** [of the 12th month] ***when ye Cartteel*** (Cartel) ***was come to passage. We returned to Beyon*** (Bayonne) ***and so to this place*** [San Sabastian]. ***We hope to embark for England tomorrow if ye wind is fare.****[50, in Appendix-A]* The Captain of the cartel-ship took several weeks to re-secure a crew in San Sabestian. The reason for having to re-secure a crew and for the delay in time was the

---

j *Webster's New World Dictionary of the American Language*, copyright 1963, defines cartel as a written agreement between nations at war especially as to the exchange of prisoners.

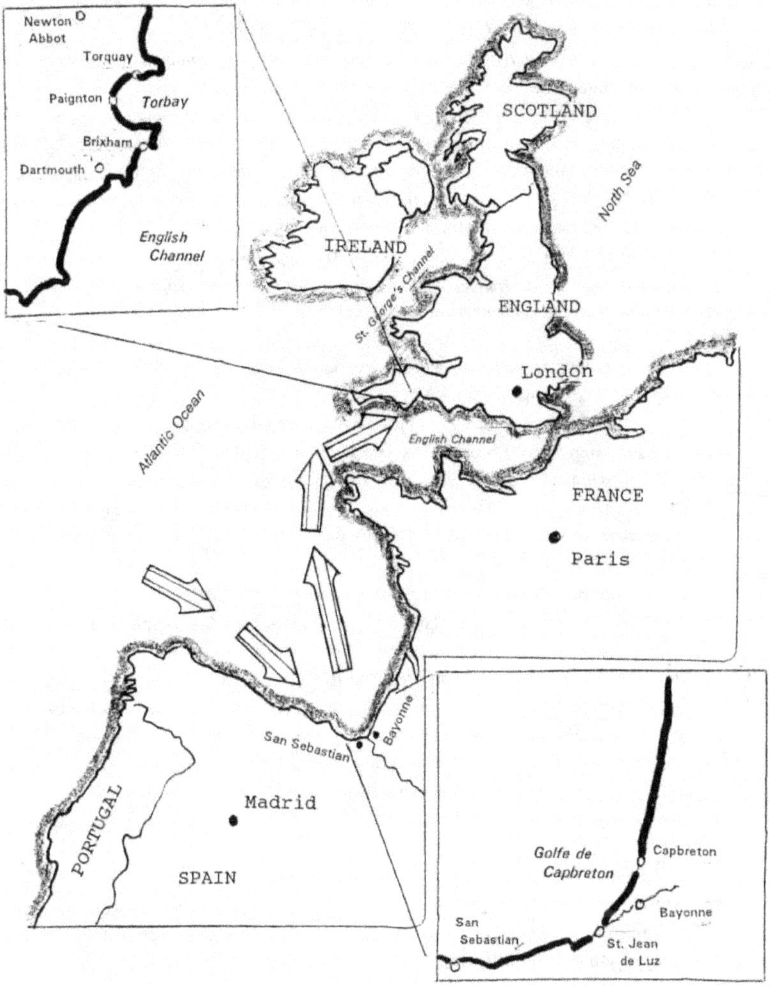


Map #9 of Spain, France and the British Isles

destination, England, and the route, up the England Channel. On the 21th of March the ministers boarded that same cartel-ship bound for England.

The journey proved difficult for the ministers; bad weather and mutinous strife on-board the ship. The weather was very stormy but the crew had their own stormy attitude. The ship was bound for Plymouth within the channel between France and England. Many of the ship's crew had been prisoners in France (or in the French Navy) and felt that if they continued sailing up the channel, more than likely, they would be captured again. Therefore, without spilling any blood, the crew mutinied. The captain pleaded with the crew telling them mutiny was punishable by death, but to no avail.

John Griffith's Journal confirms this, ***The ship was bound for Plymouth, but the sailors, who had been prisoners in France, being in fear of another confinement, by being pressed on board of the men of war, took the command of her from the captain, by something, in appearance at least, like force.*** */44/*

This predominately Spanish crew now had two enemies, the French because they were at war, and the British because they mutinied. So, because of this mutiny, the crew anchored a considered distance from the town of Brixham, England just outside of Torbay Bay (see Map #8). This was on the 26th of the 1st month 1748 (26 March), after a passage of only 5 days. Again because the ship was under the control of a mutinous crew, the ministers still had the problem of getting ashore. Over objections of several crew members, the ministers (Thomas, John Griffith, Peter Davis and one non-minister, Isaac Greenleaf) were put ashore to find some religious relief.

By inquirer in Brixham, Thomas found a meeting of Friends was held near a place called Newton-Bushel some ten miles inland. */44/* This was small Meeting but the Friends showed much love toward the captured ministers. On their second day of freedom in England, the four set out for London. They only travelled to Exeter, under 24 kilometers, because of the declining health of Peter Davis. Some Friends at Exeter took them into their homes, fed them, and allowed them to bed-down for the night. Those same Friends expressed much concern over the health of Peter Davis. The next day Thomas, John Griffith and Isaac Greenleaf again set out for London on horseback leaving behind the ancient Friend, Peter Davis. They soon parted company at Honiton, England */24/* and Thomas went on to London while the others went to Bridgeport. */44/*

Thomas writes to Israel Pemberton of Philadelphia from London on the 8th day of the 2nd month 1748 (8 April) and again from Warrington, England on the 19th day of the 2nd month 1748 (19 April) while on the return trip home after being captured. */51, 52, in Appendix-A/* The letters reiterated the account of their capture and subsequent release. However, the Post Script (P.S.) in the London letter gives a hint of Thomas' concern about the warrent that he purchased from Isaac Greenleaf for a tract of land in West New Jersey. Thomas felt, because of their capture and the delay it caused, that John Hunt might not honor the agreement.

Thomas writes from his home on the 27th day of September 1748 to Israel Pemberton. He says, ***...I gave thee account that I. Greenleaf can't make any title of ye land. J. Hunt having soul*** (sold) ***it to E. Lar***[gg [k]] ***who was unwilling to give up ye part of ye bargan*** (sic) ***tho I have good reson*** (sic) ***to think their contact was not fully complete till some time after I had bought and pade*** (paid) ***for it. I was sorry for I. Greenleaf for either he had a right to sell or not. J. Hunt said he had none*** [the right to sell] ***and that seems to fix it.*** *[53, in Appendix – A]*

Thomas travelled from his home to London in 1753 for the Yearly Meeting of Ministers and Elders. At the same time in London there was the Yearly Meeting of Women Friends. He writes to Israel Pemberton Jr. concerning those meetings. The P.S. gives some more details about the Warrent for 1728 acres in West Jersey that Thomas thought he had bought from Isaac Greenleaf. Thomas writes, ***P.S. May just give thee ye hint last night I spoke with J. Hunt conserning*** (sic) ***ye warrent*** (sic) ***thou advised*** [me] ***to buy. He sade*** (said) ***he would give me 20 Gunies*** (sic) ***for releasing ye bargin*** (sic) ***which will in full satisfy me when it coms*** (sic) ***to my hands.*** [J. Hunt] ***shall give thee advise to draw for ye same from E. Largg. J. Hunt saith*** [he] ***disputes ye paying for ye lands alltho*** (sic) ***he hath given his bond for ye money, ...*** *[54, in Appendix-A]*
John Hunt had valid reasons for his doughts; the transaction entered into was on Thomas' and Isaac Greenleaf's voyage and eventual capture in 1747. Hunt probably did not receive any money for the property because, although the captains allowed the prisoners to keep their clothes, papers and money, the money went quickly to bribe guards. There is also a chance that Hunt did not know that the property was sold because of the lengthy incarceration of Isaac Greenleaf.

## 1754/1755

In the Preston Patrick Men's Preparative Meeting, Thomas was chosen to represent the meeting on several occasions:-

- -on the 31st day of the 5th month 1754 (31 May*[37]*) with George Crosfield (his Brother-in-law),
- -on the 21st day of the 6th month 1754 with Thomas Newby,
- -on the 28th day of the 5th month 1755 with Richard Sill,
- -on the 18th day of the 6th month 1755 with Edward Sill.

George Crosfield, Thomas Newby, Richard Sill and Edward Sill were all prominent people within the Quaker establishment in Preston Patrick.*[55]* There is no way to tell who was more dominate; it may have just been age in those days that sets ministers apart from others in the ministry or it may have been the person who felt the Spirit of God within himself or herself.

In the Preparative Meeting held on the 20th day of the 9th month 1754, ***Thos Gawthrop***

---

k Thomas refers to an "E. Largg" in the postscript of a letter written from London, June 17, 1753. It is therefore assumed that E. Lar is really "E. Largg."

***and George Crosfield are desired to collect the Sufferings of Friends belonging to this meeting and advise therupon*** (sic) ***as they may see occacion*** (sic).*[55]*

In the Preparative Meeting held on the 21th day of the 9th month 1755, Thomas advised this Meeting that he wishes to go to America. The Meeting Minutes read, ***Our Friend Thomas Gawthrop hath this day aquainted*** (sic) ***us that for several years he has had drawings on his mind to pay a religious visit to friends in America ...****[55]* The minutes go on to say ...***this Meeting hath solidly weighd*** (sic) [the request] ***and gives him to this liberty, and appoints Rich Sill, Thomas Sill, and George Crosfield to prepare a few lines by way of Certificate to be laid before said Monthly Meeting.****[55]* Benjamin Ferris remember five English Friends at the Yearly Meeting in Philadelphia on the 17th day of the 9th month, 1757. He writes in his Journal, ***Five European Friends attended this meeting, namely, Thomas Gawthrop, John Hunt, Christopher Wilson, Wm. Reckitt and Samuel Sparvold.****[56]* Benjamin Ferris also remembers the counsel and love delivered by Thomas, ***In the 10th month*** [1757], ***being in Philadelphia, I attended at a meeting where Thomas Gawthrop attend, and it was a tendering time for me, under a renewed visitation of Divine Love. In the evening I went to see T. Gawthrop, who was about departing for England.****[56]*

## 1756/1757

Undeterred by his former experience at the hands of the French, Thomas again visited America. He writes from Liverpool on the 25th day of Jan. 1756 (where he was bound for America) that, ***Our Cap***–[tain] ***has great markets hear for provistions*** (sic) ***it's likly*** (sic) ***we must stay hear 2 to 3 days.****[57, in Appendix-A]* The voyage took about 3 months because he landed at Rhoade Island on April 25, 1756. There is a record of his visiting Newport (Rhode Island) in the 5th month 1756.*[43]* He also visited Nantucket Island (Mass) Meeting in 1756.*[42]* He stayed in New England visiting different Friends until the Yearly Meeting at Portsmouth, Road Island. Thomas had heard rumors about the lack of English ministers visiting the Virgin Islands. There was a period between 1750 to 1756 that no travelling Friend visited Tortola. Thomas Gawthrop chose to visit the Virgin Islands in the early spring in 1756, as is quoted in the *Tortola, a Quaker experiment of long ago in the tropics,* ***A Friend reached Tortola, in the person of Thomas Gawthrop, of Westmoreland, England.****[31]* When Thomas returned to America, he wrote to Israel Pemberton Jr. from Rhode Island saying he was appalled that some English Friends had returned home without stopping in the Virgin Islands. He writes, ***Have been at Tortola*** [Virgin Islands] ***and if I had thoughts our English Friends had not been gone home*** [they] ***should have been glad to have seen or at least writ to them ...****[58, in Appendix-A]* Thomas goes to say that the Virgin Islands are worthy of a visit from any English Friends. The Indians there believing that The Load had sent the English ministers to preach His almighty word. Thomas says that if the Virgin Islands were on the Continent and if the people were not just West Indians, they would get visitors from England much more often.

Thomas writes in that same letter to Israel Pemberton Jr., ***I left Tortola near four week ago.****[58, in Appendix-A]* He visited the West Indies and Tortola about the third or fourth week in March 1756. He gave encouragement the small group of Friends that made the islands their home. He was developing a genuine concern for any negro slave in any location but he was particularly concerned with the suffering and hard life of the poor individuals that he found there on the islands. The people on the Island respected him because of his wonderful sermons, so that when he left for America he was asked to take the Torlota Monthly Meeting minutes dated the 29th day of the 3rd month 1756 to be recorded by the ***Friends and Brethren at Barbadoes*** (sic)...*[31]* However, Thomas could not find passage, he writes, ... ***could meet with no passage to Barbados nor yeat*** (sic) ***to Antegue*** (sic).*[58]*

***H***e left the West Indies bound for America in the later part of March 1756. After about a month's journey along the coast of America, he land at Rhoade Island. He spent about ¼ of that year on the water; departed England via ship in late January 1756, departed the West Indies via ship in late March 1756 and arrived in Rhoade Island in late April 1756. In the Biographical Sketches and Anecdotes of Members of Religious Society of Friends, Thomas Gawthrop is referred to as ... ***that honest old seaman ...****[23]* This allusion of him as a seaman is, apparently, an indication that, in order to make his third religious visit to America, he worked his passage as a sailor.*[23]*

***A***lthough Thomas was viewed as an honest sailor, he still was a staunch Quaker. In an expression of today, he was a conscientious objector. In a letter written in Blackwater, VA to Samuel Fothergill on the 8th day of the 12th month 1756, he writes, ... ***Friends were much distressed about training*** [of troops], ***in New England and New York governments; and though some could not suffer, yet a good number were faithful in the testimony they were called to bear on behalf of their Load; who said, "My kingdom is not of this world; if it were, then would my servants fight, that I should not be delivered to the Jews;" so that if, as servants of Christ, they could not fight for their Master's life, much less for their own lives; and if not fight, not train, nor pay others to do that for them, which they believe they should not do either for their Master or themselves.****[34]* In that same letter he writes, ***I hope thou wilt sometimes remember me, a poor traveller in these perilous times, with desires that fortitude and wisdom from on high may be my armour, whilst I have to pass through the broken ranks of these hosts, where sword is set against sword, and the divisions are so great, even amongst the first born of the son of Jacob; for which my heart and bowels are pained within me.****[35]*

***T***homas left New England in 1757 for the Yearly Meeting in Burlington, NJ. The first Yearly Meeting of the Friends on the Delaware River began in Burlington in 1681, and held there alternately with Philadelphia from 1685 to 1760.*[36, 59]* Also that same year of 1681, William Penn was granted the piece of property known as Pennsylvania and under his direction, Pennsylvania had a large influx of Quakers and Quaker settlements. So in 1757, by numbers alone, Burlington/Philadelphia was the center of Quaker society in the new world.

***T***here is no record found of Thomas Gawthrop speaking in the minutes of Yearly Meeting at Bulington in 1757. However, as Samuel Fothergill remembers early in Thomas' ministry and as John Griffith remembers later in Thomas' ministry, Thomas may have sat through the entire meeting in silence and then afterward giving counsel to some close friends.

Although no record was found in the minutes of Yearly Meeting, Thomas must have had an impact on John Pemberton. A letter is added from John Pemberton to Samuel Fothergill showing the character and great respect in which Thomas Gawthrop was held:

***Philadelphia, First Mo. 11th, 1757.***

> ***Our Yearly Meeting at Burlington was a time of great favour to the upright. Honest Thomas Gawthrop was there, and had some very satisfactory opportunities in public. In the meeting of ministers John Churchman told me he thought him equal at least to any he had ever heard. In the meetings for discipline, he was several times singularly favoured; but it is not often he is permitted thus to ascend; his path is trodden by few, and he is often reduced so low, both in body and mind, as to be scarcely able to keep on his feet.*** *[28]*

With the Yearly Meeting complete, Thomas travelled down the Delaware River to Wilmington. His whereabouts are stated in the minutes of the Wilmington Monthly Meeting, ***Thomas Gawthrop, from Westmoreland, Eng., visited the meeting in 1757.*** *[28]* There is no record of his stopping in or around the Philadelphia area; however, many of his close friends lived in that area. In all likelihood he could have stayed with Friends like Israel Pemberton or Israel Pemberton Jr. or John Pemberton or John Griffith or perhaps he stayed with more then one Friend.

Thomas writes to Israel Pemberton Jr. from Cape May on-broad ship, *The Snow Bunbar,* bound for Barbados on the June 12, 1757. He writes ... ***this is writ about ye midel*** (middle) ***of ye Bay*** [Delaware Bay] ***we were across*** [from] ***New Castle yesterday morning about 9 o'clock ...*** *[60, in Appendix-A]* He must have felt strongly about visits from English Friends to the West Indies because this was his second trip visiting there on his third visit to America. After staying for a few months with Friends in Barbados, Thomas came back to the Philadelphia area. On October 24, 1757 he writes from on-broad ship, *The Philadelphia*, bound for Liverpool. In his letter he thanks Israel for the articles (presumable clothes, necessaries, etc.) that Israel sent to him via the Captain of the shuttle (pilot boat). Thomas bids Israel and family farewell and hope to hear of him when he arrives in England. *[61, in Appendix-A]*

The following anecdote is from the "Life of George Dillwyn" (again found in the Biographical Sketches and Anecdotes of Members of Religious Society of Friends):

> ***When Thomas Gawthrop, that honest old seaman, was on his second[1] religious visit to this country, in the year 1755, or 6; he was sitting at the dinner-table in a Friends' house, when George Dillwyn entered the room whistling in his usual thoughtless manner. Thomas ceased eating, laid down his knife, and in accents of strong feeling, said, "I wished for the wings of a dove to be with you; and now you make my heart sick." This short sermon made a powerful impression on the lad to whom it was addressed, and it was remembered and repeated by him in very advanced life.*** *[24]*

There are two letters written by Thomas Gawthrop on Nov. 13th, 1757 and Nov. 19th, 1757 from the Isle of Ely, West of Scotland to Israel Pemberton Jr. and John Pemberton, both of Philadelphia.*[Appendix-A]* Thomas travelled throughout England, Ireland and Scotland for the next several years.

On December 5th, 1759, there is a reference in the Preston Patrick Preparative Meeting of Thomas Gawthrop, the younger (Thomas' first son). The reference says that Thomas Gawthrop, the younger removed to Settle Monthly Meeting in Settle, England to apprentice in the capacity of a servant.*[55]* Settle, England is in the southeast direction from Gatebeck less than 23 miles away. Thomas Gawthrop, the younger, was 22 years old when this move as a servant is made. { To find out more about Thomas Gawthrop, the younger, review the Quaker records for Settle, England starting in 1759/1760. }

In 1762, Thomas writes from England to Friend Israel Pemberton Jr. concerning his second son, Hugh, his mental condition/capacity (he contracted the measles) and the effect that Hugh might have on his younger brothers. He writes, ***My second son, after I came home, was very sober and well inclined of whom I flatered*** (sic) ***myself with in having much comfort in being like a tree promising for much good fruit, but alas is more like one plucked up by ye roots. Having lost his understanding in ye great measure and at times even much*** [like a] ***lunatick*** (sic). ***He had ye measals*** (sic) ***very sore and we thought he would have fallen into consumtion*** (sic), ***but what shall we say save this ye Lord hath permitted or done it.*** *[62, in Appendix-A]* He continues saying ***Many fears distresseth me confirming him*** [Hugh's age was 21 years] ***as also what he may do to younger brothers that's daily and nightly with him.*** *[62, in Appendix-A]* The mental state of Hugh may be just one of the many factors that caused Thomas to advise his two youngest sons, James and George, to emigrate to America about 1769.

On the 28th day of the 11th month 1762, according to the Preston Patrick Men's Preparative Meeting, Thomas signed the distribution of monies at the Meeting on the same

---

1 Although this quote talks of Thomas' second visit to America, in the book by R.M. Jones entitled *The Quakers in the American Colonies*, there is strong evidence to suggest that this was in fact his third visit.

date.[55] Apparently, he spent more time at his home in England and only travelled locally during the years of 1758 - 1765.

In a letter written by Thomas Gawthrop at his home in England on January 5th, 1765 to Israel Pemberton in Philadelphia, he writes of his friendship for Israel. Also, the P.S. gives an indication that Thomas' land near Nottingham, PA did not sell. The P.S. says, ***I resevd*** (received) ***thy letter & was much pleased to be rememberd*** (sic) ***by thee and thy near simpathy*** (sic) ***with poor unworthy me*** [over Thomas' second son who had the measles]. ***Thou gave me account*** [that] ***thou had not disposed of ye land but had sum*** (some) ***mony*** (sic) ***of mine in thy hand, if it is sould*** (sold) ***it is well, if it not*** [sold] ***may let it alone till thou receives further*** [word] ***from me.***[63, in Appendix-A] The P.S. goes on to read that if Israel does have any of Thomas' money could he take the first opportunity to send that money because his second son, Hugh, was feeling like a dead weight on his shoulders.[63, in Appendix-A]

It appeared that when Thomas was in America on one of his earlier trips that he bought some property near Nottingham, PA. He had wished to sell this piece of property because he needed the money. Thomas may have asked Israel Pemberton, because Israel made his home in America, to be his agent. Now, apparently, Thomas does not wish to sell this property and he asked Israel to take no further action regarding this land. He may have been planning to give this land to one of his sons. One has to remember, that English Quakers were looked on as religious dissenters throughout most of the 18th century.

The Westmoreland County records give Thomas as son of Thomas "first entered" (first born). Thomas (1709-1780) had four sons, Thomas, Hugh, James (q.v.) and George (q.v.) and two girls, Ann and Ruth. There is little record of Thomas' son, Thomas (1737 - ) in England except that in 1759 in the Preston Patrick Preparative Meeting a reference to Thomas Gawthrop, the younger, removed to Settle Monthly Meeting in the capacity of a servant.[55] However, it may be wondered if he emigrated to Virginia and is same Thomas mentioned in "Apple Ridge", Virginia.[64] Thomas' son, Hugh, as mentioned earlier, had the measles and, for all intensive purposes, lost his mind. Thomas' son, James, who married Patience Allen (niece of John Woolman) and eventually migrated to Virginia, is the father of the Virginia and West Virginia branch of the Gawthrops. Thomas' son, George, who married Jane Allen (first cousin of Patience[84]), stayed in Pennsylvania and is the father of the Pennsylvania and Delaware branch of the Gawthrops.

## 1766

During his fourth visit, ***he was particularly concerned on account of the hard and suffering state of the poor negroes, and we believe his labours on behalf of that oppressed people were of service.***[65] John Griffith, in his journal on June 12th, 1766 at the yearly-meeting in Portsmouth, Rhode Island, states that he met Friend Thomas Gawthrop who was visiting

Friends for a third time[m] and we both sat in silence throughout the entire meeting.*[45]* Another reference verifies his visiting the Newport (Rhode Island) in the 6th month 1766.*[43]* Thomas also visited Nantucket Island (Mass) Meeting in 1766.*[42]*

Thomas seemed to be a visionary or a prophet about the American Revolution. John Hunt of New Jersey mentions in Thomas' 1766 public testimony at the Quaker meeting in Moorestown, New Jersey, writes of what Thomas said, ***I am not come the third time*[n] *into this wilderness country to sew pillows to the armholes of the people [Ezekiel. xiii.18.]. No, I am not come to cry peace, but a sword. There is a bright, polished, glittering sword prepared for this nation.*** *[66]*

Thomas developed a friendship with John Woolman, the journalist and Quaker minister. John Woolman writes that Thomas' voyages of late were ... ***mainly engaged in efforts to relieve the sufferings of the negro slaves.*** *[20]* An account of this emancipation trait is expressed by Edward Stabler when he wrote to John Pemberton from Petersburg, Virginia in 1767, ***Our esteemed Friend Thomas Gawthrop left us about three weeks ago in good health. He hath been instrumental in giving such a stroke to the practice of slave keeping in this province as, I believe, will not be forgot in this age.*** *[67]*

John Griffith notes in his Journal that the minutes of the Wilmington Monthly Meeting on the 11th day of the 3rd month, 1767, ...***our esteemed Friend, Thomas Gawthrop, from England, attended this meeting, whose company and service was acceptable.*** *[28]* There are several more signs that Thomas travelled to the mid-Atlantic region as early as the third month 1767. There is a reference about Thomas in Ephraim Tomlinson's Journal that reads, ***On the 21st of 3rd month*** [1767], ***began our Spring meeting at Philadelphia. ... In those meetings, we were favoured with the company of our friend Thomas Gawthrop, from England, and other good friends ...*** *[69]* There is another reference about Thomas in a list of yearly stock transactions for Pennsylvania & New Jersey, the 1st day of the 5 month 1767.*[68]* On the 29th day of the 5th month 1767, there is yet another reference in the Philadelphia Monthly Meeting of his being granted a "Certificate of Removal" to Kendal Monthly Meeting, Westmoreland County, England.*[59]*[o] Thomas travelled throughout most of the mid-central and the New England parts of America (New Jersey, Delaware, Pennsylvania, Virginia, Rhoade Island and Mass.) on his fourth visit.

In a letter written by Thomas Gawthrop in London to Israel Pemberton Jr., in Philadelphia, PA on June 27th, 1767, of Thomas' arrival in England and that how he (Thomas)

---

m Although this reference speaks of Thomas' third visit to America, in *The Quakers in the American Colonies*, there is evidence that this was in fact Thomas' fourth visit.

n Thomas must not be counting his visit in 1739. The visit was to Philadelphia and he may not have been on a religious visit. It may be wondered if he felt that he was not recognized as a minister, yet. He may not have been given any church monies for his travels.

o A quote from the Philadelphia Monthly Meeting as expressed in Volume II of the *Encyclopedia of American Quaker Genealogy* is, ***Gawthrop, Thomas granted certificate of removal to Kendal, England, 1767, 5, 29.***

In a letter written by Thomas Gawthrop in London to Israel Pemberton Jr., in Philadelphia, PA on June 27th, 1767, of Thomas' arrival in England and that how he (Thomas) might send some of his children to settle on his land in Pennsylvania.*[70, in Appendix-A]* This is the second reference to a piece of land in America that Thomas owned. Thomas travelled extensively over much of America and it is believed that the reason he purchased this land was because it was in William Penn's Quaker State. Perhaps he had at one time envisioned moving his family from England to the American Quaker State of Pennsylvania.

In a letter about Thomas Gawthrop that was written by John Griffith to John Pemberton, June 31th, 1767, upon Thomas' arrival in England. This letter speaks of Thomas' plan for several of his children to settle in Pennsylvania. This letter speaks of some of John Griffith's children that also may settle in Pennsylvania.*[71]*

In a letter written in Philadelphia by Rachel Wilson to Isaac Wilson, her husband, in Kendal on the 22nd of the 6 month 1769 she says, ... ***Sarah Bonney is now by me, a Friend that travelled with Jane Crosfield, who desires to be remembered to her & Thos. Gawthrop, and many more enquire after them in these parts. The remembrance of them seems pleasent*** (sic), ***they have left a sweet savour*** (sic) ***behind them, and some seals of their Ministry.****[72]*

In a letter written in Preston Patrick by Thomas Gawthrop to John Pemberton in Philadelphia on the 30th day of December 1769, Thomas says ...***I send my two youngest sons which intend to settle on ye lands in Notingham*** (sic) ***ye which I have given to them.****[73, in Appendix-A]* Thomas decided to send his 3rd and 4th son to live on his property in Nottingham, PA that he had given to his sons. Sometime in the year of 1770, Thomas' sons arrived with the intent to settle in Pennsylvania. James (unmarried) was in his 28 year when he emigrated. George (unmarried) was one year younger than his brother when he emigrated.

In 1772, John Woolman writes of being in England at George Grosfield's (Sr.'s) house. He writes of attending the Preston Patrick meeting where Jane Crosfield, the wife of the George, was a prominent minister in the Society of Friends. Jane Crosfield presided over the Preston Patrick meeting. It was in the home of George Crosfield that John Woolman ...***rested a few days in body and mind.****[20]* John Woolman had family ties to the Gawthrop family; Woolman's niece was Patience Allen, wife of Thomas' son, James Gawthrop (married in 1771). Probably, in his travels, John Woolman was asked to carried messages back and forth between the two Gawthrop sons in America and their parents in Gatebeck, England.

In a letter written by Thomas Gawthrop in Preston Patrick to Israel Pemberton Jr., in Philadelphia on July 6th, 1774, which states that he is sending his son, George, in America, a Bible.[p] ***My son George in his last letter desires me to send him a Bible. Having sent one with a***

---

p This Bible (referred to as the 1700-1800 Bible) is in the procession of Raymond and Patricia Gawthrop, 855 Nights Lane, Engelwood, FL 34223, as of September 1993. Ray and Pat also, have a Bible (referred to as the 1800-1900 Bible) that was given to Ray by his father, Laurence Brown Gawthrop, which may have been given to Laurence by his father, Evan B. Gawthrop.

***concordance directed to thy care ye troble*** (sic) ***of which I hope thou will exquse*** (sic). ***Ra-***[q] ***Wilson informed me of thy remembering of me as also of our sons welfare which was very acceptable. Was also glad to hear that ye indians is likely to be visited with ye Light of ye Glorious Gospell*** (sic) ***power ... Jane Crosfield hath been very unwell this winter and spring past, but has got better ...*** *[74, in Appendix-A]* The letter goes on to say, ***I am much affected with ye rumatisam*** (sic) ***ernestly*** (sic) ***suffering.*** *[74, in Appendix-A]* Thomas' age at this point was 65 years and being exposed to the elements as he was throughout most of his life it is no wonder he had rheumatism. Also, there is a brief inquiry concerning John Woolman's Journal on the "fold over" address page under who the letter came from, that being Thomas Gawthrop.

**1775**

Israel Pemberton Jr. must have sent Thomas the Journal of John Woolman because Thomas drafted a letter from his home in Preston Patrick to Israel Pemberton Jr. dated March 14th, 1775, thanking him for John Woolman's Journal. *[75, in Appendix-A]* This letter goes on to say, ***Sister Jane Crosfield hath been but poorly this Winter but is now got better. Rachel Wilson*** (sic) ***is at London ... My Dear Wife was taken from me about 2 weeks since and*** [being] ***by myself*** [I am feeling] ***but very poorly*** [so] ***I hope thy favor will Exquse*** (sic) ***my not inlarging*** (sic) ***at presant*** (sic). *[75, in Appendix-A]* He must have been in shock because this letter shows little emotion, almost an indifference. He wrote of things in general before telling of his loss. He thanked Israel for John Woolman's journal, told of the health of a prominent minister and told the whereabouts of a minister before he got to something that should have been foremost in his mind, the fact that his wife died.

His last visit was in 1775 when he was ***deeply dipped in sympathy with Friends there*** *[76]* because of their sufferings from the War of Independence ***so that in consideration of their distress and famine, he could not eat a pleasant meal himself.*** *[76]* He also may have been sorrowful about the loss of his wife. So, on his return home applied 50 pounds that his daughter had saved for him to the American Quakers relief. There is a record of Thomas' visiting Nantucket Island (Mass.) in 1775. *[42]* Two letters from Thomas to his daughter, Ann and Ruth, dated about 1776, are found in the Friends House in London. { However, they were not attainable. }

There is a record of Thomas visiting Newport (Rhode Island) Meeting in the first month 1776. *[43]* There is also a record of Thomas' booking passage to England after his fifth visit to America, ... ***Decemr 2, 1777, Rec'd of Mr Thomas Gawthrop and George Napper the sum of forty seven pounds, five shillings for a passage to England in the Eagle Packet pr me, Edmund Spence.*** *[68]*

---

q It is believed that Thomas was referring to **Rachel** when he used "Ra-". This may have been a way to protect Rachel Wilson from the persecution at home in England if this letter fell into the wrong hands. However, in "Isaac and Rachel Wilson - Quakers of Kendal 1714 - 1785", by John Somervell, published 1924, Isaac Wilson recounts how Rachel Wilson's Ministry was missed, especially as so many others were away on concerns in different parts, Jane Crosfield, Thos. Gawthrop, Alice Rigge, etc, ...

*O*n his way to the docks to make passage home from Philadelphia on the 1st day of the 12 month 1777, he reportedly said, ***Master said thou came poor among them, be content to leave them so. I have taken their crown from off their heads. Let them wear dust and ashes the appointed time; then shall their light break forth as brightness, and my glory be their crown and diadem.*** *[78]* In appendix A, reference 77, Thomas reportedly said those same (similar) words but he went further, ***I am glad I have been amongst you, I have seen His protecting Providence over this City, but the People do not see it, neither are they humble and grateful for His Mercy.*** *[77, in Appendix-A]* In Samuel Fothergill's journals, again there are many of the same words that Thomas Gawthrop reportedly said just before he left Philadelphia.*[35]* If he was so feeble and could not use his right hand, would he have made such a strong statement. There is a strong possibility that he knew he would never return to America because of his age. One would think he was in sound health because of this powerful statement; however, the statement (reference 77, page A – 65 in the appendix) is not in his own handwriting.

*T*his extract of a letter by George Crosfield (Sr.) [George Sr. & Isabel were siblings*[28]*] written at the time of Thomas Gawthrop's last return from America in 1778 - ***William Dillworth, brought my brother, Thomas Gawthrop*** [actually, his brother-in-law], ***home in a chaise; he was very feeble, he can neither write, nor in any way use his right hand. He says he was twenty seven days on his passage from Philadelphia to Falmouth; he was in the former place when Washington and his army were in it, also after he left it, William Howe took possession of it without any opposition, many of the inhabitants rejoicing, though they had little left to give them, wanting almost everything necessary for the support of the body. Beef and mutton sold at half-a-crown and three shillings per pound, and other things in proportion ...*** (Letter from Geo. Crosfield, Westmoreland, to his son Geo. Crosfield, Warrington, 1778, also, see Friends Quarterly Examiner*[28]*) More than likely, Thomas had a stroke or heart attack either just prior to his return to England or on the voyage back to England. Probably just prior to the voyage back he had a mild stoke. The reason for this assumption can be ascertained in Crosfield's letter, ... ***Thomas Gawthrop, home in a chaise; he was very feeble...*** and apparently paralyzed on his right side. George goes on to say, ***He*** (Thomas) ***says his son James, who is settled in Virginia, suffered much, and for refusing to muster when required by the Provincials he was taken and marched two hundred miles to Philadelphia with his hands tied behind him and a gun on his back; he was not kept long, but sent home again, but was not allowed to see his father, though then in Philadelphia.*** (George Crosfield letter, 1778, also, see Friends Library, vol ix., published Philadelphia, 1845, f. 191.*[28]*)

*H*enry Gawthrop in a 1903 article in Friends Quarterly Examiner writes about Thomas Gawthrop; ***Thomas survived the hardships of his last American experiences for nearly three years, and, "though under great bodily infirmity," was diligent in his attendance of Preston Patrick Meeting till he met with a fall and fracture which kept him a prisoner to his room.*** *[28]* This fall is again seen in another journal, the *Memoirs of Sarah Stephenson* who writes, ***We next went again to Kendal, calling by the way to see our ancient friend, Thomas Gawthrop, who was confined to his bed, by an accident. We sat by him to satisfaction. The heavenly frame of his spirit was such, as was to me truly comfortable; and a belief was fixed with me, that he would soon be removed from works, to a*** *joyful reward. We afterwards heard that he remained about two months, and then sweetly departed.*[79]

***He departed this Life the 29th of Ninth Month, 1780, aged about seventy-one, a minister forty-seven years.***[35] Thomas ***was decently interred the 4th of 10th month following in Friends' Burying Ground at Preston Patrick.***[23]

Thomas Gawthrop married Isabel Crosfield [r] on 31 x. [Dec.] 1735 [20, 29] or the 31st day of the 10mth [Dec.] 1735[16, 19, 23].[s] Isabel died about Feb. 28, 1775 [75] and is buried 1 March 1775.[30] They had six children:

| | |
|---|---|
| **151241,** | Ann, born 6 Oct. 1736, [born 6 viii. 1736[29]], [8-6-1736[23]] |
| **151242,** | Thomas, born 23 Jan. 1737, [born 23 xi. 1737[29]], [11-23-1737[23]] |
| **151243,** | Ruth, born 1 Nov. 1739, [born 1 ix. 1739[29]], [9-1-1739[23]], died 31 Sept. 1813[29] |
| **151244,** | Hugh, born 15 May 1741, [born 15 iii. 1741[29]], [3-15-1741[23]], died 11 May 1773[29] |
| **151245,** | James (q.v.), born 4 July 1742, [born 4 v. 1742[29]], [5-4-1742[23]], died sometime after the 6th month of 1807[80] |
| **151246,** | George (q.v.), born 17 Dec. 1743 [t], [born 17 x. 1743[29]], [10-11-1743[23]], died 27 Aug. 1795[17, 18] |

Thomas had no brothers and four sisters. The four sisters were **1)** Mary birth: the 13th day of the 4th month [June] 1700[17], **2)** Rebekkay baptized: the 3rd day of the 3rd month [May] 1702[15, 17], **3)** Ruth baptized: the 17 day of the 9th month [Nov.] 1703[15, 17] and **4)** Jane born circa: 1715/16; buried at Skipton on the 24th June 1726[15].

---

r With regard to the spelling of her last name; with one "s" vs two "ss". Five references (*Dictionary of Quaker Biography*), (Family tree prepared for Everard Conard Gawthrop by G. Cope), (Thomas Carr Gawthrop's genealogical work), (George Crosfield's letter { believe to be her brother }) and (the *Preston Patrick Men's Preparative Meeting*) have Crosfield spelled with one "s". Whereas, another reference, (Henry Gawthrop's work, ..., *The Emigrate*) spells Crossfield with two "ss". Therefore, the conclusion drawn; the spelling of Crosfield should have only one "s".

s With regard to Thomas and Isabel's marriage date. Three references, (Our Childrens Ancestors by Brown), (the Gawthrop Family Tree by Allen Gawthrop) and (the unfinished manuscript by Horace Henry Gawthrop) all have the same date [10mth 31dy 1735]. Also, three other references, (the Journal of John Woolman), (the Tortola Experiment), and (the Dictionary of Quaker Biography) have the same date although slightly different in form. The conclusion drawn: the best record of their marriage date should be 31 Dec. 1735.

t With regard to George's birth and death dates: a record of George's birth and deathdates are found in the work of Henry Gawthrop, (*GEORGE GAWTHROP, The Emigrate*). This work is about George and is more believable than other works. Therefore, the conclusion drawn is that *GEORGE GAWTHROP, The Emigrate* supplies the best record of his birth and deathdates; b: 17 December 1743, d: 27 August 1795.

REFERENCES:

SOURCE [15]: Letter/Chart dated 11 Jan. 1993 from Brian Clayton, Ilkley, West Yorkshire, England to Philip E. Gawthrop. Follow-on letter from same source dated 5 Feb. 1993.

SOURCE [16]: A handwritten family tree, *"OUR CHILDREN'S ANCESTORS,"* compiled by Rev. Darward and Dorothy Brown for their children and grandchildren, no date was available; however, Rev Darward Belmont Brown was born on 12 January 1897.

SOURCE [17]: Genealogy work compiled by Thomas Carr Gawthrop. This manuscript was not published by a publisher; however, Thomas Carr Gawthrop was born Jan. 1938 and died Sept. 1966.

SOURCE [18]: A handwritten family tree prepared for Everard Conard Gawthrop by G. Cope of Pittsburgh, PA done in the mid 1920's. Philip Evan Gawthrop (Grandson of Everard) has the original work on this family tree.

SOURCE [19]: A handwritten family tree prepared by Allen Gawthrop in 1871. The son of Allen and Mary Ann (Newlin) Gawthrop, Henry Gawthrop, collected data from Allen's work along with the assistance of several family members to generate another work entitled *GEORGE GAWTHROP, The Emigrate*, dated Christmas 1900. Henry's work (in typescript, not published by a publisher) is available from the Friends Historical Lib., Swarthmore College, Swarthmore, PA.

SOURCE [20]: A.M. Gummere (edition) [BX7743A41922] *The Journal and Essays of John Woolman*, (Philadelphia & London 1922), pages 171 and 577.

SOURCE [21]: R.M. Jones, et. al, *THE QUAKERS in the AMERICAN COLONIES*, W.W. Norton & Company, Inc., copyright 1911 & 1966, Introduction to the 1966 edition by Frederick B. Tolles, Swarthmore, PA, Preface by Haverford College, PA, when it was first published in 1911.

SOURCE [22]: E.H. Milligan & M.J. Thomas, *My Ancestors were Quakers, How can I find out more about them?*, published by Society of Genealogists, London, England, copyright 1983, (Reprinted 1990).

SOURCE [23]: In an unfinished manuscript by Horace Henry Gawthrop called *"GAWTHROP", Chapter III, entitled Thomas Gawthrop - Life - Memorial*, pages 10 & 19, written at Christmas 1902. It is believed that he obtained much of the information about Thomas' death from the Testimony of Kendal Monthly Meeting in *Testimonies Concerning Ministers Deceased*, Vol 3.

SOURCE [25]: Thomas Gawthrop's birth is not in *Yorks QM Birth digest*.

SOURCE [26]: *Westmoreland QM Marriage digest supp.*

SOURCE [27]: *Bulletin of Friends Historical Society*, page 136, no date available.

SOURCE [28]: *The Friends' Quarterly Examiner*, Vol. 37 (1903), pages 238-243.

SOURCE [29]: *Dictionary of Quaker Biography*, (typescript, similar to a manuscript, not published by a publisher but is referenceable), only two copies exist; copies from both sources; Religious Society of Friends, London, England and Haverford College, Haverford, PA.

SOURCE [30]: *Westmoreland QM Marriage digest supp.* Simon Crosfield is described as a weaver, of Kendal. NOTE: Isabel Crosfield birth is not in the Westmoreland QM Birth digest. However, she died in 1775 and was buried 1 March 1775 according to the Westmoreland QM Burials digest.

SOURCE [31]: C.F.Jenkins, *Tortola, a Quaker experiment of long ago in the tropics*, (London, supplement to the *Journal of Friends Historical Society*, 1903), p.40.

SOURCE [32]: Cumbria Records Office (Kendal), Historical Research Service, research conducted by Mrs. V.M. Gate, *Map of Preston Patrick Survey of Estates, 1771*, WD/AG (Map Box)(ACC.1219), research carried out in September 1993.

SOURCE [33]: *Record of Friends travelling in Ireland 1656-1756*, found in the *Journal of Friends Historical Society*, Vol. 10 (1913), pages 243-244. Obtained in 1992 from the Quaker Collection, at the Library in Haverford College, Haverford, PA.

SOURCE [34]: *Record of Friends travelling in Ireland 1756-1861*, found in the *Journal of Friends Historical Society*, Vol. 15 (1918), page 18. Obtained in 1992 from the Quaker Collection, at the Library in Haverford College, Haverford, PA.

SOURCE [35]: George Crosfield (editor), *Memoirs of the Life and Gospel Labours of Samuel Fothergill & c.*, (New York 1844), pages 286-289.

SOURCE [36]: Ezra Michener, *A Retrospect of Early Quakerism,* Published by T.Ellwood Zell, copyright 1860, Reprinted by Cool Spring Publishing Company, 1991, Washington, D.C.

SOURCE [37]: April 13, 1986 letter to Philip E. Gawthrop from Mrs. Nancy P. Speers, Assistant Librarian for the Friends Historical Library (Quakers), Swarthmore College, PA concerning the Julian vs. the Gregorian Calendar.

SOURCE [38]: Cumbria Archive, Historical Research Service, research conducted by Mrs. V.M. Gate, *Preston Patrick Preparative Meeting, Men's Meeting Minute Book 1724 - 1754,* WDFC/F1 - 10/1, research carried out in September 1993.

SOURCE [40]: William Wade Hinshaw and Thomas Worth Marshall, *ENCYCLOPEDIA OF AMERICAN QUAKER GENEALOGY*, Volume VI (Virginia), Genealogical Publishing Co., Baltimore, MD, 1977.

SOURCE [41]: Letter from Thomas Gawthrop to Israel Pemberton Jr., at Philadelphia from New York, dated 5 month 3 day 1747 [July 3, 1747], obtained from the *PEMBERTON PAPERS*, Vol. 4, page 70.

SOURCE [42]: L.S. Hutchinson, *Early Settlers of Nantucket,* (2nd ed., Philadelphia 1901), pages 321-323.

SOURCE [43]: *Record of Public Friends Visiting Newport Meeting, 1665-1838,* in the Quaker Collection at the Library in Haverford College, Haverford, PA.

SOURCE [44]: *A JOURNAL of the Life, Travels and Labours in the WORK of the MINISTRY of JOHN GRIFFITH,* London, Printed and Sold by James Phillips, M.DCCLXXIX (London 1779), pages 71-74, 76-77 and 99.

SOURCE [45]: For an account of their voyage and stay in France, v. *A Journal of the Life, Travels and Labours ... of John Griffith*, (London 1779). [BX7735.G84A31779]

SOURCE [46]: Letter from Thomas Gawthrop to Israel Pemberton Jr. at Philadelphia while on-board the "Widow," dated December 1, 1747, obtained from the *PEMBERTON PAPERS*, Vol. 4, page 82.

SOURCE [47]: Letter from Thomas Gawthrop to Israel Pemberton Jr. at Chester or Philadelphia from Reedy Island, dated 4 day 10 month 1747 [December 4, 1747], obtained from the *PEMBERTON PAPERS*, Vol. 4, page 83.

SOURCE [48]: Promissory letter from Isaac Greenleaf to Thomas Gawthrop, dated 2 day 10 month 1747 [December 2, 1747], obtained from the *PEMBERTON PAPERS*, Vol. 4, page 83.

SOURCE [49]: M.S. Wood, *Society hours with Friends,* taken from *Capture of Four Friends by a French Privateer,* Abridged from John Griffith { *Journal* }, (New York 1867), pages 133-139.

SOURCE [50]: Letter from Thomas Gawthrop written in San Sebastians via Lisbon to Israel Pemberton Jr., Philadelphia, PA, dated 6th mo. 25th, 1748, obtained from the *PEMBERTON PAPERS*, Vol. 4, page 130.

SOURCE [51]: Letter from Thomas Gawthrop written in Warrington, England to Israel Pemberton, Philadelphia, PA, dated 2nd mo. 19th, 1748, obtained from the *PEMBERTON PAPERS*, Vol. 4, page 100.

SOURCE [52]: Letter from Thomas Gawthrop written in London, England to Israel Pemberton Jr., Philadelphia, PA, dated April 8th, 1748, *Of being carried into France and now arriving in England and of the title to land in New Jersey*, obtained from the *PEMBERTON PAPERS*, Vol. 4, page 97.

SOURCE [53]: Letter from Thomas Gawthrop from Stenton (sic), England to Israel Pemberton Jr., Philadelphia, PA, dated September 27, 1748, obtained from the *PEMBERTON PAPERS*, Vol. 4, page 116.

SOURCE [54]: Letter from Thomas Gawthrop from London to Israel Pemberton Jr., Philadelphia, PA, dated June 17, 1753, obtained from the *PEMBERTON PAPERS*, Vol. 9, page 20.

SOURCE [55]: Cumbria Archive, Historical Research Service, research conducted by Mrs. V.M. Gate, *Preston Patrick Preparative Meeting, Men's Meeting Minute Book 1754 - 1766,* WDFC/F1 - 10/2, research carried out in November 1993.

SOURCE [56]: FRIENDS' MISCELLANY, No. 6, Vol.XII, Sixth Month, 1839, *A JOURNAL Of the Life and Travels of Benjamin Ferris, son of David Ferris, of Wilmington, Delaware,* Edited by John and Isaac Comly (common referred to as Comly's Miscellany), Byberry, PA, page 249, obtained in 1992/95 from the Religious Society of Friends in Britain, Friends House, London, England.

SOURCE [57]: Letter from Thomas Gawthrop written in Eustatia (Liverpool) to Israel Pemberton Jr., Philadelphia, PA, dated Jan. 25, 1756, obtained from the *PEMBERTON PAPERS*, Vol. 11, page 69.

SOURCE [58]: Letter from Thomas Gawthrop from Road Island to Israel Pemberton Jr., Philadelphia, PA, dated April 26, 1756, obtained from the *PEMBERTON PAPERS*, Vol. 11, page 72.

SOURCE [59]: William Wade Hinshaw and Thomas Worth Marshall, *ENCYCLOPEDIA OF AMERICAN QUAKER GENEALOGY*, Vol. II, Genealogical Publishing Co., Baltimore, MD, 1969.

SOURCE [60]: Letter from Thomas Gawthrop bound for Barbados to Israel Pemberton Jr., Philadelphia, PA, dated 6 mo., 25, 1757, obtained from the *PEMBERTON PAPERS*, Vol. 12, page 31.

SOURCE [61]: Letter from Thomas Gawthrop on-board the ship, the Philadelphia, to Israel Pemberton Jr., Philadelphia, PA, dated October 24, 1757, obtained from the *PEMBERTON PAPERS*, Vol. 12, page 77.

SOURCE [62]: Letter by Thomas Gawthrop on April 10, 1762 written near Kendal, England to Israel Pemberton Jr. concerning Thomas' son who had lost his mind due to the measles. This letter was obtained from The Historical Society of Pennsylvania in the *PEMBERTON PAPERS,* Vol. 15, page 133.

SOURCE [63]: Letter from Thomas Gawthrop to Israel Pemberton, in Philadelphia, PA, dated January 5, 1765, obtained from the *PEMBERTON PAPERS*, Vol. 17, page 124.

SOURCE [64]: Draft genealogy work compiled by Wm. A.A. Gawthrop, *GAWTHROP GENEALOGY,* U.S. Congressional Library, CS71.G277, 1986.

SOURCE [65]: "*Piety Promoted,*" (1854 ed.), Vol. 3, pages 119-121, Philadelphia edition.

SOURCE [66]: *Friends' Miscellany*, Sixth Month 1831, No. 3, Vol. 1, page 9, Extracted from the writings of John Hunt, who resided near Moorestown, New Jersey.

SOURCE [67]: Letter from Edward Stabler to John Pemberton. Letter dated Petersburg, VA, 3mth 2dy 1767.

SOURCE [68]: John Reynell, Treasurer, to the *Yearly Meeting Stock for Pennsylvania & New Jersey Dr.,* 1767 5mo. 1st, To(tal) cost of Wine, Rum, Beer & Cider for Sea Stores of Thos. Gawthrop...(Pounds).. 4.16.2 3/4; Cost of Sheep and a Groat..... 1.13.4, Corn, Bran, & packing hay..... 10.8; Biscuit..... 6.8.

SOURCE [69]: FRIENDS' MISCELLANY, No. 4, Vol.III, Eleventh Month, 1832, *EPHRAIM TOMLINSON'S JOURNAL, John Hunt's Testimony concerning Ephraim Tomlinson, and Reflections on reading his Journal,* Edited by John and Isaac Comly (common referred to as Comly's Miscellany), Byberry, PA, pages 172 and 173, obtained in 1992/95 from the Religious Society of Friends in Britain, Friends House, London, England.

SOURCE [70]: Letter from Thomas Gawthrop written in London, England to Israel Pemberton, in Philadelphia, PA, dated June 27, 1767, obtained from the *PEMBERTON PAPERS*, Vol. 19, page 95.

SOURCE [71]: Letter about Thomas Gawthrop written by John Griffith to John Pemberton, in Philadelphia, PA on June 31, 1767, obtained from the *PEMBERTON PAPERS*, Vol. 19, page 97.

SOURCE [72]: *Isaac and Rachel Wilson - Quakers of Kendal 1714 - 1785*, by John Somervell, published 1914, research conducted by Mrs. V.M. Gate, research carried out in September 1993.

SOURCE [73]: Letter from Thomas Gawthrop written in Preston Patrick, England to John Pemberton, in Philadelphia, PA, dated December 30, 1769, obtained from the *PEMBERTON PAPERS*, Vol. 21, page 96.

SOURCE [74]: Letter from Thomas Gawthrop written in Preston Patrick, England to Israel Pemberton, in Philadelphia, PA, dated July 6, 1774, obtained from the *PEMBERTON PAPERS*, Vol. 26, page 117.

SOURCE [75]: Letter from Thomas Gawthrop written in Preston Patrick, England to Israel Pemberton Jr., Philadelphia, PA, dated March 14, 1775, obtained from the *PEMBERTON PAPERS*, Vol. 27, page 96.

SOURCE [76]: M. Leadbeater, *Memories and Letter of Richard and Elizabeth Shackleton & c.,* (New edition, London 1849), page 110.

SOURCE [77]: Two packages (no dates) *The Quaker Collection*, Haverford, PA and *The Historical Society of Pennsylvania*, Philadelphia, PA, containing handwritten material (not in Thomas Gawthrop's handwriting) concerning what Thomas reportedly said when leaving America for the last time.

SOURCE [78]: FRIENDS' MISCELLANY, No. 4, Vol.I, 1831, *John Pemberton's Journal*, Edited by John and Isaac Comly (common referred to as Comly's Miscellany), Byberry, PA, pages 74 and 75, obtained in 1992/95 from the Religious Society of Friends in Britain, Friends House, London, England.

SOURCE [79]: *Memoirs of the life and travels of Sarah Stephenson*, (London 1807), page 50.

SOURCE [80]: Letter from the Clerk's Office, Frederick County Circuit Court, George B. Whitacre, Clerk, Winchester, VA, post marked April 15, 1994, containing the Will of JAMES GAWTHROP (1742-1807).

SOURCE [84]: Letter dated 13 April 1986 from Mrs. Nancy Speers, assistant librarian of the Friends Historical Library, Swarthmore College, PA.

# Chapter 6

6th Generation

## 151245, JAMES GAWTHROP ( 1742 – 1807 )

*J*ames Gawthrop, the fifth child and third son of Thomas Gawthrop (1709-1780) and Isabel Crosfield (          -1775), was born on 4 July 1742[a] in Stainton,[b] near Kendal, Westmoreland, England.*[16, 17, 19, 29]* He was a Friend very early in his life because his father was a travelling Friend. (a Quaker minister). His father travelled back from Ireland for his birth. He died sometime after the 6th month of 1807[c] in Frederick County, Virginia[d] and [is buried in an unidentified cemetery plot in Bunker Hill, West Virginia.*[64]*] He is the ancestor of the Virginia and West Virginia Gawthrop Families.

*I*n a letter written by his father from his home in England to John Pemberton in Philadelphia on the 30th day of December 1769, ***...I send my two youngest sons which intend to settle on ye lands in Notingham which I have given to them.****[73-Appendix A]* James and his younger brother, Gawthrop, were going to settle on the property in Nottingham, PA that their father had given them.

*S*ometime in 1770, James and George arrived in America with the intent to settle on their property in Nottingham, PA.[e] They probably sailed up the Delaware Bay and then up the Delaware River and disembarked at New Castle, Delaware or Wilmington, Delaware or Chester, Pennsylvania (see Map #10). If they went straight to Nottingham the best route

---

a *Egle's Notes and Queries*, Annual Volume 1900, page 51, says that he was born on, ***5 May 1742, in England***, other references such as 16, 17, 20, 23, and 29 shows 4 July.

b Stainton, England and Gatebeck, England are within a 1½ miles of each other (see Gatebeck land plat in the chapter on *Thomas Gawthrop (1709-1780), the Travelling Friend*). His parents moved to Gatebeck around 1735/6 and were still there in 1771. Therefore, the location of Stainton as to where he was born is believed to be in error unless they travelled to a mid-wife in Stainton.

c Based on the last paragraph in his Last Will and Testament, which says, ***6th Mo 11th – 1807, Signed Sealed and Delivered in the presence of Jacob Jenkins*** [and] ***George Dawson {signature} James Gawthrop {seal}***, James had to live at least until that date. (Date of comment April 1994)

d ***Based on Jan. 1807 estate appraisal of James' property***, probably in a tax assessor ledger someplace in Frederick County, VA, that gives a hint as to where he died. However, this action may have been James' way to prepare his Last Will and Testament, which he prepared five months later. (Date of comment April 1994)

e John V. Hollingsworth in a letter written sometime in the later 19th or early 20th century to Charlotte W. Maule of West Grove, PA he says, ***...possibly sometime after the middle of the 18th century, two brother, James and George came to America from Westmoreland, England, and took up residence in the vicinity of Nottingham in Chester County.***

would have been to disembark at New Castle and travel almost due West. There is a western road from New Castle, DE to Newport, DE to London Britain, PA to New London Cross Roads, PA to Oxford, PA. Then travel South for about 6 miles to Nottingham, PA. If they wanted to go through Wilmington, DE, they would have to travel West to New Garden, PA than to West Grove, PA. Once in West Grove, they would have to travel Southwest to New London Cross Roads than almost due West to Oxford, PA then South to Nottinghan, PA. If their father had advised them disembark at Chester, PA, which was a more formally route and one he knew well, they would travel West to Concord and Kennett, PA. Once in Kennett, they would travel in a Southwest direction to London Grove, West Grove, and New London Cross Roads, PA. Once in New London Cross Roads, they would travel almost due West to Oxford, PA then South for about 6 miles to Nottingham, PA all the time travelling through Quaker surroundings in Pennsylvania.

James was unmarried in his 28 year when he emigrated. Perhaps when James left England, his father and John Woolman, a close friend of his fathers*[20]* and a Quaker Minister/journalist and her uncle, may have arranged the marriage between Patience Allen and him. Patience was born in West Nottingham, PA on the 3rd day of the 10th month [Dec.] 1746. She was the daughter of John Allen (b: 1725) and Esther (Woolman) Allen (b: 1707). Patience died sometime prior to 1796 (see footnote k, this chapter). Patience's mother, Ester (Woolman) Allen, was the sister of John Woolman, the Quaker minister from Mount Holly, N.J.*[81]* Patience was 24 years of age and living with her parents in West Nottingham when she married James.*[82]* [f] On page 168 of the East Nottingham Monthly Meeting's Marriage Book, James Gawthrop and Patience Allen were orderly married and a copy of their certificate follows: ***James Gawthrop of the township of Little Brittain in the County of Lancaster & province of Pennsylvania, son of Thomas Gawthrop of Westmoreland in Old England and Isabel, his wife, and Patience Allen daughter of John Allen of the township of West Nottingham in the County of Chester & province of Pennsylvania aforesaid and Esther, his wife ... On 9th. day of 5th. mo., 1771 ... In the public meeting house at East Nottingham. And the signors who considered themselves relatives were, Esther Allen, William Allen, John Churchman, James Allen, George Gawthrop, Joseph Coulson, Hannah Allen, Rachel Allen, Anne Kirk, Jane Allen, William Allen Jr., and Nathan Allen.*** *[83]* This marriage took place in Cecil County, MD on 9 May 1771.*[17, 82, 83]* James and his brother, George, married first cousins, Patience and Jane Allen.*[84]* James' marriage occurred about 1 year after he emigrated to America which could have meant the marriage was pre-arranged by his father and her uncle.

---

f In the *Maryland Marriage, 1634 – 1777*, there appears to be an error. This publication shows that John Gawthrop and Patience Allen were married on 9 May 1771. There appears to be a discrepancy with James' first name and the first name associated with this marriage, which is John. However, the marriage date and the bride's name are the same, therefore, it is believed that ***John*** is in error. (Date of comment Jan. 1990)

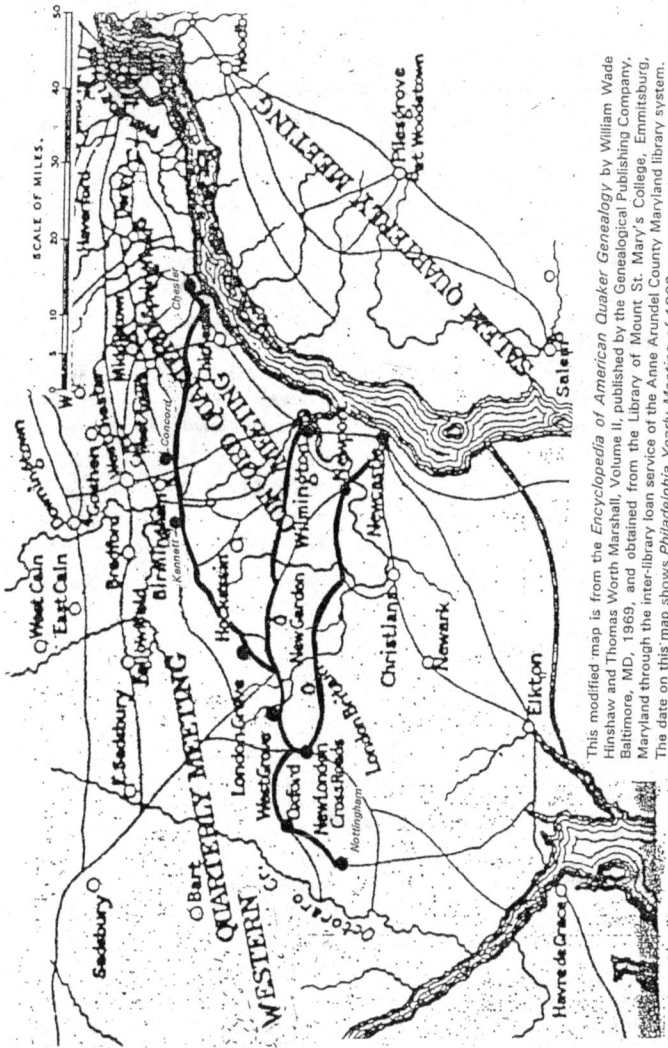

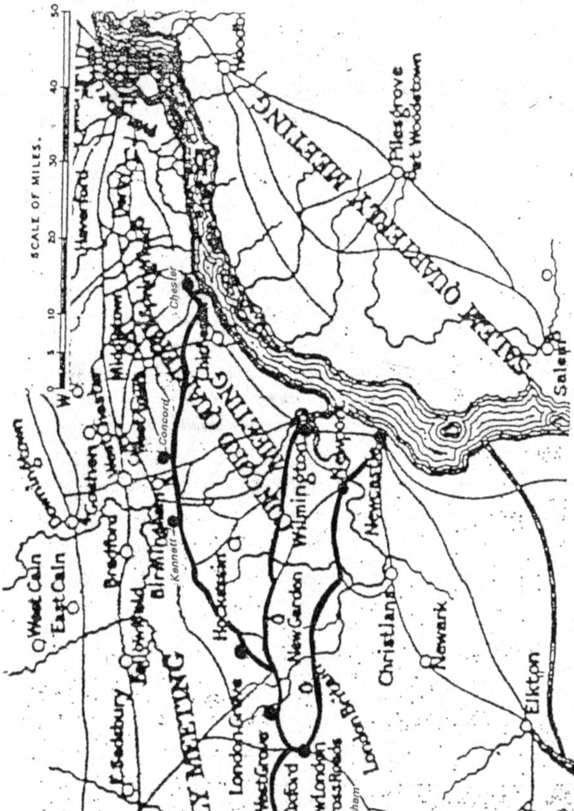


This modified map is from the *Encyclopedia of American Quaker Genealogy* by William Wade Hinshaw and Thomas Worth Marshall, Volume II, published by the Genealogical Publishing Company, Baltimore, MD, 1969, and obtained from the Library of Mount St. Mary's College, Emmitsburg, Maryland through the inter-library loan service of the Anne Arundel County Maryland library system. The date on this map shows *Philadelphia Yearly Meeting of 1838*.

Map #10 of Chester, Wilmington, Newcastle, Oxford, Nottingham, etc

*J*ames and his wife, who was pregnant at the time,[g] moved to Hampshire County, VA.[h] ***Jas. Gawthrop & w. Patience*** received a ***Hopewell Certificate Of Membership*** from ***E. Nottingham*** Monthly Meeting to ***Hopewell*** Monthly Meeting on ***6 12*** (Feb.) ***1773.*** *[85]* James, being the older brother, probably decided to give up the land his father had given to both he and George before travelling to Virginia. There are records of James' residences as: in the vicinity of Nottingham in Chester County, PA*[83]*; Little Britainy Township, Lancaster County, PA*[20]*; and Hampshire County, VA.*[85]*

*J*ames was in Hampshire County, VA at the time of the Revolutionary War but did not fight. He refused to muster as ordered by the Provincials. The information about James' refusal to fight is contained in a letter by George Crosfield Sr. at the time of the Revolution. George, in England at the time in 1778, writes of what Thomas Gawthrop told him, ... ***James, who is settled in Virginia, suffered much, and for refusing to muster when required by the Provincials he was taken and marched 200 miles to Philadelphia with his hands tied behind him and a gun on his back; he was not kept long, but sent home again, but was not allowed to see his father, though then in Philadelphia.*** *[35]*[i]

*J*ames owned 200 acres in Lost Run, Harrison County, WV which is recorded in the 1793, Book 4, page 1.*[86]* James Gawthrop was active early in his time spent at Hopewell Friends Society.[j] James showed his passion almost as soon as he became a member of the Hopewell Friends Society by becoming an overseers for the poor.[k] James Gawthrop's Last

---

g If the removal from East Nottingham, PA M.M. to the Hopewell, VA M.M. in Feb. 1773 and her daughter's birthdate of 25 March 1773 are accurate, then Patience would have been in the 8th month of pregnancy. (Date of comment December 1993)

h Hampshire County, Virginia became Hampshire County, West Virginia when the State split during the Civil War. Hampshire County, WV has a northern boarder of Washington County, Maryland.

i The information pertaining to James' refusal to fight is referred to in a letter from George Crosfield, Westmoreland, England to his son, George Crosfield, Warrington, VA in 1778. This letter is contained in Samuel Fothergill memoirs. Also see Friends' Library, vol ix., published Philadelphia, 1845, p. 191. (Date of comment November 1990)

j ***James Gauthrop*** became a member in the Hopewell Friends Society. ***COMMITTEE MEMBERS, In Hopewell Book 1, 1759-1776.***

k According to Hopewell records on page 530, ***James Gawthrop*** was on the committee for the ***OVERSEERS FOR THE POOR, 1759-1851.***

Will and Testament is recorded in the Fredrick County, Virginia Book of Wills.[l] The Will synopsis has the following information:

*Gawthrop, James - Will: 11 Jun 1807/30 Nov 1807.*
*Wife: Patience.*
*Sons: James and Thomas.*
*Daughters: Edith Taylor, Hannah Jenkins, and Rachel Gawthrop.*
*To Wife: two thirds of profits from plantation during her lifetime and chaste widowhood.*
*To son James: land known as Plummer's Survey, deeded to me by Henry Lee, Esq., Governor, dated 1 July 1793. To son Thomas: my watch.*
*To daughters: monies divided among the daughters.*
*Executors: David Lupton and David Barrett, sons of Benjamine Barrett dec'd.*
*Witnesses: Jacob Jenkins and George Dawson.*
*Sec. Thomas Barrett, Jacob Rinker, Benjamine Barrett [Jr.], Thomas Gawthrop, David Barrett, Daniel Wade, Jacob Taylor and James Gawthrop.[86]*

A handwritten copy of James Gawthrop's Will was obtained from the Clerk's Office in the Frederick County Circuit Court House.*[80]* This Last Will and Testament of James Gawthrop has been transcribe at the end of this chapter.

James Gawthrop (Sr.) apparently married a second time because he was disowned by Hopewell Monthly Meeting for marriage contrary to discipline on 1 Feb. 1796.*[85]* [m] [This person is also identified as John Gawthrop in the Nottingham Monthly Meeting Records.*[86]*]

James and Patience had 8 children as follows:

**1512451,** Esther b: 25 March 1773, d: 12 May 1773*[17]*

---

l The Fredrick County, Virginia, Will Book, Number 8 for 1804 - 1810, gives a brief synopsis of Will. This information is found in the draft of *The Descendants of Thomas Gawthrop*, by Wm. A.A. Gawthrop, dated 23 Sept. 1993.

m The Hopewell Monthly Meeting History indicates that James married again. However, nothing is known about his 2nd wife. Basis for the assumption that James married again - James and Patience were granted a *"Certificate of Removal"* to Hopewell from East Nottingham on 6 Feb. 1773 indicating that they both were Friends. When James was disowned for marriage contrary to discipline on 1 Feb. 1796, Patience would have been 50 years of age. Although it is not known when she died, there is a good possibility she died prior to 1796 and that James married again. Noting: His son, James Jr. would have been only 15 years of age on this date (1796). (Date of comment March 1991)

1512452, Thomas[n] *[17]* William*[64]*; Thomas William*[87]* (q.v.) b: 22 Feb. 1776, d: 26 Dec. 1832, married Elizabeth Hiett about 1797)*[17]*

1512453, Isabella*[17]* b: 16 Feb. 1778*[64]* [o], married Daniel Wade on 19 June 1806*[date from 89]* [p]

1212454, James*[17]* Jr.*[85]* [q] b: 21 Oct. 1781*[85]*

twin 1512455, Edith b: 6 Aug. 1783, married Mr. Taylor about 1806*[85]* [r]

twin 1512456, Rachel b: 6 Aug. 1783, married Mr. [William*[86]*] Davis about 1812*[85]* [s] [1 Feb. 1812 in Fredrick County, VA*[86]*]

1512457, Hannah b: 1788, married Jacob Jenkins on 8 April 1807*[85]* [t]

1512458, Ruth b: 27 Feb. 1791*[85]*

---

n According to Hopewell records on page 390, ***1798, 9*** (Sept.), ***3 Thomas [ Gauthrop ] rpd;*** (reported) ***mcd;*** (married contrary to discipline) ***dis*** (disowned for) and on page 511, ***4 Day 2 Mo. 1799 Yr.*** Person Disowned ***Thomas Gauthrop*** Reason for Disownment ***Married contrary to discipline.***

o *Egles Notes and Queries*, Annual Volume 1900, page 51 (reference 90), says Isabella's birth was 8 Feb. 1778, born at West Nottingham, PA; however, if her parents were granted a "Certificate of Removed" from West Nottingham PA to Hopewell, VA in 1773, then the location of her birth is believed to be in error. (Date of comment March 1993)

p According to Hopewell records on page 390, ***1806, 11*** (Nov.) ***3. Isabella Wade (form Gawthrop) rpd;*** (reported) ***mcd;*** (married contrary to discipline) ***dis*** (disowned for). Therefore she could have married in the 6th month of that year as David Carl Gawthrop has indicated.

q According to Hopewell records on page 390, ***1806, 1*** (Jan.), ***6. James Jr. dis*** (disowned for) ***disunity.*** Which meant marriage outside of their faith.

r According to Hopewell records on page 390, ***1806, 11*** (Nov.), ***3. Edith Taylor (form Gawthrop) rpd*** (reported) ***mcd*** (married contrary to discipline) ***dis*** (disowned for) and on page 515, ***2 Day 3 Mo. 1807 Yr.*** Person Disowned ***Edith (Gawthrop) Taylor*** Reason for Disownment ***Married contrary to discipline.***

s According to Hopewell records on page 390, ***1812, 11*** (Nov.), ***5 Rachel Davis (form Gawthrop) rpd;*** (reported) ***mcd;*** (married contrary to discipline) ***dis*** (disowned for) and on page 517, ***10 Day 12 Mo. 1812*** Person Disowned ***Rachel Davis (formerly Gawthrop)*** Reason for Disownment ***Married contrary to discipline.***

t According to Hopewell records on page 390, ***1807, 4*** (April), ***8. Hannah, dt*** (daughter of) ***James & Patience*** (Gawthrop) ***m*** (married) ***Jacob JENKINS*** and on page 332 of the Hopewell Friends History, ***JENKINS – GAWTHROP, Jacob Jenkins, of the State of Virginia in the County of Frederick, son of Jonathan Jenkins (Deceased) of the County of Hampshire and state aforesaid and Ann his Wife, and Hannah Gawthrop, daughter of James Gawthrop and Patience his Wife; 8th day of the 4th month, 1807; "At the upper meeting on appe-pye ridge."*** Apparently only two of her sisters came to the wedding, Rachel Gawthrop and Edith Taylor.

*J*ames had 3 brothers and 2 sister. The three brothers were **1)** Thomas b: 23 Jan. 1737. There are little records found in England on Thomas (1737 - )*[55]* [u] or elsewhere; however, it may be wondered if he emigrated to Virginia and is same Thomas as mentioned in "Apple Ridge", Virginia.*[64]* **2)** Hugh b: 15 May 1741, d: 11 May 1773 *[29]* and **3)** George (q.v.) b: 17 Dec. 1743, d: 27 Aug. 1795. The two sisters were **1)** Ann b: 6 Oct. 1736 and **2)** Ruth b: 1 Nov. 1739, d: 31 Nov. 1813.

### *James Gawthrop's Will is in the form following[80]*

*1st – I leave to my beloved Wife, Patience Gawthrop two thirds of the Neat profits of the Plantation on which I live after the Taxes and Repairs are deducted during her natural life and chaste Widowhood.*

*2nd – I Will to my three Daughters, Rachel, Edith and Hannah the $ incum* (sic) *of the Annual Rent of the Lotts in Keff's Town to them or the survivors of them.*

*3rd – I give to my Son, James, Two Hundred Acres of Land on the Drains of Lost Run known by the Name of Plummers Survey, a Deed Signed to me from Henry Lee, Esq. Governor will fully scrific* (sic) *my Right dated the first Day of July 1793 – To him and his Heirs.*

*4th – at the Decease of my Wife, I Will that the Whole of my Property Be Sold or Rented for the Use of my children at the election of my executors, David Lupton & David Barrett (son of Benjamin Barrett, Deceased). I Will to Each of them Ten dollars.*

*5th – I Will to my Son, Thomas Gawthrop, my watch and as many of my wearing clothes as he chooses to accept after.*

*6th – I Will that the Plantation on Which I now reside may Be sold or Rented after my Wife Death as per above and Equally Divided amongst the survivors of my Living Children –*

*The Lotts in Keff's Town may be held by them or sold at their choosing, and My Executors and if any cost is on hand or out of hand in a Debts to be collected & Equally divided between Rachel Gawthrop, Edith Taylor & Hannah Jenkins.*

*Laying aside all former Wills and Testaments and I Acknowling* (sic) *this to be my Last Will –*

*6th Mo 11th – 1807, Signed Sealed and Delivered in the presence of Jacob Jenkins*
*George Dawson* *{signature of} James Gawthrop {seal}*

REFERENCES:

---

u In the Preston Patrick Preparative Meeting of Dec. 5th, 1759, Thomas Gawthrop, the younger, removed to Settle Monthly Meeting in the capacity of a servant.

SOURCE [16]: A handwritten family tree, *"OUR CHILDREN'S ANCESTORS,"* compiled by Rev. Darward and Dorothy Brown for their children and grandchildren, no date was available; however, Rev Darward Belmont Brown was born on 12 January 1897.

SOURCE [17]: Genealogy work compiled by Thomas Carr Gawthrop. This manuscript was not published by a publisher; however, Thomas Carr Gawthrop was born Jan. 1938 and died Sept. 1966.

SOURCE [19]: A handwritten family tree prepared by Allen Gawthrop in 1871. Allen was the son of Thomas and Elizabeth (Thompson) Gawthrop. The son of Allen and Mary Ann (Newlin) Gawthrop, Henry Gawthrop, collected data from Allen's work along with the assistance of several family members to generate another work entitled *GEORGE GAWTHROP, The Emigrate*, by Henry Gawthrop, dated Christmas 1900. Henry's work (in typescript, not published by a publisher) is available from the Friends Historical Library, Swarthmore, PA.

SOURCE [20]: A.M. Gummere (ed) *The Journal and Essays of John Woolman*, (Philadelphia & London 1922), pages 171 and 577.

SOURCE [23]: In an unfinished manuscript by Horace Henry Gawthrop called *"GAWTHROP", Chapter III, entitled Thomas Gawthrop - Life - Memorial*, pages 10 & 19, written at Christmas 1902. It is believed that he obtained much of the information about Thomas' death from the Testimony of Kendal Monthly Meeting in *Testimonies Concerning Ministers Deceased*, Vol. 3.

SOURCE [29]: *Dictionary of Quaker Biography*, (typescript, similar to a manuscript, not published by a publisher but is referenceable), only two copies exist; copies from both sources; Religious Society of Friends, London, England and Haverford College, Haverford, PA.

SOURCE [35]: G. Crosfield (ed), *Memoirs of the Life and Gospel Labours of Samuel Fothergill & c.*, (New York 1844), pages 286-287.

SOURCE [55]: Cumbria Archive, Historical Research Service, research conducted by Mrs. V.M. Gate, *"Preston Patrick Preparative Meeting, Men's Meeting Minute Book 1754 - 1766,"* WDFC/F1 - 10/2, research carried out in November 1993.

SOURCE [64]: Draft genealogy work compiled by Wm. A.A. Gawthrop, *"GAWTHROP GENEALOGY,"* U.S. Congressional Library, CS71.G277, 1986.

SOURCE [73]: Letter from Thomas Gawthrop written in Preston Patrick, England to John Pemberton, in Philadelphia, PA, dated December 30, 1769, obtained from the *PEMBERTON PAPERS*, Vol. 21, page 96.

SOURCE [80]: Letter from the Clerk's Office, Frederick County Circuit Court, George B. Whitacre, Clerk, Winchester, VA, post marked April 15, 1994, containing the Will of JAMES GAWTHROP (1742-1807).

SOURCE [81]: Letter/package containing a draft of Gawthrop Genealogy dated 2 June 1992 from Charles (Chuck) D. Thornton, Cape Coral, Fl.

SOURCE [82]: *Maryland Marriage, 1634 – 1777*, compiled by Robert Barnes of Genealogical Publishing Company, Inc., Baltimore, MD, publication date 1975.

SOURCE [83]: Vault - Gawthrop, misc-data of the J.V. Hollingsworth Collection, Chester County Historical Society, Letter from John V. Hollingsworth to Charlotte W. Maule in the late 18th century.

SOURCE [84]: Letter dated 13 April 1986 from Mrs. Nancy Speers, assistant librarian of the Friends Historical Library, Swarthmore College, Swarthmore, PA.

SOURCE [85]: *Hopewell Friends History 1734-1934, Frederick County, VA*, Records of Hopewell Monthly Meeting & meetings reporting to Hopewell, Compiled from Offical Records and Published by a Joint Committee of Hopewell Friends, printed by Shenandoah Publishing House, Inc., Strasburg, VA, pages 332, 390, 411, 511, 514, 517, 524, 530.

SOURCE [86]: Draft of the *Descendants of Thomas Gawthrop*, by Wm. A.A.Gawthrop, September 1993.

SOURCE [87]: Letter/package containing a draft #2 of *Gawthrop Genealogy* dated 15 Sept. 1993 from Charles (Chuck) D. Thornton, Cape Coral, Fl.

SOURCE [89]: Letter/package dated 7 April 1992 from David Carl Gawthrop, Charlottesville, VA.

SOURCE [90]: *"Egles Notes and Queries"*, Annual Volume 1900, page 51.

# Chapter 7

6th Generation

## 151246, GEORGE GAWTHROP ( 1743 – 1795 )

**G**eorge Gawthrop, the sixth child and fourth son of Thomas Gawthrop (1709-1780) and Isabel Crosfield (      -1775), was born on 17 Dec. 1743 in Stainton,[a] near Kendal, Westmoreland, England and died 27 Aug. 1795, in London Grove, Pennsylvania.*[17, 18, 19, 29]* He settled in Chester County, PA and became the ancestor to the Pennsylvania and Delaware Gawthrop Families. A copy of the Last Will and Testament of George Gawthrop has been transcribed at the end of this chapter.[b]

**I**t is known that George had several residences: in the vicinity of Nottingham in Chester County*[83]*; near Avondale, Chester County, PA; and London Grove Township, Chester County, PA. George attended Quaker meetings in East Nottingham, Monthly Meeting, MD; Kennet Square Monthly Meeting, PA; New Garden Monthly Meeting, PA.

***I***n a letter written by his father from his home in England to John Pemberton in Philadelphia on the 30th day of December 1769, ***...I send my two youngest sons which intend to settle on ye lands in Nottingham which I have given to them.****[73]* [c] George and his older brother, James, were going to live on their new found property in Nottingham that their father had given them.

***S***ometime in 1770, James and George emigrated from Gatebeck, Yorkshire, England*[17]* to America with the intent to settle on this property at Nottingham, PA.*[83]* [d] They probably sailed up the Delaware Bay then up the Delaware River and disembarked at New Castle,

---

a  Stainton, England and Gatebeck, England are within a 1 ½ miles of each other (see Gatebeck land plat in the chapter on *Thomas Gawthrop (1709-1780), the Travelling Friend*). His parents moved to Gatebeck around 1735/6 and his parents were still at Gatebeck in 1771. Therefore, the location of Stainton as to where George was born is believed to be in error unless they travelled to a Mid-wife in Stainton.

b  Several copies of this Will are available; 1.) Chester County Historical Society; 2.) George Gawthrop of Winchester, KY ( direct descendant and from which it was transcribed ); 3.) Major William A.A. Gawthrop, Glen Burnie, MD ( mother's address ) and 4.) P.E. Gawthrop, 1538 Endsley Pl., Crofton, MD.

c  A. M. Gummere (ed) in *The Journal and Essays of John Woolman*, verifies that Thomas Gawthrop was in the colonies in 1766; however, nothing is written concerning the actual date his two sons who emigrated to his piece of property in America.

d  John V. Hollingsworth in a letter written sometime in the later 19th or early 20th century to Charlotte W. Maule of West Grove, PA says, ***...possibly sometime after the middle of the 18th century, two brother, James and George came to America from Westmoreland, England, and took up residence in the vicinity of Nottingham in Chester County.***

Delaware or Wilmington, Delaware or Chester, Pennsylvania (see Map #10). If they went straight to Nottingham, the best route would have been to disembark at New Castle and travel almost due West. There is a western road from New Castle, DE to Newport, DE to London Britain, PA to New London Cross Roads, PA to Oxford, PA. Then travel South for about 6 miles to Nottingham, PA. If they wanted to go through Wilmington, DE, they would travel West to New Garden, PA then to West Grove, PA. Once in West Grove, they would travel Southwest to New London Cross Roads then almost due West to Oxford, PA then South to Nottingham, PA. If their father had advised them disembark at Chester, PA, which was a more formally route and one he knew well, they would travel West to Concord and Kennett, PA. Once in Kennett, they would travel in a Southwest direction to London Grove, West Grove, and New London Cross Roads, PA. Once in New London Cross Roads, they would travel almost due West to Oxford, PA then South for about 6 miles to Nottingham, PA all the time travelling through Quaker surroundings in Pennsylvania.

**G**eorge was unmarried in his 27 year when he emigrated. He attended the East Nottingham Monthly Meeting until 1772 when he wished to marry Jane Allen[e] of Kennett Monthly Meeting. According to custom, he told of his request to marry Jane to East Nottingham and requested a "Certificate of Removal" from East Nottingham. Also, according to custom, he appeared at the Kennett Monthly Meeting to tell of their plans to wed with a "Certificate of Removal" that read,

> ***George Gawthrop and Jane Allen appeared here and said they continued their intentions of marriage with each other, and the young man hath produced a Certificate as desired, they are left to their Liberty to Accomplish their Marriage orderly, James Wickersham and Isaac Bailey are appointed to oversee the same and make report to our next Meeting also bring the marriage certificate to be recorded.*** *[83]*

**G**eorge and Jane were orderly married and a copy of their certificate follows:*[83]*

***Whereas George Gawthrop of the Township of East Nottingham in the County of Chester & province of Pennsylvania, son of Thomas Gawthrop of Westmoreland in Old England and Isabel, his wife and Jane Allen daughter of James Allen of the Township of East Marlborough Township in the County of Chester & Province of Pennsylvania aforesaid and Jane his wife, Having declared their Intentions of Marriage before several Monthly Meetings of the People of God Called Quakers held at Kennett Center according to the Good order Used amongst them and having after deliberate Consideration they appearing Clear of all others were***

---

e They probably met at the wedding of James Gawthrop, his brother, and Patience Allen on 9 May 1771 (see previous chapter, page 58).

*approved of by the Said Meeting ... Now these are to Certify all whom it May Concern that for the full accomplishing their said intentions this thirty first day of the twelfth mo. in the Year of our Load one thousand seven hundred & seventy two, they the said George Gawthrop and Jane Allen appeared in a public Meeting of the People called Quakers and others in a Meeting house in Kennett where the said George Gawthrop taking her the said Jane Allen by ye hand did in a solemn Manner openly declare that he took her to be his Wife promising throw Divine Assistance to be unto her a loving & faithful husband until death should Separate them. And then & there in ye same Assembly She said Jane Allen did in like manner declare that she took him the said George Gawthrop to be her husband promising throw Divine Assistance to be unto him a loving and faithful wife until death shall Separate them ... Moreover the said George Gawthrop and Jane Allen, she according to ye custom of Marriage, assuming the name of her husband as a further Confirmation thereof did then and there to those present Sett their hands .... And we being present at the Solemnization of the said Marriage and subscription in manner aforesaid do as witnesses hereunto Sett our Names,*

*George Gawthrop*
*Jane Gawthrop*

| | | |
|---|---|---|
| *Thomas Carleton* | *Rachel Peirce* | *James Gawthrop* |
| *Wm. Harvey* | *Jane Temple* | *James Allen* |
| *Caleb Peirce* | *Ann Peirce* | *Jane Allen* |
| *William West* | *Rachel Marshall* | *William Allen* |
| *Amos Davis* | *Abigail Cloud* | *Hannah Allen* |
| *Thomas Milhous* | *Mary Way* | *Nathan Allen* |
| *Isaac Bailey* | *Sarah Bailey* | *Dinah Allen* |
| *Joshua Peirce* | *Esther Temple* | *Isaac Allen* |
| *Sampson Wickersham* | *Hannah Bailey* | *Wm. Cloud* |
| *Samuel Marshall* | *Fanny Dowdle* | *John Pugh* |
| *James Wickersham* | *Priscilla Wickersham* | *Hannah Pugh* |
| *Richard Barker* | *Rebekah Grubb* | *John Churchman Jr.* |
| *Abel Wickersham* | *David Bailey* | *Zebeda Hollingsworth* |
| | | *Rachel Baker* |
| | | *David Brown* |
| | | *Elizabeth Brown* |

NOTE: the signors in the right hand column, consider themselves to be the relatives of the couple that have just been married.

The marriage occurred on 31 Dec. 1772 and took place at the Kennet Square Meeting House, PA.*[83]* ***...shortly after their union they took up their residence in London Grove township, Chester county.****[91]* Jane was born 15 Jan. 1753 and died 30 Sept. 1821. George and his brother, James, married first cousins, Jane and Patience Allen.*[84]* George's father, Thomas, and a Quaker minister/journalist, John Woolman, developed a close friendship in their time spent in

America.[20] Therefore, this marriage may have been arranged by George's father and John Woolman.

***S***ome 14 years later, on the 18th of January 1786, George purchased a farm at West Grove (Deed Book Vol. 54, page 162, Chester County deeds). He purchased 3 tracts of land totaling 256 3/4 acres from the estate of James Greenfield for the sum of £450 cash and assuming £350 mortgage held in Philadelphia by Benjamin Chew. His adjoining property holders are mentioned in the deed as William Miller, Jeremiah Starr, William Miller Jr., Jonathan Lindley, Caleb Harlan, William Jackson, and John Allen the son-in-law to the former owner, James Greenfield.[83]

**J**ane is referred to as "Jane Jr." in the records of Kennet meeting.[92] George received a "Certificate of Removal" from East Nottingham Monthly Meeting to Kennet Monthly Meeting on 24 July 1773.[92] George and Jane received a "Certificate of Removal" from Kennet Monthly Meeting to New Garden Monthly Meeting on 13 June 1782.[93]

***G***eorge and Jane had 9 children[17] as follows:

**1512461,** Thomas (q.v.) b: 10 March 1774, d: 2 March 1851; He married Elizabeth Thompson[93] [f] on 13 Nov. 1800. {It should be noted that Elizabeth's brother married Thomas' sister, Jane.}

**1512462,** Hannah[93] [g] b: 24 Oct. 1776; She married Smithin Shortledge on 19 Dec. 1799. The marriage took place at New Garden Meeting House.

**1512463,** Isabella b: 18 July 1779, d: 1847.

**1512464,** James (q.v.) b: 25 Dec. 1781, d: 1 Aug. 1858; He married Hannah Marshall on 2 Feb. 1808.

**1512465,** George (q.v.) b: 19 Feb. 1784, d: 24 Sep. 1865; He married Amy Chambers[92] on 20 Jan. 1813.

**1512466,** Jane b: 22 May 1786, d: 1 June 1859; She married Daniel Thompson[92] [h] on 11 Jan. 1810. He was the son of Daniel & Elizabeth (Chambers) Thompson of Mill Creek, New Castle County, DE. The marriage took place at New Garden Meeting House. {It should be noted that Jane's brother, Thomas, married Daniel Thompson's sister, Elizabeth.}

**1512467,** William (q.v.) b: 1 March 1789, d: 13 Jan. 1856 in Baltimore, MD; He married Mary Griffith on 4 Aug. 1818.

---

f NG, PA #1, ***Gawthrop, Thomas married Elizabeth Thompson, 1800, 11, 13.***

g NG, PA #3, ***Gawthrop, Hannah married Smithin Shortlegde, 1799, 12, 19.***

h NG, PA #3, ***Gawthrop, Jane married Daniel Thompson, 1810, 1, 10.***

1512468, Allen born 15 Nov. 1792 – [died circa 1794, in London Grove, PA/86/][i],

1512469, Elizabeth b: 27 Aug. 1795, d: 1860; She married Nicholas W. Taylor of Baltimore, MD on 14 May 1818. He was the son of Thomas & Sarah Taylor of York, PA. The marriage took place at New Garden Meeting House.

George had 3 brothers and 2 sister. The three brothers were **1)** Thomas (b: 23 Jan. 1737). There is little record of Thomas (1737 - ) in England*/55/* [j] or elsewhere; however, it may be wondered if he emigrated to Virginia and is same as mentioned at "Apple Ridge", Virginia.*/64/* **2)** Hugh (b: 15 May 1741, d: 11 May 1773*/29/*) and **3)** James (q.v.)(b: 4 July 1742, d: sometime after 6th month 1807*/80/*). The two sisters were **1)** Ann (b: 6 Oct. 1736) and **2)** Ruth (b: 1 Nov. 1739, d: 31 Nov. 1813).

### *WILL OF GEORGE GAWTHROP, LONDON GROVE, PA/94/*

***I, GEORGE GAWTHROP, of the township of London Grove, County of Chester, and State of Penna. Being sick and weak of body, but of sound mind and memory, thanks be given to God, Therefore and calling to mind the uncertainty of life for setting my outward estate, do make this present writing my last will and testament, hereby revoking, annulling and making void all other wills by me heretofore made either by word or writing.***

***FIRST: My will is and I order that all my just debts and funeral expenses be paid out of my personal estate by my executors thereinafter named.***

***SECONDLY: I give devise and bequeath my well beloved wife, JANE GAWTHROP, one hundred acres of land off the east side or end of this my plantation, including the old mansion house wherein I now dwell with all the buildings, orchards, improvements and appliances thereunto belonging, to be divided and laid off by three judicious men chosen for that purpose to have and to hold during the term of her natural life, and this is intended as her full dower of my estate in full trust and confidence with the injunction that she shall neither waste or destroy the timber, orchards, fences, or other improvements and that at her decease the said plantation of one hundred acres be disposed of and equally by my surviving children, and further it is my will and desire that my said wife keep and bring up, educate and school my minor children at her own expense. The boys until they are of the age of 16 years, at which time, they are to be put to trades of their own choice, the girls until the are of***

---

i His father, Thomas, did not mention Allen in his Last Will and Testament which might be another indication that Allen may have died young.

j In the Preston Patrick Preparative Meeting of Dec. 5th, 1759, Thomas Gawthrop, the younger, removed to Settle Monthly Meeting in the capacity of a servant.

*the age of 18 years. Also I leave unto her the cart, harrow, and her choice of the plows, a full set of plow gears for two horses, the cart saddle and one pair of cart chains, two horses, four cows, two calves, six sheep, and four swine, all of her own choice. My silver during her life, afterwards to go to my son Thomas. All my household goods and furniture (except what is hereinafter excepted) for her own use and behoof and to be at her disposal as she pleases.*

*THIRDLY: I give and bequeath unto my son Thomas, The taether bed and bed steds with the clothing and furniture thereunto belonging, now standing in the little back room below the stairs. Four sheep of his choice after my wife, and this is intended for his services since he was of age, The young stone horse named TOGUE, and fifty pounds in cash, to be paid unto him one year after my decease and an equal share with the other children.*

*FOURTHLY: I give and bequeath unto my daughter Hannah, one feather bed and short bed steds now standing in the front room below the stairs with the furniture and clothing thereunto belonging, one cow of her choice of what remains, and the heifer that is called hers, and fifteen pounds in cash for her service since she was of age, to be paid unto her within one year after my decease, and an equal share with the other children.*

*FIFTHLY: It is my will and I order that the remaining part of this my said plantation to be sold at public sale within one year after my decease, and upon such conditions as shall be judged by the three friends chosen to divide the land, to be most advantageous and the moneys arising therefrom, as also from remaining part of my personal estate, to be equally divided between my children, Namely: Thomas, Hannah, Isabel, James, George, Jane, William, and if there should be one more, that it also have a share and part alike with the other surviving children, and they to have and be entitled to the increase and issue there of paid unto them with the principal as they come of age.*

*LASTLY: I nominate, constitute and appoint my beloved wife JANE GAWTHROP executrix and my son THOMAS GAWTHROP, executors of this my last will and testament. Signed with my hand and seal this 26th day of the eighth month in the year of our Lord 1795. GEORGE GAWTHROP (Seal)*

*Signed, Sealed, Published, Pronounced and Declared by the said GEORGE GAWTHROP as his last will and testament in the presence of us: Samuel Sharp, Jane Jackson, Isaac Wilson of West Chester, September 23rd, 1795.*

*Then personally appeared Samuel Sharp and Isaac Wilson who on their solemn affirmations according to law did severally declare, affirm and say that they were present and did see and hear GEORGE GAWTHROP the testator within named, sign, publish, pronounce and declare the within instrument appointing as and for his last will and testament and that the doing thereof, he was sound disposition of mind and memory to the best of their understandings. Affirmed before John Hannum, REGISTER.*

*Be it remembered that on the 23rd day of Sept. The last will and testament of GEORGE GAWTHROP deceased was proven in due form of law and testamentary were granted to James Gawthrop and Thomas Gawthrop sole executors herein named, They begin solely affirmed well and truly to administer and bring in an inventory into the registers office for the County of Chester on or before 23rd day of September next and in make a just and true account of their administration within one year or when thereunto lawfully required. Given under my hand and seal of the office.*

*John Hannum, REGISTER*

After the death of Jane Gawthrop on September 30, 1821, the 100 acres was transferred to her son, George Gawthrop. The heirs giving up their clam to the property and signing the deed were: Thomas Gawthrop *[George & Jane's first child]* and his wife, Elizabeth (Thompson); Smithin Shortledge and his wife, Hannah (Gawthrop) *[their second child]*; Isabel Gawthrop *[their third child]*; James Gawthrop *[their fourth child]* and his wife, Hannah (Marshall); Daniel Thompson and his wife, Jane (Gawthrop) *[their sixth child]*; and William Gawthrop *[their seventh child]*. *[*Do not know why Mary (Griffith), William's wife was not listed, they married 1818 and the year was 1821.*]* *[*Do not know why the signors did not include Nicholas W. Taylor and his wife, Elizabeth Gawthrop [their ninth child*]*.

REFERENCES:


SOURCE [17]: Genealogy work compiled by Thomas Carr Gawthrop. This manuscript was not published by a publisher; however, Thomas Carr Gawthrop was born Jan. 1938 and died Sept. 1966. This compiled work was obtained from Mary Virginia (Merrifield) Gawthrop wife of Wilbur Edmond Gawthrop (deceased) and her son, Richard Carr Gawthrop in early 1992. Thomas Carr Gawthrop was her nephew and Richard's cousin.

SOURCE [18]: A handwritten family tree prepared for Everard Conard Gawthrop by G. Cope of Pittsburgh, PA done in the mid 1920's. Philip Evan Gawthrop (Grandson of Everard) has the original work of this family tree.

SOURCE [19]: A handwritten family tree prepared by Allen Gawthrop in 1871. Allen was the son of Thomas and Elizabeth (Thompson) Gawthrop. The son of Allen and Mary Ann (Newlin) Gawthrop, Henry Gawthrop, collected data from Allen's work along with the assistance of several family members to generate another work entitled *GEORGE GAWTHROP, The Emigrate*, by Henry Gawthrop, dated Christmas 1900. Henry's work (in typescript, not published by a publisher) is available from the Friends Historical Library, Swarthmore College, PA.

SOURCE [20]: A.M. Gummere (ed) *The Journal and Essays of John Woolman*, (Philadelphia & London 1922), pages 171 and 577.

SOURCE [29]: *Dictionary of Quaker Biography*, (typescript, similar to a manuscript, not published by a publisher but is referenceable), only two copies exist; copies from both sources; Religious Society of Friends, London, England and Haverford College, Haverford, PA.

SOURCE [55]: Cumbria Archive, Historical Research Service, research conducted by Mrs. V.M. Gate, *"Preston Patrick Preparative Meeting, Men's Meeting Minute Book 1754 - 1766,"* WDFC/F1 - 10/2, research carried out in November 1993.

SOURCE [64]: Draft genealogy work compiled by Wm. A.A. Gawthrop, "GAWTHROP GENEALOGY," U.S. Congressional Library, CS71.G277, 1986.

SOURCE [73]: Letter from Thomas Gawthrop written in Preston Patrick, England to John Pemberton, in Philadelphia, PA, dated December 30, 1769, obtained from the *PEMBERTON PAPERS*, Vol. 21, page 96.

SOURCE [80]: Letter from the Clerk's Office, Frederick County Circuit Court, George B. Whitacre, Clerk, Winchester, VA, post marked April 15, 1994, containing the Will of JAMES GAWTHROP (1742-1807).

SOURCE [83]: Vault - Gawthrop, misc-data of the J.V. Hollingsworth Collection, Chester County Historical Society, Letter from John V. Hollingsworth to Charlotte W. Maule in the late 18th century. John V. states that this is from the Quaker records and Chester County Deeds and Wills, no date is on this document.

SOURCE [84]: Letter dated 13 April 1986 from Mrs. Nancy Speers, assistant librarian of the Friends Historical Library, Swarthmore College, Swarthmore, PA.

SOURCE [91]: Chester and Delaware Counties, Vol 2, by Gilbert Cope and Henry Graham Ashmead, page 577, obtained from Chester County Historical Society, West Chester, PA.

SOURCE [92]: Kennett Square Monthly Meeting, PA records.

SOURCE [93]: New Garden Monthly Meeting, PA records.

SOURCE [94]: A letter from George Gawthrop Jr. dated sometime in 1992 had a copy of The Last Will and Testament of George Gawthrop (1743 - 1795) or A package dated Dec. 24, 1993 mailed from the Chester County Historical Society contains a typed copy of The Last Will and Testament of George Gawthrop, obtained from the Chester County Historical Society, West Chester, PA.

# Chapter 8

7th Generation

## 1512452, THOMAS GAWTHROP ( 1776 - 1832 )

Thomas/17/ or Thomas William/64, 87/ Gawthrop, the second child and the first son of James Gawthrop (1742-1807) and Patience Allen (1746- ), was born on 22 Feb. 1776 and died on 26 Dec. 1832 in Taylor County, WV./location 87/ [a] Thomas married Elizabeth Hiett about 1797./81/ Elizabeth was the daughter of Rev. Evan Hiett and Sarah Smith of Hampshire County, VA. Elizabeth was born on 6 Jan. 1779 at Hampshire Co., VA[b] and died on 17 Aug. 1873 (94 years 7 months 11 days) in Taylor County, WV./17/ Thomas was a Quaker/81/ and was disowned by Hopewell Monthly Meeting for marriage contrary to discipline on 4 Feb. 1799./81/ [c] Their family moved from Winchester, VA to Pruntytown, WV about 1798/1800./20/ Spouses Note: The Waldo Book[d] states that the Hyat's (Hiett's) were Quakers and spells Elizabeth's last name as "Hyat" but does not give any birth or deathdates./81/

Panther Story: Elizabeth (Hiett) Gawthrop, daughter of Evan Hiett and Sarah Smith, married Thomas Gawthrop and they removed to one of the western counties of VA (now called West VA) the part of the state that is wilderness. One day while the men were away, she heard the stock making some unusual outcries, so went to investigate, fearing to find Indians, but instead, a panther caught her eye; it had attacked a hog in the pen. She hurried back, took down the gun from its hook and noiselessly returned to the pen, took aim and fired at the panther, killing it instantly. She had the skin tanned to prove her prowess. (authority for this story-her great nephew; Mr. A.C. Cowgill)./95/

Thomas and Elizabeth's children follow:

**15124521**, James (q.v.) b: 16 Oct. 1798; d: 10 Sept. 1883; married Hulda Waldo on 9 Jan. 1824,

---

a In 1861 when the Virginia delegates voted to secede from the Union the delegates from the northwestern counties rebelled and set up their own restored Government of Virginia. Congress voted to admit West Virginia on 20 June 1863.

b Hampshire County, Virginia became Hampshire County, West Virginia when the State split during the Civil War. Hamsphire County, WV has a northern bourder of Washington County, Maryland.

c *Hopewell Friends History 1734-1934*, p. 511 and p. 524.

d Charles D. Thornton, 1226 S.W. 18th Terrace, Cape Coral, FL 33991, has a copy of the "Genealogy of the Waldo Family."

**15124522,** Hiet (q.v.) b: 1807 at Taylor County, WV; d: no date but know where he died, Pruntytown, Taylor County, WV; married Mary Pool on 15 Feb. 1827 and after his death, Mary Pool Gawthrop married John Guines,*/64/*

**15124523,** Evan (H.*/81/*) b: 1810 at Taylor County, WV*/81/* (In the research of Thomas Carr Gawthrop, there is a reference that states "He went West unmarried about 1838. He was near Galena, Illinois when last heard from."*/17/*)

**15124524,** John (q.v.) b: 8 Dec. 1803 in Taylor County, WV; d: 25 April 1881; **1M**-Josinah Corbin on 22 May 1825; **2M**-Kathrine Radabaugh in 1871,

**15124525,** Thomas (q.v.) b: 7 April 1806 in Taylor County, WV; d: 4 Feb. 1876; He married Elizabeth Wiseman on 2 Feb. 1832.

**15124526,** Allen B. (q.v.) b: 1 March 1808 in Taylor County, WV; d: 10 Dec. 1887; He married Elizabeth H. Corder on 26 Sept. 1833.

**15124527,** Enos D. (q.v.) b: 6 March 1810in Taylor County, WV; d: 27 Oct. 1843; He married Ruth Wiseman on 28 Dec. 1831.

**15124528,** Sarah b: 3 Oct. 1812, (letter from David C. Gawthrop on 7 April 1992 places date of birth at Nov. 1918*/89/*), d: unmarried on 14 Oct. 1881 at Taylor County, WV and is buried in the Gawthrop Cemetery, Taylor County, WV,

**15124529,** Mary b: 6 Feb. 1815*/16/*, d: 11 Dec. 1902*/16/* in Taylor County, WV; married Wilson Boyle Brown (b: 26 June 1818, d: 7 Nov. 1898*/16/* in VA*/81/*) on 2 June 1840 in Taylor Co., WV*/81/*; Mary is buried at the Webster Cemetery for Quakers.*/16/* Wilson was a tanner and a farmer.*/81/*

**15124521.0** Elizabeth*/17, 89/* b: 23 June 1813 at Taylor County, WV*/89/* and d: 19 June 1910. She was married on 17 Nov. 1836 to John Shroyer. John was born on 29 Aug. 1811. John was a Gunsmith.*/89/*

**15124521.1** Margaret*/17, 89/* b: 12 Oct. 1818*/89/* and d: unmarried on 27 Feb. 1888 at age 70 years,*/89/*

**15124521.2** Isabella*/17, 89/* d: unmarried 8 Oct. 1863.*/89/*

Thomas had 1 brother and 6 sisters. The brother was **1)** James Jr. (b: 21 Oct. 1781, who was disowned for disunity by the Hopewell Monthly Meeting on 3 March 1806.*/85/*) The 6 sisters were **1)** Ester (b: 25 March 1773, d: 12 May 1773), **2)** Isabella (b: 16 Feb. 1778) was disowned for disunity by Hopewell Monthly Meeting on 3 Nov. 1806*/85/*, **3)** Edith (b: 6 Aug. 1783) married Mr. Taylor about 1806 and was disowned by the Hopewell Monthly Meeting for marriage contrary to discipline on 3 March 1807*/85/*, **4)** Rachel (b: 6 Aug. 1783) married Mr. [William*/86/*] Davis and was disowned by the Hopewell Monthly Meeting for marriage contrary to discipline on 11 Dec. 1812*[85]*. **5)** Hannah[e] (b: approx. 1788) married Jacob Jenkins, son of Jonathan Jerkins and Ann Hoge, and **6)** Ruth (b: 27 Feb. 1791.

REFERENCES

SOURCE [16]: A handwritten family tree, *"OUR CHILDREN'S ANCESTORS"*, compiled by Rev. Darward and Dorothy Brown for their children and grandchildren, no date was available; however, Rev Darward Belmont Brown was born on 12 January 1897. It is thought that the Brown Family Tree and the Everard C. Gawthrop Family Tree were commissioned approximately the same time. Philip E. Gawthrop has the original work of the Everard C. Gawthrop family tree prepared by genealogist G. Cope in the early to mid 1920's.

SOURCE [17]: Genealogy work compiled by Thomas Carr Gawthrop. This manuscript was not published by a publisher; however, Thomas Carr Gawthrop was born Jan. 1938 and died Sept. 1966. This compiled work was obtained from Mary Virginia (Merrifield) Gawthrop wife of Wilbur Edmond Gawthrop (deceased) and her son, Richard Carr Gawthrop in early 1992. Thomas Carr Gawthrop was her nephew and Richard's cousin.

SOURCE [20]: A.M. Gummere (ed) *The Journal and Essays of John Woolman*, (Philadelphia & London 1922), pages 171 and 577.

SOURCE [64]: Draft genealogy work compiled by Wm. A.A. Gawthrop, "GAWTHROP GENEALOGY," U.S. Congressional Library, CS71.G277, 1986.

SOURCE [81]: Letter/package containing a draft of Gawthrop Genealogy dated 2 June 1992 from Charles (Chuck) D. Thornton, Cape Coral, Fl.

SOURCE [85]: *Hopewell Friends History 1734-1934, Frederick County, VA*, Records of Hopewell Monthly Meeting & meetings reporting to Hopewell, Compiled from Offical Records and Published by a Joint Committee of Hopewell Friends, printed by Shenandoah Publishing House, Inc., Strasburg, VA, pages 332, 390, 411, 511, 514, 517, 524, 530.

SOURCE [87]: Letter/package from Charles D. Thornton, Cape Coral, FL on September 15, 1993.

SOURCE [89]: Letter from David Carl Gawthrop, Charlottesville, VA on 7 April 1992.

SOURCE [95]: Charles D. Thornton visited the Orlando Public Library on 26 Aug. 1993 in the WV section. He came across the "Capon Valley Pioneers & Their Descendants," 1698-1940, Volume I & II, by Maud Pugh - the Panther Story was on page 132.

---

e ***Jacob Jenkins, of the State of Virginia in the County of Frederick, son of Jonathan Jenkins (Deceased) of the County of Hampshire and the State aforesaid and Ann his Wife, and Hannah Gawthrop, daughter of James Gawthrop and Patience his Wife; 8th day of 4th month, 1807; "At the upper meeting on appe-pye ridge." Jacob Jenkins*** and ***Hannah Jenkins.*** *[85]* Only two sisters apparently attended the wedding, Rachel Gawthrop and Edith Taylor.

# Chapter 9

7th Generation

## 1512461, THOMAS GAWTHROP ( 1774 - 1851 )

Thomas*/16, 19/* Gawthrop, the first child and the first son of George Gawthrop (1743-1795) and Jane Allen (1753-1821), was born on 10 March 1774 at London Grove, PA*/91/* and died 2 April 1851 at his residence in London Grove, PA.*/96/* Thomas was buried in the New Garden Friends (Hicksite) Meeting Cemetery.*/97/* The grave stone inscriptions from that cemetery reads, ***THOMAS GAWTHROP, Age 77 years, 1851.****/98/* In the newspaper, American Republican, dated October 21th, 1851, there is an estate sale that in part reads, ***Real Estate at Public Sale. Pursuant to the last will and testament of Thomas Gawthrop, deceased, will be sold at public sale, ...****/99/* Thomas married Elizabeth Thompson on 13 Nov. 1800*/64, 100/* at New Garden Monthly Meeting, PA.[a] Elizabeth was the daughter of Daniel and Elizabeth (Chambers) Thompson of Mill Creek, New Castle County, DE. Elizabeth was born on 15 Nov. 1779 at Mill Creek and died on 16 April 1864 at New Garden, PA. Elizabeth is buried in the New Garden Friends (Hicksite) Meeting Cemetery.*/97/* The grave stone inscriptions from that cemetery reads, ***ELIZABETH GAWTHROP, Aged 85, 1864.****/101/*

Thomas was a gentleman farmer and a Quaker throughout his life.*/81/* Thomas was an executor to his father's Will along with his mother.*/94/* Thomas is bequeathed some furniture, some stock, and some cash by his father, George Gawthrop in 1795. The part of his father's Will that relates to Thomas is as follows:

> .... ***THIRDLY: I give and bequeath unto my son Thomas, The taether bed and bed steds with the clothing and furniture thereunto belonging, now standing in the little back room below the stairs. Four sheep of his choice after my wife, and this is intended for his services since he was of age, the young stone horse named TOGUE, and fifty pounds in cash, to be paid unto him one year after my decease and an equal share with the other children.****/94/*

Thomas and Elizabeth lived in London Grove Township, Chester County, PA (near Avondale) throughout their lifetime. Apart of the homestead was divided off for him and they lived for a time in a log house. He built the stone house in the west end in 1808, and in the east end

---

a According to the New Garden M.M., PA record, #1, ***Gawthrop, Thomas married Elizabeth Thompson 1800, 11, 13.***

in 1816.*[102]* A copy of the Last Will and Testament of Thomas Gawthrop has been transcribed at the end of this chapter.[b]

Thomas and Elizabeth's children follow *[17, 19, 102]*:

**15124611,** Sarah b: 14 Sept. 1801 at London Grove, PA, d: in July 1887, She married Joseph Seal of Philadelphia, PA on 13 March 1823*[93]* [c] in West Grove, PA. Joseph, the son of Benjamin and Phebe Seal of New Garden, PA, was born on 20 Nov. 1788 and died on 17 June 1842. Sarah's funeral was at the residence of her daughter Phebe S. Bailey.*[81]* Sarah was buried on 13 July 1887*[81]* in West Grove, PA.

**15124612,** Ann b: 9 Sept. 1803 at London Grove, PA, d: at the home of her widowed mother in London Grove, PA on 9 Oct. 1857 at age 54 years.

**15124613,** Daniel (q.v.) b: 12 July 1805 at London Grove, PA, d: 16 March 1838, He married Elizabeth Mitchell on 16 Dec. 1830 at Hockessin, DE.

**15124614,** Jane b: 29 Sept. 1807 at London Grove, PA, d: 9 Jan. 1837, She married Hibberd Moore on 14 Oct. 1830 at New Garden, PA. Hibberd was the son of David and Martha (Sharpless) Moore. They had one child, Gilpen Moore b: 27 Oct. 1831. They moved from eastern Pennsylvania to Rock Island, Illinois.[d]

**15124615,** Allen (q.v.) b: 22 June 1810 at London Grove, PA, d: 23 June 1885, He married Mary Ann Newlin on 31 July 1833.

**15124616,** Lydia b: 12 Feb. 1813 at London Grove, PA, d: 30 July 1842 at age 29 years 5 months 18 days.

**15124617,** Elizabeth b: 16 July 1815 at London Grove, PA, d: 20 Oct. 1819.

**15124618,** James T. b: 20 Sept. 1819 at London Grove Township, PA, d: 23 July 1889 at his home in Avondale, PA age 69 years, He married Priscilla Peirce on 24 May 1855. Priscilla was the daughter of Gideon and Rebecca (Lukens) Peirce of Ercild, PA. The marriage took place at Gideon Peirce's home. Priscilla was born 1 Dec. 1829 and died on 11 June 1860. She is buried at New Garden, PA. They lived in the "brick"

---

b Several copies of Thomas' Will are available; 1.) Chester County Historical Society; and 2.) a copy of that said Will is at the home of Philip E. Gawthrop, 1538 Endsley Place, Crofton, MD.

c According to New Garden M.M. record #3, ***Gawthrop, Sarah married Joseph Seal on 1823, 3, 13.***

d There is conjecture that something happened to his parents in Illinois and he came back to live with his grandparents or when his parents moved to Illinois that they left him behind with his grandparents until he could be sent for (apparently something happened such that he was never sent for). The reason for this conjecture is an item in Thomas' Will. He bequeaths 500 dollars to Sarah, Lydia Ann, Amy, Emmor, and Gilpen. Gilpen's parents may also have died. More research is needed to be sure about this.

house at the homestead near Avondale (southern part of) Chester County, PA. James is buried at New Garden Cemetery on 26 July 1889. They had two daughters; Ella R. and Lucy.

In 1838 when Daniel and his wife, Elizabeth, died suddenly, somebody had to look after their 4 children, Sarah M., Emmor, Lydia Ann, and Amy. Two of their children, Sarah Mitchell and Emmor, were taken in by their Grandparents on the father's side, Thomas and Elizabeth (Thompson) Gawthrop. Sarah was just over 7 years old and Emmor was only 8 months old when they came to live with their Grandparents. For more than 15 years, Sarah and Emmor were the children in their Grandparents home.

**151246131**, Sarah Mitchell (called Sallie) b: 20 Nov. 1831 and is recorded in the New Garden Monthly Meeting, Chester County, PA, d: [ 23 Oct. 1886 in Oxford, Chester County, PA*(81)*], married William Henry Way (b: 27 March 1829*(81)*, d: 21 March 1910*(81)*) on 17 April 1862 in Avondale, Chester County, PA. Sarah and William had 4 children: James Allen, Elizabeth H. (called Lizie), Charles Henry, and Amy Anna.

**151246134**, Emmor D. (q.v.) b: 31 Aug. 1837 in London Grove, PA, d: 25 Dec. 1920 in PA, He married Phebe Thompson on 29 Jan. 1863. He was in the Civil War-87th Pennsylvania Volunteers under the command of Colonel Murphy.

Lydia Ann was taken in by the Grandparents on the mother's side, Joseph & Sarah Mitchell.

**151246132**, Lydia Ann b: 27 June 1833 recorded at New Garden, PA, d: 26 Dec. 1907 at Hochessin, DE, buried at New Castle County, DE, unmarried.

Amy was taken in by her Grandfather Thomas Gawthrop's brother and his wife, George & Amy (Chambers) Gawthrop.

**151246133**, Amy b: 10 Dec. 1835, d: in Lancaster County, PA, married Alexander N. Turner of Colerain, Lancaster County, PA on 12 April 1862.

Thomas had 4 brothers and 4 sisters. The four brothers were **1)** James (q.v.) b: 25 Dec. 1781, d: 1 Aug. 1858, married Hannah Marshall on 2 Feb. 1808, **2)** George (q.v.) b: 19 Feb. 1784, d: 24 Sept. 1865, married Amy Chambers on 20 Jan. 1813, **3)** William (q.v.) b: 1 March 1789, d: 13 Jan. 1856, married Mary Griffith on 4 Aug. 1818, **4)** Allen b: 15 Nov. 1792. The four sisters were: **1)** Hannah b: 24 Oct. 1776, married Smithin Shortledge (b: 4 Oct. 1772, d: 16 Aug. 1822) on 19 Dec. 1799 at New Garden Monthly Meeting, PA*(93)*[e], **2)** Isabella b: 18 July 1779, d: 24 Dec. 1847 at London Grove Township, Chester County, PA, **3)** Jane b: 22 May 1786, d: 1 June 1859, married Daniel Thompson (b: 10 March 1782, d: 14 June 1837) on 11 Jan. 1810 at New Garden Monthly Meeting, PA. Daniel was the son of Daniel and Elizabeth (Chambers) Thompson. Daniel and Jane lived at

---

e According to New Garden M.M. record #3, ***Gawthrop, Hannah married Smithin Shortledge, 1799, 12, 19.***

Mill Creek, New Castle County, DE. Jane is buried at Mill Creek Hundred, New Castle County, DE. **4)** Elizabeth b: 27 Aug. 1795, d: 1860, married Nicholas W. Taylor (b: 8 Aug. 1794, d: 26 Dec. 1826) of Baltimore on 14 May 1818 at the New Garden Monthly Meeting, PA. Nicholas was the son of Thomas and Sarah Taylor of York, PA. He is buried in Baltimore, MD. They lived in Baltimore, then after the death of Nicholas, afterwhich Elizabeth moved to a farm on the state road near New West Grove, PA.

### *WILL OF THOMAS GAWTHROP, LONDON GROVE, PA[103]*

*I, THOMAS GAWTHROP, of the township of London Grove, County of Chester, and state of Pennsylvania being advanced in years but in health of body and of sound mind, memory and understanding and considering the uncertainty of this transitory life do make and publish this my last will and testament in manner and form as follows:*

*FIRST: I order and direct that all my just debts and funeral expenses be first paid by my executors (herein after name) as soon after my decease as can conveniently be done.*

*ITEM: I give and devise unto my beloved wife, ELIZABETH GAWTHROP, all that plantation on which I now reside situate in the township of London Grove, County of Chester and state of Pennsylvania (except that part on which the brick buildings are erected and which I will herein after direct to be sold) together with all my live stock, farming utensils, household and kitchen furniture which I may have at my decease; all and every of which property both real and personal (with the profits thereof) she shall have and hold as her own for and during her natural life which is to be in lieu of her dower at common law.*

*ITEM: I give and devise unto my son JAMES GAWTHROP at the decease of my said wife (but not till then) all that plantation or tract of land (which I have bequeathed unto my said wife during natural life) to hold the said plantation or tract of land to him the said JAMES GAWTHROP his heirs and assigns forever he paying to my grandson GILPEN MOORE at the decease of my aforesaid wife or when he the said GILPEN MOORE arrives at the age of twenty one years the sum of four hundred dollars (which sum I will hereinafter bequeath to him the said GILPEN MOORE) and further it is my will that my daughter ANN GAWTHROP shall have the privilege of a home with him the said JAMES GAWTHROP if it be her choice. I also bequeath to my said son JAMES GAWTHROP all the stock and farming utensils which my said wife may have at her decease also the desk and clock.*

*ITEM: I give and bequeath to my two sons ALLEN GAWTHROP and JAMES GAWTHROP all my wearing apparel to be divided between them equally share and part alike.*

*ITEM: I give and bequeath to my daughter ANN GAWTHROP (at the decease of my wife) her first choice of the feather beds, bedsteads and bedclothing* (sic) *for the same also the bureau that was her sister JANE MOORE'S also her first choice of the other bureaus.*

*ITEM: I give and bequeath to my two daughters SARAH SEAL and ANN GAWTHROP (at the decease of my aforesaid wife) all the residue and remainder of my household and kitchen furniture that may be remaining to be divided between them equally share and part alike.*

*ITEM: I give and bequeath to my five grandchildren namely SARAH GAWTHROP, LYDIA ANN GAWTHROP, AMY GAWTHROP, EMMOR GAWTHROP, and GILPEN MOORE five hundred dollars each to be paid to them as they severally arrive at the age of twenty one years by my executors herein after named.*

*ITEM: I also give and bequeath unto my grandson GILPEN MOORE four hundred dollars to be paid to him when he arrives at the age of twenty one years by my son JAMES GAWTHROP as I before mentioned or directed but not to be paid until after the decease of my wife or the farm comes into his possession.*

*ITEM: It is my will and I direct that the aforesaid part of my farm on which the brick building stands shall be sold at public sale by my executors as soon after my decease as can properly be done which said (Northern) part is divided from the whole by a line beginning at a stone at a south east corner of the land of the heirs of ISRAEL JACKSON deceased thence S. 19° & dis 21.2P to a stone thence N. 84° & dis. 2.68P to a stone thence S. 19.6° & dis 23.3 per to a stone thence N. 83 3/4° & dis 39.4P to a stone thence 69 1/2 ° & dis 8.28P to a stone thence N. 70 1/2° & dis. 66.68P to a stone a corner of GEORGE GAWTHROP's land. The proceeds of which sale together with all the residue and remainder of my estate shall be equally divided between my three children namely SARAH SEAL, ANN GAWTHROP and ALLEN GAWTHROP share and part alike.*

*LASTLY: I nominate constitute and appoint my two sons ALLEN and JAMES GAWTHROP executors of this my last will and testament hereby revoking all wills by me at any time heretofore made and declaring this and no other to be my last will and testament. In witness whereof of I have here unto set my hand and seal this nineteenth day of ninth month in the year of our Lord one thousand eight hundred and forth three.*

*Thomas Gawthrop {Seal}*

*Signed sealed published and declared by the said Testator as his last will and testament in the presence of us who in his presence and as his request have subscribed our names as witnesses therto* (sic).

*Benjamin West*
*George Gawthrop Jr.*

## REFERENCES


SOURCE [16]: A handwritten family tree, *"OUR CHILDREN'S ANCESTORS,"* compiled by Rev. Darward and Dorothy Brown for their children and grandchildren, no date was available; however, Rev Darward Belmont Brown was born on 12 January 1897.

SOURCE [17]: Genealogy work compiled by Thomas Carr Gawthrop. This manuscript was not published by a publisher; however, Thomas Carr Gawthrop was born Jan. 1938 and died Sept. 1966. This compiled work was obtained from Mary Virginia (Merrifield) Gawthrop wife of Wilbur Edmond Gawthrop (deceased) and her son, Richard Carr Gawthrop in early 1992. Thomas Carr Gawthrop was her nephew and Richard's cousin.

SOURCE [19]: A handwritten family tree prepared by Allen Gawthrop in 1871. Allen was the son of Thomas and Elizabeth (Thompson) Gawthrop. The son of Allen and Mary Ann (Newlin) Gawthrop, Henry Gawthrop, collected data from Allen's work along with the assistance of several family members to generate another work entitled *GEORGE GAWTHROP, The Emigrate*, by Henry Gawthrop, dated Christmas 1900. Henry's work (in typescript, not published by a publisher) is available from the Friends Historical Library, Swarthmore College, PA.

SOURCE [64]: Draft genealogy work compiled by Wm. A.A. Gawthrop, "GAWTHROP GENEALOGY," U.S. Congressional Library, CS71.G277, 1986.

SOURCE [81]: Letter/package containing a draft of Gawthrop Genealogy dated 2 June 1992 from Charles (Chuck) D. Thornton, Cape Coral, Fl.

SOURCE [91]: Chester and Delaware Counties, by Gilbert Cope and Henry Graham Ashmead, Vol. 2, page 577, obtained from Chester County Historical Society, West Chester, PA.

SOURCE [93]: New Garden Monthly Meeting, PA records.

SOURCE [94]: A letter from George Gawthrop Jr. dated sometime in 1992 had a copy of The Last Will and Testament of George Gawthrop (1743 - 1795), or a package dated Dec. 24, 1993 mailed from the Chester County Historical Society contains a typed copy of The Last Will and Testament of George Gawthrop, obtained from the Chester County Historical Society, West Chester, PA.

SOURCE [96]: Package dated Nov. 13, 1991 mailed from the Chester County Historical Society, West Chester, PA, contains a newspaper article, *Village Record*, dated 15 April 1851, on the death of Thomas Gawthrop (1774 - 1851).

SOURCE [97]: The New Garden Friends (Hicksite) Meeting Cemetery records for Thomas (1851) and Elizabeth (1864) Gawthrop, obtained from the Chester County Historical Society, West Chester, PA.

SOURCE [98]: Grave Stone inscriptions from the New Garden Friends (Hicksite) Meeting Cemetery, C-4-24 New Gar. Hicksite for Thomas Gawthrop 1851, obtained from the Chester County Historical Society, West Chester, PA.

SOURCE [99]: The American Republican, a newspaper, 21 October 1851, ***Real Estate at Public Sale.***, obtained from the Chester County Historical Society, West Chester, PA.

SOURCE [100]: Package dated 24 Dec. 1990 obtained from the Chester County Historical Society, West Chester, PA, contains a copy of *History of Chester County Pennsylvania*, by J. Smith Futhey & Gilbert Cope, I. Evert (editor), 1881, page 563.

SOURCE [101]: Grave Stone inscriptions from the New Garden Friends (Hicksite) Meeting Cemetery, C-4-25 New Gar. Hicksite for Elizabeth Gawthrop 1864, obtained from the Chester County Historical Society, West Chester, PA.

SOURCE [102]: Package dated Nov. 13, 1991 mailed from the Chester County Historical Society contains a handwritten copy about Thomas Gawthrop (b: 1774-3-10) from the work by Henry Gawthrop called *GAWTHROP Genealogy*, File-Gawthrop 1-35, written about 1900, obtained from the Chester County Historical Society, West Chester, PA.

SOURCE [103]: Package dated Nov. 13, 1991 mailed from the Chester County Historical Society contains a handwritten copy of The Last Will and Testament of Thomas Gawthrop (1774 - 1851), obtained from the Chester County Historical Society, West Chester, PA.

# Chapter 10

7th Generation

## 1512464, JAMES GAWTHROP ( 1781 - 1858 )

*J*ames*/17, 19/* Gawthrop, the second child and the fourth son of George Gawthrop (1743-1795) and Jane Allen (1753-1821), was born on 25 Dec. 1781 and died 1 Aug. 1858 (77 years 7 months 6 days) at Marlborough, PA. James married Hannah Marshall of West Bradford, PA on 2 Feb. 1808 at Bradford Monthly Meeting House, PA. Hannah was the daughter of Samuel and Rachel Marshall of West Bradford, PA. Hannah was born on 1 Aug. 1784 and died on 29 Sept. 1862 (77 years 10 months 21 days). They both are buried at Marlborough, Chester County, PA.*/81/* They lived in London Grove Township, Chester County, PA (near Avondale).

*J*ames and Hannah's children follow */17, 19/*:

**15124641,** Mary b: 9 Nov. 1809 recorded at Kennet Square Monthly Meeting, Chester County, PA, married Caleb J. Hoopes on 12 April 1837*/92/* [a] at Marlborough, Chester County, PA.*/81/* Caleb was the son of Abner and Sarah Hoopes of Thronbury, Delaware County, PA. Caleb was born on 4 April 1792 and died on 14 June 1865,*/81/*

**15124642,** Jane b: 16 Aug. 1812, married Joshua H. Moore,

**15124643,** George (q.v.) b: 29 April 1815 at Chester County, PA, d: 26 Nov. 1877 (62 years 6 months 27 days) at Marlboroville, PA, married Mary Jane Woodward.

**15124644,** Rachel b: 25 Nov. 1817 recorded at Kennett Square M.M., Chester County, PA, married Thomas [Wistar*/81/*] Parker on 13 March 1839 at Marlborough Monthly Meeting, Chester County, PA. Thomas was the son of Benjamin and Sarah Parker of East Marlborough, PA. After Thomas died, Rachel lived in Philadelphia, PA with her daughter Hannah.

**15124645,** Hannah [Hanna */64/*] b: 3 Nov. 1821 at Marlborough, PA*/81/*, d: 17 Dec. 1849 (28 years old) at Marlborough, PA, and is buried at Marlborough, PA.*/92/* [b]

**15124646,** James Jr. (q.v.) b: 14 Jan. 1825 at Chester County, PA, d: 2 March 1869 at Kennett Square, PA, married Sarah C. Ridgway on 15 Feb. 1849.

---

a According to the Kennett Monthly Meeting, as delineated by Wm Hinshaw in his notes, KP-44-2.

b According to Kennett Monthly Meeting, as delineated by Wm Hinshaw in his notes, KP-458-3.

*J*ames had 4 brothers and 4 sisters. The four brothers were: **1)** Thomas (q.v.) b: 10 March 1774, d: 2 March 1851, married Elizabeth Thompson, **2)** George (q.v.) b: 19 Feb. 1784, d: 24 Sept. 1865, married Amy Chambers, **3)** William (q.v.) b: 1 March 1789, d: 13 Jan. 1856, married Mary Griffith, **4)** Allen b: 15 Nov. 1792. The four sisters were: **1)** Hannah b: 24 Oct. 1776, married Smithin Shortledge (b: 4 Oct. 1772, d: 16 Aug. 1822) on 19 Dec. 1799 at New Garden Monthly Meeting, PA*[93]* [c], **2)** Isabella b: 18 July 1779, d: prior to 26 Jan. 1848 at London Grove, Chester County, PA, **3)** Jane b: 22 May 1786, d: 1 June 1859, married Daniel Thompson (b: 10 March 1782, d: 14 June 1837) on 11 Jan. 1810 at New Garden Monthly Meeting, PA. Daniel was the son of Daniel and Elizabeth (Chambers) Thompson. Daniel and Jane lived at Mill Creek, New Castle County, DE, **4)** Elizabeth b: 27 Aug. 1795, d: 1860, married Nicholas W. Taylor (b: 8 Aug. 1794, d: 26 Dec. 1826) of Baltimore on 14 May 1818 at the New Garden Monthly Meeting, PA. Nicholas was the son of Thomas and Sarah Taylor of York, PA and is buried in Baltimore, MD. They lived in Baltimore, then after the death of Nicholas, Elizabeth moved to a farm on the state road near New West Grove, PA.

REFERENCES


SOURCE [17]: Genealogy work compiled by Thomas Carr Gawthrop. This manuscript was not published by a publisher; however, Thomas Carr Gawthrop was born Jan. 1938 and died Sept. 1966. This compiled work was obtained from Mary Virginia (Merrifield) Gawthrop wife of Wilbur Edmond Gawthrop (deceased) and her son, Richard Carr Gawthrop in early 1992. Thomas Carr Gawthrop was her nephew and Richard's cousin.

SOURCE [19]: A handwritten family tree prepared by Allen Gawthrop in 1871. Allen was the son of Thomas and Elizabeth (Thompson) Gawthrop. The son of Allen and Mary Ann (Newlin) Gawthrop, Henry Gawthrop, collected data from Allen's work along with the assistance of several family members to generate another work entitled *GEORGE GAWTHROP, The Emigrate*, by Henry Gawthrop, dated Christmas 1900. Henry's work (in typescript, not published by a publisher) is available from the Friends Historical Library, Swarthmore College, PA.

SOURCE [64]: Draft genealogy work compiled by Wm. A.A. Gawthrop, "GAWTHROP GENEALOGY," U.S. Congressional Library, CS71.G277, 1986.

SOURCE [81]: Letter/package containing a draft of Gawthrop Genealogy dated 2 June 1992 from Charles (Chuck) D. Thornton, Cape Coral, Fl.

SOURCE [92]: Kennett Square Monthly Meeting, PA records.

SOURCE [93]: New Garden Monthly Meeting, PA records.


---

c According to New Garden Monthly Meeting, #3, ***Gawthrop, Hannah married Smithin Shortledge, 1799, 12, 19.***

# Chapter 11

7th Generation

## 1512465, GEORGE GAWTHROP Jr.*[Jr. in 100, 104]*( 1784 - 1865 )

George Gawthrop, the fifth child and the third son of George Gawthrop (1743-1795) and Jane Allen (1753-1821), was born on 19 Feb. 1784. This birth is recorded in the New Garden Monthly Meeting, Chester County, PA.*[93]* George died on 24 Sept. 1865 at London Grove Township, PA. George is buried in the New Garden Friends (Hicksite) Meeting Cemetery.*[105]* The grave stone inscription from that cemetery reads, ***GEORGE GAWTHROP, 1865.****[106]* In the newspaper, American Republican, dated February 20th, 1866, there is an estate sale that reads, ***Estate of George Gawthrop, Deceased. All persons indebted to the Estate of Gawthrop, late of the township of London Grove, county of Chester, deceased, will come forward and settle the same and those having claims against said Estate, will present them for settlement. THOS.GAWTHROP, GEO.GAWTHROP, WM.GAWTHROP.****[107]* George and Amy Chambers announced to the Kennett Monthly Meeting of their plans to wed on 8 Dec. 1812.*[108]* They announced their plans a second time, as is customary, on 5 Jan. 1813.*[109]* George married Amy Chambers on 20 Jan. 1813 *[92]* [a] at Old Kennett Square Monthly Meeting House, PA. As is customary, they were reported as married to the Kennet Monthly Meeting on 2 Feb. 1813*[110]* Amy was the daughter of Joseph and Amy (Thompson) Chambers of New Castle County, DE. Amy was born on 4 May 1787 and died on 11 Oct. 1851 probably in her home in London Grove Township. Amy is buried in the New Garden Friends (Hicksite) Meeting Cemetery.*[111]* They lived in London Grove Township (near Avondale), PA. Again, as is customary, Amy received a "Certificate of Removal" from Kennett Monthly Meeting to New Garden Monthly Meeting on April 6th, 1813 so she could join her husband's meeting.*[92]* [b]

George and Amy had 10 children: 7 sons and 3 daughters. Their children follow:

**15124651,** Ruth b: 11 Nov. 1813, d: unknown, married Isaac Moore (b: 21 March 1810 @ London Grove, PA) son of Joseph and Beulah Moore on 18 Nov. 1841 (marriage is recorded in the New Garden Monthly Meeting*[93]*). They lived on a farm at West Grove, Chester Co., PA and operated a mill.

**15124652,** Joseph C. b: 29 Jan. 1815, d: unmarried on 26 June 1892, had what appeared to be polio (leg paralyzed*[17]*), lived with sister, Elizabeth (Gawthrop) Hughes. He was a tinsmith (pot-maker).

---

a According to the Kennett Monthly Meeting, as delineated by Wm Hinshaw in his notes, KP-481-4.

b According to the Kennett Monthly Meeting, as delineated by Wm Hinshaw in his notes, KP-183-2.

George Gawthrop Jr., b: 19 Feb. 1784, d: 24 Sept. 1865

and

Amy (Chambers) Gawthrop, b: 4 May 1787, d: 11 Oct. 1851

[Obtained from Ethel (Stahl) Gawthrop's picture collection. In Ethel's handwriting, in pencil, on the back of this picture, there are two names; George Gawthrop and Amy (Chambers) Gawthrop. Also, in pencil, George and Amy are linked to William (their son), to Evan (their grandson), to Everard (their great grandson), and to Arthur (their great, great grandson)].

**15124653,** son that was a twin, unknown name because he died in infancy/17/, b: 29 Dec. 1816, d: 30 Dec. 1816.

**15124654,** daughter that was a twin, unknown name because she died in infancy/17/, b: 29 Dec. 1816, d: 29 Jan. 1817.

**15124655,** Thomas (q.v.) b: 7 Feb. 1818, d: 25 Jan. 1864, married twice to sisters, Lydia and Susanna Conard.

**15124656,** Elizabeth b: 15 Feb. 1820 (birth is recorded in the New Garden Monthly Meeting, Chester County, PA/93/), d: 31 Dec. 1897, married William Hughes (b: 10 April 1819, d: 9 May 1894) on 20 May 1841. William was the son of Mark and Lydia Hughes (marriage is recorded in the New Garden Monthly Meeting/93/). They both died at the residence of their daughter and son-in-law, Amy Anna (Hughes) and Dr. Milton E. Conard, in West Grove, PA. They both are buried at West Grove, PA.

**15124657,** George W. (q.v.) [William /81/] b: 29 Aug. 1822, d: 23 Jan. 1892, married Louisa Way.

**15124658,** Evan b: 5 March 1824, d: 9 July 1824.

**15124659,** William (q.v.) b: 9 Sept. 1825, d: 31 March 1882, married Sarah Brown.

**15124651.0,** Jessie b: 7 April 1828 (birth is recorded in the New Garden Monthly Meeting/93/), d: 27 Aug. 1828.

With the sudden death of his nephew, Daniel and his wife, Elizabeth, in 1838 somebody had to look after their 4 children. One of their children, Amy, was taken in by her Grandfather's brother and his wife, George and Amy (Chambers) Gawthrop. Amy was just over 3 years old when she came to live with their George and Amy. The other children were looked after by his parents (Sarah M. and Emmor) and her parents (Lydia Ann).

**151246133,** Amy b: 10 Dec. 1835; d: in Lancaster County, PA; married Alexander N. Turner of Colerain, Lancaster County, PA on 12 April 1862.

*G*eorge had 4 brothers and 4 sisters. The four brothers were: **1)** Thomas (q.v.) b: 10 March 1774, d: 2 March 1851, married Elizabeth Thompson on 13 Nov. 1800, **2)** James (q.v.) b: 25 Dec. 1781, d: 1 Aug. 1858, **3)** William (q.v.) b: 1 March 1789, d: 13 Jan. 1856, and **4)** Allen b: 15 Nov.1792. The four sisters were: **1)** Hannah b: 25 March 1773 at London Grove Township, Chester Co., PA, married Smithin Shortledge on 19 Dec. 1799 (marriage is recorded in the New Garden Monthly Meeting/93/), **2)** Isabella b: 18 July 1779, d: 24 Dec. 1847 at London Grove, PA, **3)** Jane b: 22 May 1786, d: 1 June 1859, She married Daniel Thompson (b: 10 March 1782, d: 14 June 1837) son of Daniel and Elizabeth (Chambers) on 11 Jan. 1810 (marriage is recorded in the New Garden Monthly

Meeting*(93)*. They lived and both are buried at Mill Creek, New Castle Co., DE, and 4) Elizabeth b: 27 Aug. 1795, d: 1860, She married Nicholas W. Taylor of Baltimore (b: 8 Aug. 1794, d: 26 Dec. 1826 at Baltimore, MD) son of Thomas and Sarah Taylor of York, PA (marriage is recorded in New Garden Monthly Meeting*(93)*. They lived in Baltimore and then after Nicholas died, Elizabeth moved to a farm on state road near New West Grove, PA.

REFERENCES

SOURCE [17]: Genealogy work compiled by Thomas Carr Gawthrop. This manuscript was not published by a publisher; however, Thomas Carr Gawthrop was born Jan. 1938 and died Sept. 1966. This compiled work was obtained from Mary Virginia (Merrifield) Gawthrop wife of Wilbur Edmond Gawthrop (deceased) and her son, Richard Carr Gawthrop in early 1992. Thomas Carr Gawthrop was her nephew and Richard's cousin.

SOURCE [64]: Draft genealogy work compiled by Wm. A.A. Gawthrop, "GAWTHROP GENEALOGY," U.S. Congressional Library, CS71.G277, 1986.

SOURCE [81]: Letter/package containing a draft of Gawthrop Genealogy dated 2 June 1992 from Charles (Chuck) D. Thornton, Cape Coral, Fl.

SOURCE [92]: Kennett Square Monthly Meeting, PA records.

SOURCE [93]: New Garden Monthly Meeting, PA records.

SOURCE [100]: Package dated 24 Dec. 1990 obtained from the Chester County Historical Society, West Chester, PA, contains a copy of *History of Chester County Pennsylvania*, by J. Smith Futhey & Gilbert Cope, I. Evert (editor) 1881, page 563.

SOURCE [104]: Package dated Dec. 24, 1990 obtained from the Chester County Historical Society, West Chester, PA, contains a letter written by George Gawthrop Jr. to the *Hon. Townsend Haines & Associates Judges of the Court of Common Pleas of the County of Chester*, written about 1850.

SOURCE [105]: The New Garden Friends (Hicksite) Meeting Cemetery Records, page 9, *Gawthrop, Geo. 1865 C-5-36*, obtained from the Chester County Historical Society, West Chester, PA.

SOURCE [106]: Grave Stone inscription from the New Garden Friends (Hicksite) Meeting Cemetery, C-5-36 New Gar. Hicksite for George Gawthrop 1865, obtained from the Chester County Historical Society, West Chester, PA.

SOURCE [107]: The American Republican, a newspaper, dated Feb. 20, 1866, ***Estate of George Gawthrop, Deceased***, obtained from the Chester County Historical Society, West Chester, PA.

SOURCE [108]: Package dated Dec. 24, 1990 obtained from the Chester County Historical Society (CCHS), West Chester, PA, contains two records of Kennett Monthly Meeting that read, ***P. 114-4, 1812-12-8 Gawthrope, George (s of George & Jane) and Amy Chambers (dt of Joseph and Amy); ami*** *(announced marriage intentions), and* ***p. 114-4, 1812-12-8, Chambers, Amy (dt of Joseph & Amy) and George Gawthrop (s of George & Jane); ami.***

SOURCE [109]: Package dated 24 Dec. 1990 obtained from the CCHS, West Chester, PA, contains two records of Kennett Monthly Meeting that read, ***P. 115-4, 1813-1-5 Gawthrop, George & Amy Chambers amist ma*** (announced marriage intentions 2d time; married), and ***p. 115-4, 1813-1-5, Chambers, Amy & George Gawthrop amist, ma.***

SOURCE [110]: Package dated 24 Dec. 1990 obtained from the CCHS, contains two records of Kennett Monthly Meeting that read, ***P. 119-4, 1813-2-2 Gawthrop, George & Amy Chambers rm*** (reported married), and ***p. 119-4, 1813-2-2, Chambers, Amy & George Gawthrop rm.***

SOURCE [111]: The New Garden Friends (Hicksite) Meeting Cemetery Records, page 9, ***Gawthrop, Amy 1851 C-5-37***, obtained from the CCHS, West Chester, PA.

# Chapter 12

7th Generation

## 1512467, WILLIAM GAWTHROP ( 1789 - 1856 )

William Gawthrop, the seventh child and the fourth son of George Gawthrop (1743-1795) and Jane Allen (1753-1821), was born on 1 March 1789 in PA*[location 81]* and died on 13 Jan. 1856 in Baltimore, MD. William married Mary Griffith on 4 Aug. 1818 recorded at Gunpowder Monthly Meeting House, MD. Mary was the daughter of Abraham and Rachel Griffith. Mary was born on 29 Oct. 1790. They first lived in Marlborough next farm south of his brother, James Gawthrop, who was 7 years William's senior.*[100]* A Certificate of Removal was granted to William, Mary and a daughter from Kennett Square Monthly Meeting to Nottingham Monthly Meeting on 2 May 1820.*[92]* Then a Certificate of Removal was granted to William, Mary and a son, Thomas T., from Nottingham Monthly Meeting to Baltimore Monthly Meeting on 4 July 1843.*[92]* When William moved to Baltimore, Maryland, he became a business man in the grain business.*[100]*

William and Mary had 3 children: 1 son and 2 daughters. Their children follow*[17]*:

**15124671,** Rachel Mott b: 25 Sept. 1819 in PA, d: 20 Feb. 1882 in PA, married James Huey of Willistown, PA (b: 19 March 1804, d: 20 Feb. 1862) on 13 Nov. 1839. James was the son of William and Lydia Huey of Chester County, PA (marriage is recorded in the Marlborough Monthly Meeting*[92]* [a]). They lived in Baltimore, MD and Philadelphia, PA. Rachel is buried at the Fairchild, Friends Burial Grounds, Philadelphia, PA. They had 4 children: William G. (b: 21 Dec. 1840), James Thomas (4 Sept. 1842-3 April 1889), Lydia (17 Aug. 1845-26 May 1846), and Mary Jane (b: 19 Nov. 1848).

**15124672,** Jane b: 23 May 1822, married Thomas J. Lovegrove (b: 13 Nov. 1819) on 12 March 1846. Thomas was the son of James and Lydia Lovegrove. They lived in Baltimore, MD and Philadelphia, PA. They had 7 children: Ross W. (28 July 1847-24 June 1848), William G. (25Oct. 1848-30 July 1849), Mary Lydia (b:25 Aug. 1850), Thomas G. (b: 24 Sept. 1852), James (b: 27 Jan. 1855), William (b: 19 Aug. 1858), and Rachel (b: 11 June 1863).

**15124673,** Thomas T. b: 3 June 1824, d: no date known, however, he died in Church Hill, MD, married Mary T. Trenchard of Queen Ann's County,

---

a According to the Kennett Monthly Meeting, as delineated by Wm Hinshaw in his notes, KP-54-2.

MD on 8 April 1846 in Philadelphia, PA. The Mayor of Philadelphia performed their marriage. They lived in Church Hill, MD. No children resulted from this marriage.

**W**illiam had 4 brothers and 4 sisters. The four brothers were: **1)** Thomas (q.v.) b: 10 March 1774, d: 2 March 1851, married Elizabeth Thompson, **2)** James (q.v.) b: 25 Dec. 1781, d: 1 Aug. 1858, married Hannah Marshall, **3)** George (q.v.) b: 19 Feb. 1784, d: 24 Sept. 1865, married Amy Chambers, and **4)** Allen b: 15 Nov.1792. The four sisters were: **1)** Hannah b: 25 March 1773 at London Grove Township, Chester Co., PA, married Smithin Shortledge (b: 4 Oct. 1772, d: 16 Aug. 1822) on 19 Dec. 1799 (marriage recorded at New Garden Monthly Meeting, PA,*[93]* [b] **2)** Isabella b: 18 July 1779, d: 24 Dec. 1847 at London Grove, Chester County, PA, **3)** Jane b: 22 May 1786, d: 1 June 1859, married Daniel Thompson (b: 10 March 1782, d: 14 June 1837) on 11 Jan. 1810 (marriage recorded at the New Garden Monthly Meeting). Daniel was the son of Daniel and Elizabeth (Chambers). Daniel and Jane lived at Mill Creek, New Castle County, DE. They both are buried at Mill Creek, New Castle County, DE and **4)** Elizabeth b: 27 Aug. 1795, d: 1860, married Nicholas W. Taylor of Baltimore (b: 8 Aug. 1794, d: 26 Dec. 1826 at Baltimore, MD) (marriage recorded at the New Garden Monthly Meeting*[93]*). Nicholas was the son of Thomas and Sarah Taylor of York, PA. Nicholas and Elizabeth lived in Baltimore and then, after Nicholas died, Elizabeth moved to a farm on state road near New West Grove, PA.

REFERENCES


SOURCE [17]: Genealogy work compiled by Thomas Carr Gawthrop. This manuscript was not published by a publisher; however, Thomas Carr Gawthrop was born Jan. 1938 and died Sept. 1966. This compiled work was obtained from Mary Virginia (Merrifield) Gawthrop wife of Wilbur Edmond Gawthrop (deceased) and her son, Richard Carr Gawthrop in early 1992. Thomas Carr Gawthrop was her nephew and Richard's cousin.

SOURCE [81]: Letter/package containing a draft of Gawthrop Genealogy dated 2 June 1992 from Charles (Chuck) D. Thornton, Cape Coral, Fl.

SOURCE [92]: Kennett Square Monthly Meeting, PA records.

SOURCE [93]: New Garden Monthly Meeting, PA records.

SOURCE [100]: Package dated 24 Dec. 1990 obtained from the Chester County Historical Society, West Chester, PA, containing a copy of *History of Chester County Pennsylvania*, by J. Smith Futhey & Gilbert Cope, L. Evert (editor), 1881, page 563.


---

b According to New Garden M.M. record #3, ***Gawthrop, Hannah married Smithin Shortledge, 1799, 12, 19.***

# Chapter 13

8th Generation

## 15124521, JAMES GAWTHROP ( 1798 - 1883 )

James Gawthrop*(16, 81)*, the first child and first son of Thomas William Gawthrop (1776-1832) and Elizabeth Hiett (1779 - 1873), was born 16 Oct. 1798 at Hampshire County, VA[a] and died 10 Sept. 1883 in Philippi, Barbour County, WV.*(81)* James married Huldah Waldo on 9 Jan. 1824 [b] at Bridgeport, VA.[a] Hulda (b: 18 March 1804 in Bridgeport, Harrison County, VA[a] d: 25 April 1894 near Philippi, WV) was the daughter of Dr. John J. Waldo and Peace Bull of the State of Vermont. James was a Baptist Minister for 50 years and is buried at the burial grounds, Mt. Olive, WV.*(81)* [c] Huldah is buried at Mt. Olive Cemetery, Philippi, Barbour County, WV. James' gravestone reads, ***Rev. James Gawthrop Born Oct. 16, 1798 Died Sep 10, 1883 age 84 yrs 10 ms 24 Days.****(87)* Huldah's gravestone reads, ***Huldah Waldo wife of Rev. James Gawthrop Born Mar. 18, 1804 Died Apr. 25, 1894 age 90 Yrs 1 Ms 7Ds.****(87)* In the research of Thomas Carr Gawthrop, there is a reference that states, ***For the 42 Grandchildren of James and Hulda, see the Waldo Genealogy at the Lincoln Historical Society of PA.****(17)* [d] A copy of the Last Will and Testament of James Gawthrop has been transcribed at the end of this chapter.*(88)*

James and Hulda's children*(17, 81)* follow:

---

a In 1861 when the Virginia delegates voted to secede, the delegates from the Unionist northwestern counties rebelled and set up their own restored Government of Virginia. This arrangement lasted until Congress voted to admit West Virginia into the union as the 35th state on 20 June 1863. Therefore, Hampshire County, Virginia became Hampshire County, West Virginia with the final split during the Civil War. Hamsphire County, WV has a northern bourder of Washington County, Maryland.

b In the Sept. 1993 draft of the *Descendants of Thomas Gawthrop*, their marriage date is 8 Jan. 1824.

c As described in the *Ninteeth Annual Session of the Baptist General Association of West Virginia*, held at Clarksburg, WV, 8-11 Nov. 1883, ***Rev. James Gawthrop is also numbered among the dead of 1883. Born in Hampshire Co., VA* during the last century, he was, at the time of his death, in the eighty-fifth year of his age and was probably the oldest member of our denomination in this state. When twenty three years old, he was baptized at Pruntytown, and seven years afterwards he was ordained to the work of the ministry. During his long period of active service he preached for churches in Lewis, Harrison, Marion, Taylor, Preston, Barbour, and Urcher counties. For a time he was a missionary of the General Association of Virginia, his labors were abundant, his ministry faithful in conversions and his pecuniary compensations pitifully meager. He was a most exemplary man, and one of the most faithful Christian workers West Virginia ever had. Old age compelled him to spend his last years in retirement; but his heart never grew old, and he never outlived his interest in education, and any branch of Christian work.***

d Charles D. Thornton has an original book of the "Genealogy of the Waldo Family", as the letter of September 15, 1993 specifies.

**151245211,** Lucinda Ann b: 30 April 1825 in Pruntytown, VA[a] d: 1915 in Michigan, married Alpheus Zinn (b: 23 Nov. 1818 in Harrison County, VA,[a] d: 2 Nov. 1876 in Barbour County, WV) on 4 Jan. 1854 at Flemington, VA.[a] Alpheus was the son of Peter and Catherine (Criss) Zinn of Barbour County, WV. Lucinda was a teacher and a magazine writer. Alpheus was a minister and a farmer. They lived in Taylor & Barbour Counties, WV and, after her husband died, Lucinda lived at Mansfield, WV (in 1899). They both are burried in Mt. Olive Cemetery, Philippi, Barbour County, WV.*/87/* Lucinda's gravestone reads, ***Lucinda A. Zinn 1825-1915.****/87/* The insciption on Lucinda's reads, ***She hath done what she could.****/87/* Alpheus' gravestone reads, ***Rev. Alpheus Zinn Died Nov. 2, 1876 age 57 Yrs. 11 Mo. 16 Ds.****/87/* The inscription on Alpheus' reads, ***I shall be satisfied when I awake with thy likeness, Ps 17.15.****/87/* Their children were: William Davidson (b: 16 May 1857), Silvanus Waldo (b: 21 April 1859), Luella (b: 31 March 1861), and Claudius Alpheus (b: 15 Feb. 1872).

Note on Alpheus: prior to his marrying Lucinda, Alpheus & Mary Woodford were married in Barbour Co., WV[a] on 9 Oct. 1845.*/87/*

**151245212,** Thomas (q.v., Vol. 2) b: 16 March 1827, d: 1911 at Rockcave, WV, married twice: **1M**-Catharine Ann Whiting on 4 Oct. 1848 and **2M**-Mary Chatherina Chandler on 26 Feb. 1871.

**151245213,** William Gifford b: 30 Sept. 1828 at Pruntytown, VA,[a] d: 23 Nov. 1851 at Pruntytown, VA,[a] married Mary Whiting in about 1847. Mary was the daughter of Perrin Whiting and Mary Whitehead of Grafton, Upshur Co., WV. They lived in Pruntytown, WV and Thomas is buried at the Baptist Church Cemetery in Pruntytown. William Gifford was a blacksmith. William and Mary had 2 children but both died as infants. After William's death, Mary married again and moved elsewhere.*/86/*

Note: William Gifford's wife and Thomas Gawthrop's 1st wife were sisters.

**151245214,** Elizabeth Peace b: 8 May 1830 at Bulltown, Braxton County, VA,[a] d: 8 May 1921 at Bridgeport, WV. Elizabeth married twice: **1M**-John Waldo Bartlett (b: 25 Dec. 1821; d: 17 Apr. 1865) on 24 Dec. 1849. He was the son of John Barkley Bartlett of Clarksburg, WV. John and Elizabeth children*/64/* were:

Wirt (b: 5 Dec. 1850), Eoline (b: 6 Dec. 1852), Elsie (b: 18 Jan. 1854), Florida (b: 5 June 1857), Henry Clay (b: 31 March 1860), and Rue (b: 9 Jan. 1863). **2M**-Pendleton Drummond (b: 11 July 1829, d: 18 Dec. 1902) on 26 May 1870 at Clarksburg, WV. Elizabeth is buried in the Masonic Cemetery, Bridgeport, WV. Elizabeth and Pendleton's children*/64/* were: Lee (b: 10 March 1871), Cora (b: 10 March 1871) and Arthur (b: 15 July 1873).

**151245215,** Susanna W. b: 22 March 1832 at Pruntytown, VA,[a] d: unsure about death but she is buried in Stillman, Upshur County, WV. Susanna married Ramsdell Bartlett (b: Columbia, VA d: 27 Dec. 1882 in Stillman, WV) on 10 Dec. 1854 at Rockcave, VA.[a] Ramsdell was a farmer and the son of James and Sarah Elizabeth (Trooper) Bartlett of Columbia, VA. They had no children.

**151245216,** Henrietta Goff b: 23 Nov. 1833 at Pruntytown, Taylor Co., VA,[a] d: 3 June 1873 at Shinnston, Harrison County, WV. Henrietta married Elias Martin Sapp (b: 9 July 1829 at Eldora, Marion County, VA,[a] d: 1919 at Shinnston, WV) on 15 Sept. 1853 at Pruntytown, VA.[a] Elias was the son of John and Elizabeth (Mariah) Martin of Shinnston, WV. Elias was a Baptist Minister. Their children were: Sophronia Ellen (b: 19 Feb. 1853) and DeBlance (b: 22 Oct. 1863).;

**151245217,** Sarah Jane b: 23 May 1836 at Pruntytown, VA,[a] d: 28 March 1838.

**151245218,** Joseph James Wrightsman (q.v., Vol. 2)*/112/* b: 31 Jan. 1842 in Taylor County, VA,[a] d: 2 Feb. 1920*/112/*. JJW married three times: **1M**-Clarissa Alice Corbitt on 13 Oct. 1861, **2M**-Annie May Mathews on 20 Sept. 1868, **3M**-Verdilla Loretta Suder on 20 Nov. 1887.

**151245219,** Harriett Tamar b: 21 July 1844 in Pruntytown, VA,[a] d: 1 Nov. 1863 in Philippi, WV. Harriett married Israel Sears. They had 1 child, Lily, but she was trampled and killed by a horse at an early age.

**151245211.0,** Mary Frances Thomazine Victoria b: 15 Feb. 1847, married twice: **1M**-Gideon Proudfoot (b: 28 April 1847 at Belington, VA,[a] d: 1 Dec. 1872 at Upshur County, WV), Gideon fathered 3 children*/64/*: Orlena Alice (b: 27 Nov. 1866), Ethel May (b: 7 July 1869) and William Albert (b: 7 July 1871), **2M**-Isaac Willet (b:

30 July 1856), Isaac fathered 4 children*(64)*: Mary Ann (b: 12 Aug. 1875), Robert Martin (b: 12 Dec. 1877), Homer Lee (b: 10 Nov. 1878), and Edith Emeline (b: 9 Aug. 1880).

**151245211.1**, Ermeline b: 5 Oct. 1848, married three times: **1M**-Wilson Greenfield Reger (b: 16 April 1845 d: 1 Dec. 1875 *(64)*), Wilson fathered 1 child: Waldo G. (b: 1 Aug. 1868), **2M**-Joshua Wood (b: 29 Aug. 1825 *(64)*), Joshua fathered 3 children: Rosa J., French A. (b: 29 March 1881), Herbert E. (b: 11 Feb. 1889), **3M**-J.J. Jenkins (b: 1820 *(64)*).

Thomas Gawthrop (151245212) in correspondence with Charles Gawthrop, Wilmington, DE, wrote that James Gawthrop (15124521) was a Baptist Minister before Thomas was born and had the care of four churches, preaching for them monthly for better then 45 years. James spent, Thomas thought, over 50 years in the service of the church. In that long service, James never realized 100 dollars a year, but one year he averaged less than 50 dollars. General he preached about 3 days each week but he did not preach for money, he preached to persuade people to become reconciled to God. James had 60 acres of land, nearly all woods to began with, so consequently he and his family worked and lived hard. The family made everything at home but iron and salt. There were no free schools in the area because the land was too thinly settled, so they had to learn at home. Thomas, himself, learned at home until he was nearly twelve, afterwhich, in the winter months, he went to school. Thomas attended winter school until he was 18 years old (aggregating nearly 15 months of schooling). Thomas' mother was the daughter of old Dr. Waldo, a Baptisi Minister of some note. Dr. Waldo was born and resided near the Hoosac Mountains in Vermont. Thomas said that he had many cousins in Harrison, Taylor, Barbour and Randolph County, WV.*(this is quoted in 81)*

James had 6 brothers and 5 sisters. The 6 brothers were: **1)** John (q.v.) b: 8 Dec. 1803, d: 25 Apr. 1881, married twice: **1M**-Josinah Corbin on 22 May 1825, **2M**-Kathrine Radabaugh in 1871 (no children of this marriage), **2)** Thomas (q.v.) b: 7 April 1806, d: 4 Feb. 1876, married Elizabeth Wiseman on 2 Feb. 1832, **3)** Hiett (q.v.) b: 1807, married Mary Pool, **4)** Allen B. (q.v.) b: 1 March 1808, d: 10 Dec. 1887, married Elizabeth H. Corder on 26 Sept. 1833, **5)** Evan (H.*(81)*) b: 1810 in Taylor County, WV.[a] In the research of Thomas Carr Gawthrop, there is a reference that states, ***He went West unmarried about 1838. He was near Galena, Illinois when last heard from.****(17)* **6)** Enos D. (q.v.) b: 6 March 1810, d: 27 Oct. 1843, married Ruth Wiseman on 28 Dec. 1831. The 5 sisters were: **1)** Sarah b: 6 Feb. 1812*(16)* (letter from David C. Gawthrop places date of birth at Nov. 1819*(112)*), d: 14 Oct. 1881 in Taylor County, WV (died unmarried at age 69 years 11 days) and is buried in the Gawthrop Cemetery, Taylor County, WV, **2)** Mary b: 6 Feb. 1815*(16)*, d: 11 Dec. 1902 in Webster, Taylor County, WV, married Wilson Boyle Brown*[16]* on 2 June 1840 in Taylor County, WV*[location 81]*.[a] Wilson was a tanner and a farmer. Both Wilson and Mary are buried in the Quaker Cemetery, in Webster, WV. They had 6 children: James Boyle*[16]*, Virginia Jane, Christopher Columbus, Jonathan Wilson, Elizabeth Ann, George Washington, Mary Emma and [Charles Wesley*[64]*]. **3)** Elizabeth*[89]* b: 23 June 1813 in Taylor County, WV,[a] d: 19 June 1910, married John Shroyer (b: 29 Aug. 1811) on 17 Nov. 1836 in Harrison County, WV.[a] They had 6 children: Jackson, Elizabeth, Louis, Jacob B., Mary C., and Irving.*[64]* John Shroyer was a Gunsmith. **4)** Margaret b: 12 Oct. 1818 *[89]* in Taylor County, WV,[a] d: unmarried on 27 Feb. 1888 at age 70 years, **5)** Isabella d: unmarried on 8 Oct. 1863.*[89]*

### *Last Will of James Gawthrop Sr.[89]*

***In the name of God Amen. I James Gawthrop Sr. of the County of Barbour and state of West Va. being old and feable*** (sic) ***and calling to mind the mortality of man, make this my last will and testament, first I will my soul to God who gave it and my body to have a decent Christian burrial*** (sic) ***and after my debts are paid, I give and bequeath to my wife, Huldah, while she retains my name my farm lanying*** (sic) ***on the North side of the road from E---ity to Burnersville reform which I now reside at, some horse two head of cattle and all of my household.***

***Kitchen furniture wgon*** (sic) ***and all other farming utensils that she wishes to keep and 6 head of sheep and interest on all notes or bonds due me which are drawing interest. After her decease, the land and all other property to be sold by my executors on a credit or for cash as they think best. The money to be equally divided between my children according to an account kept by me which will be found in a book where I have kept an account of all advancements are to be considered in the division without interest being charged on the advancements where any of my children are dead their children are to inherit their lawful portion of my estate the same as if the parents were alive, except my granddaughter, Lilly Ann Saer*** (Sears), ***I bequeath to her twenty five dollars out of the money of the aforesaid land when sold. To my son, Thomas Gawthrop, I bequeath my watch and rifle gun without change. My plains, Augers, & chisels, I bequeath to my son Thomas and Sylvanus Zinn (my grandson) to be equally divided between them without charge. My books, I bequeath to be divided between my children as they think best. I appoint as executor and***

*executist to carry out my said Will, William D. Zinn and Luciinda A. Zinn. Witness my hand and seal this 7th day of February 1878.*

*James Gawthrop (seal)*

*Desk* (of)
*Hartsel E. Hoff*
*Annie E. Hoff*

*West Virginia,*

*Barbour County Count October 3rd 1883, The Last Will and Testament of James Gawthrop, deceased was this day presented in open Count for probate, and the same being duly praved by the oaths of the attesting witness H.E. Hoff and Annie E. Hoff. It is hereby ordered that the same be admitted to probate.*

*L.C. Elliott, Clerk*

## REFERENCES


SOURCE [16]: A handwritten family tree, *"OUR CHILDREN'S ANCESTORS,"* compiled by Rev. Darward and Dorothy Brown for their children and grandchildren, no date was available; however, Rev Darward Belmont Brown was born on 12 January 1897. It is thought that the Brown Family Tree and the Everard C. Gawthrop Family Tree were commissioned approximately the same time. Philip E. Gawthrop has the original work of the Everard C. Gawthrop family tree prepared by genealogist G. Cope in the early to mid 1920's.

SOURCE [17]: Genealogy work compiled by Thomas Carr Gawthrop. This manuscript was not published by a publisher; however, Thomas Carr Gawthrop was born Jan. 1938 and died Sept. 1966. This compiled work was obtained from Mary Virginia (Merrifield) Gawthrop wife of Wilbur Edmond Gawthrop (deceased) and her son, Richard Carr Gawthrop in early 1992. Thomas Carr Gawthrop was her nephew and Richard's cousin.

SOURCE [64]: Draft genealogy work compiled by William A.A. Gawthrop, "GAWTHROP GENEALOGY," U.S. Congressional Library, CS71.G277, 1986.

SOURCE [81]: Letter/package containing a draft of Gawthrop Genealogy dated 2 June 1992 from Charles (Chuck) D. Thornton, Cape Coral, Fl.

SOURCE [86]: Draft of the Descendents of Thomas Gawthrop, by Wm. A.A.Gawthrop, September 1993.

SOURCE [87]: Letter/package from Charles D. Thornton, Cape Coral, Fl on September 15, 1993.

SOURCE [88]: Letter from Debra Harris Talbott, Clerk of Barbour County Commission, Barbour County, Philippi, WV, to Philip Evan Gawthrop on February 8, 1995, containing a handwritten copy in book 1, pages 363 and 364, of the Last Will and Testament of James Gawthrop (1798-1883).

SOURCE [89]: Letter dated 7 April 1992 from David Carl Gawthrop, Charlottesville, VA.

SOURCE [112]: Letter dated 28 April 1992 from David Carl Gawthrop, Charlottesville, VA.

# Chapter 14

8th Generation

## 15124522, JOHN GAWTHROP ( 1803 - 1881 )

John Gawthrop[a], the second child and second son of Thomas William Gawthrop (1776-1832) and Elizabeth Hiett (1779-1873), was born 8 Dec. 1803 in Taylor County, VA[b] and died 25 April 1881 at Bridgeport, Harrison County, WV.*[81]* He is buried in the Old Baptist Cemetery, Harrison County, WV. John spent most of his life as a drover (herded cattle).*[81]* This is a quote from the Hiett Genealogy, ***He had little education but could judge the value of a steer within a few cents.****[87]* John married twice: **1M**-Josinah Corbin on 22 May 1825 *[1823 in reference 81]*. Josinah died on 28 March 1869 *[9 mth 23 dy 1869 in reference 81]*. John and Josinah had 8 children. **2M**-Kathrine Radabaugh in 1871*[May 22, 1873 in reference 86]* in Harrison County, WV (no children of this marriage). Kathrine died 7 Aug. 1911*[81]* [in WV*[86]*.] John lived in Harrison County, WV then Taylor County, WV. In Thomas Carr Gawthrop work there is a reference to a letter that states, ***John visited the Gawthrop's of Chester County, PA and gave an account of his generation and of the children of the emigrants.****[17]*[c] John had no will but the qualification of the administrator for John Gawthrop's estate, Asa G.T. Gawthrop, is transcribed at the end of this chapter.*[114]*

John and Josinah had 8 children*[17, 81]*:

**151245221** Elizabeth A.*[A. in 81]* b: 6 May 1826 in Harrison County, WV,*[location 81]*[b] d: 26 Oct. 1910, married Abel W. Shinn (1828-1888*[87]*) in WV.*[location 81]*) They had 7 children: Joseph Melville, Annetta, John Allen, Dora, Ashby, Edgar, and Ella May. Abel was imprisoned at Camp Chase during the Civil War for aiding the Confederate Army.*[113]*

**151245222** Henry Haines b: 16 Aug. 1828 in Harrison County, WV,*[location 81]*[b] died of scarlet fever.

---

a John A. Gawthrop is listed in the 1860 Census records of Taylor County, WV on page 532.

b In 1861 when the Virginia delegates voted to secede, the delegates from the Unionist northwestern counties rebelled and set up their own restored Government of Virginia. This arrangement lasted until Congress voted to admit West Virginia into the union as the 35th state on 20 June 1863. Therefore, Taylor County, Virginia became Taylor County, West Virginia with the final split during the Civil War. Other counties in western part of Virginia became counties in West Virginia during that same split.

c Thomas Carr Gawthrop makes reference to a letter that states in part "*... **the emigrants.***" Presumably that reference was James Gawthrop (1742-1806) and George Gawthrop (1743-1795) who emigrated to America about 1770.

**151245223** Sarah b: 18 June 1831 in Harrison County, WV,*[location 81]*[b] died of scarlet fever.

**151245224** Thomas Franklin b: 12 Oct. 1834 in Harrison County, WV,*[location 81]*[b] died of scarlet fever.

**151245225** Salina b: 5 Feb. 1837 in Harrison County, WV,*[location 81]*[b] d: 23 April 1907, married John L. Craig on 4 Dec. 1870 in Harrison County, WV.*[81]*

**151245226** Edith Helen Mary b: 10 Nov. 1839 in Harrison County, WV,*[location 81]*[b] d: 1916, married B.H. Cook in 1864 in WV.*[81]*

**151245227** Oline Arena*[17, 81]*, Arenal*[64]* b: 13 Jan. 1844 in Harrison County, WV,*[location 81]*[b] d: 21 Dec. 1924 in Bridgeport, Harrison County, WV, married Jessie H. Willis on 13 Oct. 1872 in Harrison County, WV and had 2 children: Walter and Carson.

**151245228** Asa Garnett Tisdale (q.v., Vol. 2) b: 29 June 1847 in Harrison County, VA,[b] d: 25 Nov. 1889 in Bridgeport, Harrison County, WV, married Cornelia Lowe (b: 14 June 1853, d: 17 Feb. 1932 in Bridgeport, WV) on 3 Jan. 1877 in Harrison County, WV.

*J*ohn had 6 brothers and 5 sisters. The 6 brothers were: **1)** James (q.v.) b: 16 Oct. 1798, married Hulda Waldo, **2)** Thomas (q.v.) b: 7 April 1806, d: 4 Feb. 1876, married Elizabeth Wiseman on 2 Feb. 1832, **3)** Hiett (q.v.) b: 1807, married Mary Pool, **4)** Allen B. (q.v.) b: 1 March 1808, d: 10 Dec. 1887, married Elizabeth H. Corder on 26 Sept. 1833, **5)** Evan (H.*[81]*) b: 1810 in Taylor County, WV, In the research of Thomas Carr Gawthrop, there is a reference that states, ***He went West unmarried about 1838. He was near Galena, Illinois when last heard from.****[17]* **6)** Enos D. (q.v.) b: 6 March 1810, d: 27 Oct. 1843, married Ruth Wiseman on 28 Dec. 1831. The 5 sisters were: **1)** Sarah b: 6 Feb. 1812*[16]* (letter from David C. Gawthrop places date of birth at Nov. 1819, *[112]*, d: 14 Oct. 1881 in Taylor County, WV (died unmarried at age 69 years 11 days) and is buried in the Gawthrop Cemetery, Taylor County, WV, **2)** Mary b: 6 Feb. 1815*[16]*, d: 11 Dec. 1902 in Webster, Taylor County, WV,[b] married Wilson Boyle Brown*[16]* on 2 June 1840 in Taylor County, WV.*[location 81]*[b] Wilson was a tanner and a farmer. Both Wilson and Mary are buried in the Quaker Cemetery, in Webster, WV. They had 6 children: James Boyle*[16]*, Virginia Jane, Christopher Columbus, Jonathan Wilson, Elizabeth Ann, George Washington, Mary Emma and [Charles Wesley*[64]*], **3)** Elizabeth*[89]* b: 23 June 1813 in Taylor County, WV,[b] d: 19 June 1910, married John Shroyer (b: 29 Aug. 1811) on 17 Nov. 1836 in Harrison County, WV.[b] They had 6 children: Jackson, Elizabeth, Louis, Jacob B., Mary C., and [Irving*[64]*]. John Shroyer was a Gunsmith. **4)** Margaret b: 12 Oct. 1818 *[83]* in Taylor

County, WV,[b] d: unmarried on 27 Feb. 1888 at age 70 years. 5) Isabella d: unmarried on 8 Oct. 1863.*[89]*

An account of the qualifications of Asa G.T. Gawthrop to be his father's executor.

> *West Virginia*
> *In the Office of the Clerk of Harrison County Court*
> *On the Occation of Wednesday, May 4th 1881,*
> *On motion of Catharine Gawthrop widow of John Gawthrop decd., the clerk of the County Count doth appoint Asa G.T. Gawthrop Administrator of the Estate of John Gawthrop, deceased. Whereupon the said Asa G.T.Gawthrop appeared before the Clerk of the said County Court and made oath accounting to law and accepted the said office or trust of Administrator aforesaid and together with Jesse H. Willis and Flocum his securities (who qualified as to their sufficincy) interest into and acknowledge a bond in the final sum of Seven Thousand Six Hundred dollars , conditional accouding to law and took the oath prescribed by law as such Admr. Certificate is therefore granted the said Asa G.T. Gawthrop upon which to obtain letters of Administration upon said estate in due form of law and motion of the said Administrator, the Clerk doth appoint Samuel Okister, Wm M. Lats & John Woffman appraisers to appraise the property of the said John Gawthrop, decd.*
>
> *James Mersor, Clerk[114]*


REFERENCES

SOURCE [16]: A handwritten family tree, *"OUR CHILDREN'S ANCESTORS,"* compiled by Rev. Darward and Dorothy Brown for their children and grandchildren, no date was available; however, Rev Darward Belmont Brown was born on 12 January 1897.

SOURCE [17]: Genealogy work compiled by Thomas Carr Gawthrop. This manuscript was not published by a publisher; however, Thomas Carr Gawthrop was born Jan. 1938 and died Sept. 1966. This compiled work was obtained from Mary Virginia (Merrifield) Gawthrop wife of Wilbur Edmond Gawthrop (deceased) and her son, Richard Carr Gawthrop in early 1992. Thomas Carr Gawthrop was her nephew and Richard's cousin.

SOURCE [64]: Draft genealogy work compiled by Wm. A.A. Gawthrop, "GAWTHROP GENEALOGY," U.S. Congressional Library, CS71.G277, 1986.

SOURCE [81]: Letter/package containing a draft of Gawthrop Genealogy dated 2 June 1992 from Charles (Chuck) D. Thornton, Cape Coral, Fl.

SOURCE [87]: Ltr/package from Charles D. Thornton, Cape Coral, Fl on September 15, 1993.

SOURCE [89]: Letter dated 7 April 1992 from David Carl Gawthrop, Charlottesville, VA.

SOURCE [112]: Letter dated 28 April 1992 from David Carl Gawthrop, Charlottesville, VA.

SOURCE [113]: Charles D. Thornton visited the Orlando Public Library on 26 Aug. 1993 in the WV section; *"Genealogical and Personal Histroy of the Upper Monongahela Valley, West Virginia,"* reprinted in 2 Volumes, Baltimore Genealogical Publishing Co., Inc., 1978, originally published in 3 Volumes, New York, copyright 1912, under the editoral supervision of Bernard L. Butcher. A collection of family histories in non-alphabetical order. He came across this imprisonment at Camp Chase for aiding the Confederates on page 602.

SOURCE [114]: Letter from Sylvia Basile, Clerk of Harrison County Commission, Harrison County, Clarksburg, WV, to Philip Evan Gawthrop post marked on February 2, 1995, containing a handwritten copy, pages 12, of Asa Gawthrop's qualification papers for the Administrator of John Gawthrop's estate. (Date entered March 18, 1995)

# Chapter 15

8th Generation

## 15124523, THOMAS GAWTHROP ( 1806 - 1876 )

Thomas Gawthrop, the third child and third son of Thomas William Gawthrop (1776-1832) and Elizabeth Hiett (1779-1873), was born 7 April 1806 in Taylor County, VA[a] and died 4 Feb. 1876 in Taylor County, WV.*[81]* Thomas married Elizabeth Wiseman on 2 Feb. 1832 in Harrison County, VA.[a] Elizabeth was born in 1811 in VA.*[location 81]* Thomas lived in Taylor County, WV.

Thomas and Elizabeth had 2 children*[17, 81, 115]*:

**151245231** John Allen (q.v., Vol. 2) b: 24 Oct. 1832 in Lost Run, Taylor County, VA,[a] d: 25 May 1919 in Harrison County, WV, married Martha Elen Knight on 25 Nov. 1858.*[81]*

**151245232** James Henry (q.v., Vol. 2) b: 15 Sept. 1834, d: 9 Sept. 1890, married Virginia Rector in March 1867.

Thomas had 6 brothers and 5 sisters. The 6 brothers were: **1)** James (q.v.) b: 16 Oct. 1798, married Hulda Waldo, **2)** John (q.v.) b: 8 Dec. 1803, d: 25 April 1881, married twice: **1M**-Josinah Corbin on 22 May 1825, **2M**-Kathrine Radabaugh in 1871, **3)** Hiett (q.v.) b: 1807, married Mary Pool, **4)** Allen B. (q.v.) b: 1 March 1808, d: 10 Dec. 1887, married Elizabeth H. Corder on 26 Sept. 1833, **5)** Evan (H.*[81]*) b: 1810 in Taylor County, WV.[a] In the research of Thomas Carr Gawthrop, there is a reference that states, ***He went West unmarried about 1838. He was near Galena, Illinois when last heard from.*** *[17]* **6)** Enos D. (q.v.) b: 6 March 1810, d: 27 Oct. 1843, married Ruth Wiseman on 28 Dec. 1831. The 5 sisters were: **1)** Sarah b: 6 Feb. 1812*[16]* (letter from David C. Gawthrop places date of birth at Nov. 1819*[112]*, d: 14 Oct. 1881 in Taylor County, WV (died unmarried at age 69 years 11 days) and is buried in the Gawthrop Cemetery, Taylor County, WV, **2)** Mary b: 6 Feb. 1815*[15]*, d: 11 Dec. 1902 in Webster, Taylor County, WV, married Wilson Boyle Brown*[16]* on 2 June 1840 in Taylor County, WV.*[location 81]*[a] Wilson was a tanner and a farmer. Both Wilson and Mary are buried in the Quaker Cemetery, in Webster, WV. They had 6 children: James Boyle*[16]*, Virginia Jane, Christopher Columbus, Jonathan Wilson, Elizabeth Ann, George Washington, Mary Emma and [Charles Wesley*[64]*]. **3)** Elizabeth*[89]* b: 23

---

a In 1861 when the Virginia delegates voted to secede, the delegates from the Unionist northwestern counties rebelled and set up their own restored Government of Virginia. This arrangement lasted until Congress voted to admit West Virginia into the union as the 35th state on 20 June 1863. Therefore, Taylor County, Virginia became Taylor County, West Virginia with the final split during the Civil War. Other counties in western part of Virginia became counties in West Virginia during that same split.

June 1813 in Taylor County, WV,[a] d: 19 June 1910, married John Shroyer (b: 29 Aug. 1811) on 17 Nov. 1836 in Harrison County, WV.[a] They had 6 children: Jackson, Elizabeth, Louis, Jacob B., Mary C., and [Irving*[64]*]. John Shroyer was a Gunsmith. **4)** Margaret b: 12 Oct. 1818 *[89]* in Taylor County, WV,[a] d: unmarried on 27 Feb. 1888 at age 70 years, **5)** Isabella d: unmarried on 8 Oct. 1863.*[89]*

REFERENCES


SOURCE [16]: A handwritten family tree, *"OUR CHILDREN'S ANCESTORS,"* compiled by Rev. Darward and Dorothy Brown for their children and grandchildren, no date was available; however, Rev Darward Belmont Brown was born on 12 January 1897. It is thought that the Brown Family Tree and the Everard C. Gawthrop Family Tree were commissioned approximately the same time. Philip E. Gawthrop has the original work of the Everard C. Gawthrop family tree prepared by genealogist G. Cope in the early to mid 1920's.

SOURCE [17]: Genealogy work compiled by Thomas Carr Gawthrop. This manuscript was not published by a publisher; however, Thomas Carr Gawthrop was born Jan. 1938 and died Sept. 1966. This compiled work was obtained from Mary Virginia (Merrifield) Gawthrop wife of Wilbur Edmond Gawthrop (deceased) and her son, Richard Carr Gawthrop in early 1992. Thomas Carr Gawthrop was her nephew and Richard's cousin.

SOURCE [64]: Draft genealogy work compiled by Wm. A.A. Gawthrop, "GAWTHROP GENEALOGY," U.S. Congressional Library, CS71.G277, 1986.

SOURCE [81]: Letter/package containing a draft of Gawthrop Genealogy dated 2 June 1992 from Charles (Chuck) D. Thornton, Cape Coral, Fl.

SOURCE [89]: Letter dated 7 April 1992 from David Carl Gawthrop, Charlottesville, VA.

SOURCE [112]: Letter dated 28 April 1992 from David Carl Gawthrop, Charlottesville, VA.

SOURCE [115]: *WEST VIRGINIA HERITAGE ENCYCLOPEDIA*, Volume 9, by William Hinshaw & Thomas Worth Marshall, Genealogical Publishing Co., Baltimore, MD, copyright 1978.

# Chapter 16

8th Generation

## 15124524, HIETT GAWTHROP ( 1807 - )

Hiett Gawthrop, the fourth child and fourth son of Thomas William Gawthrop (1776-1832) and Elizabeth Hiett (1779 - 1873), was born about 1807 in Taylor County, VA[a] and died at an unknown date in Pruntytown, WV.[b] Hiett married Mary Pool on 15 Feb. 1827 in Harrison County, VA.[a] Mary was born about 1805. In the research of Thomas Carr Gawthrop, there is a letter that states, ***Evan B. Gawthrop of West Grove in business in Pittsburg, PA made acquaintance with the Gawthrop's of West Virginia and furnished considerable data now given.*** *[17]* John Guines married Mary (Pool) Gawthrop after the death of Hiett.*[64]*

Hiett and Mary's children follow*[81]*:

**151245241**, Hulda b: 1828 in Taylor County, VA,[a]

**151245242**, Lurina b: 1829 in Taylor County, VA,[a]

twin: **151245243**, Phebe Catharine*[17]* b: 22 March 1840 in Taylor County, VA,[a] d: 1 Oct. 1903 at Cecil in Taylor County, WV, married John R. Kinsey on 29 Oct. 1875 in Taylor County, WV. Phebe and John's children were: Elizabeth (b: 1877 in Taylor County, WV), Charles Lee (b: 1878 in Taylor County, WV) and Mary L. (b: 1880 in Taylor County, WV).

twin: **151245244**, Sarah Matilda*[17]* b: 22 March 1840 in Taylor County, VA,[a] d: 5 July 1900; married William Montgomery Dabisman. Sarah and William's children were: Ira Lee Dadisman (b: 11 Oct. 1873 in Barbour County, WV) and James W. Dadisman (b: 27 Feb. 1876 in Barbour County, WV). Sarah is buried at Betheny Baptist Cemetery, Hall, Barbour County, WV.

**151245245**, Richard Hamleton (q.v., Vol. 2) b: 1848 in Taylor County, VA,[a] d: 1895, married an unknown woman.

---

a In 1861 when the Virginia delegates voted to secede, the delegates from the Unionist northwestern counties rebelled and set up their own restored Government of Virginia. This arrangement lasted until Congress voted to admit West Virginia into the union as the 35th state on 20 June 1863. Therefore, Taylor County, Virginia became Taylor County, West Virginia with the final split during the Civil War. Other counties in western part of Virginia became counties in West Virginia during that same split.

b Hyatt Gawthrop is listed in the Census of Randolph County, VA in 1840. Unsure whether or not this person is the same as Hiett Gawthrop, although, Chuck D. Thornton, Jr. has the Waldo Genealogy which tends to point in that direction.

*H*iett had 6 brothers and 5 sisters. The 6 brothers were: **1)** James (q.v.) b: 16 Oct. 1798, married Hulda Waldo on 9 Jan. 1824, **2)** John (q.v.) b: 8 Dec. 1803, d: 25 April 1881, married twice: **1M**-Josinah Corbin on 22 May 1825, **2M**-Kathrine Radabaugh in 1871 (no children of this marriage), **3)** Thomas (q.v.) b: 7 April 1806, d: 4 Feb. 1876, married Elizabeth Wiseman on 2 Feb. 1832, **4)** Allen B. (q.v.) b: 1 March 1808, d: 10 Dec. 1887, married Elizabeth H. Corder on 26 Sept. 1833, **5)** Evan (H.*[81]*) b: 1810 in Taylor County, WV,[a]. In the research of Thomas Carr Gawthrop, there is a reference that states, ***He went West unmarried about 1838. He was near Galena, Illinois when last heard from.****[17]* **6)** Enos D. (q.v.) b: 6 March 1810, d: 27 Oct. 1843, married Ruth Wiseman on 28 Dec. 1831. The 5 sisters were: **1)** Sarah b: 6 Feb. 1812*[16]* (letter from David C. Gawthrop places date of birth at Nov. 1819*[112]*, d: 14 Oct. 1881 in Taylor County, WV (died unmarried at age 69 years 11 days) and is buried in the Gawthrop Cemetery, Taylor County, WV, **2)** Mary b: 6 Feb. 1815*[15]*, d: 11 Dec. 1902 in Webster, Taylor County, WV, married Wilson Boyle Brown*[16]* on 2 June 1840 in Taylor County, WV.*[location 81]*[a] Wilson was a tanner and a farmer. Both Wilson and Mary are buried in the Quaker Cemetery, in Webster, WV. They had 6 children: James Boyle*[16]*, Virginia Jane, Christopher Columbus, Jonathan Wilson, Elizabeth Ann, George Washington, Mary Emma and [Charles Wesley*[64]*]. **3)** Elizabeth*[89]* b: 23 June 1813 in Taylor County, WV,[a] d: 19 June 1910, married John Shroyer (b: 29 Aug. 1811) on 17 Nov. 1836 in Harrison County, WV.[a] They had 6 children: Jackson, Elizabeth, Louis, Jacob B., Mary C., and [Irving*[64]*]. John Shroyer was a Gunsmith. **4)** Margaret b: 12 Oct. 1818 *[89]* in Taylor County, WV,[a] d: unmarried on 27 Feb. 1888 at age 70 years, **5)** Isabella d: unmarried on 8 Oct. 1863.*[89]*

REFERENCES


SOURCE [16]: A handwritten family tree, *"OUR CHILDREN'S ANCESTORS,"* compiled by Rev. Darward and Dorothy Brown for their children and grandchildren, no date was available; however, Rev Darward Belmont Brown was born on 12 January 1897. It is thought that the Brown Family Tree and the Everard C. Gawthrop Family Tree were commissioned approximately the same time. Philip E. Gawthrop has the original work of the Everard C. Gawthrop family tree prepared by genealogist G. Cope in the early to mid 1920's.

SOURCE [17]: Genealogy work compiled by Thomas Carr Gawthrop. This manuscript was not published by a publisher; however, Thomas Carr Gawthrop was born Jan. 1938 and died Sept. 1966. This compiled work was obtained from Mary Virginia (Merrifield) Gawthrop wife of Wilbur Edmond Gawthrop (deceased) and her son, Richard Carr Gawthrop in early 1992. Thomas Carr Gawthrop was her nephew and Richard's cousin.

SOURCE [64]: Draft genealogy work compiled by Wm. A.A. Gawthrop, "GAWTHROP GENEALOGY," U.S. Congressional Library, CS71.G277, 1986.

SOURCE [81]: Letter/package containing a draft of Gawthrop Genealogy dated 2 June 1992 from Charles (Chuck) D. Thornton, Cape Coral, Fl.

SOURCE [89]: Letter dated 7 April 1992 from David Carl Gawthrop, Charlottesville, VA.

SOURCE [112]: Letter dated 28 April 1992 from David Carl Gawthrop, Charlottesville, VA.

# Chapter 17

8th Generation

## 15124525, ALLEN B. GAWTHROP ( 1808 - 1887 )

Allen B. Gawthrop[a], the fifth child and fifth son of Thomas William Gawthrop (1776-1832) and Elizabeth Hiett (1779-1873), was born 1 March 1808 in Taylor County, VA[b] and died on 10 Dec. 1887 in Taylor County, WV. Allen B. is buried in the Gawthrop Cemetery in Taylor County, WV.*[81]* Allen B. lived in Taylor County, WV[c] and farmed the land. He owned 29 acres in Taylor County, VA[b] at Lost Creek in 1852 as recorded in Book 1, page 428 of the county land records.*[86]* Allen B. married Elizabeth H. Corder on 26 Sept. 1833 in Harrison County, WV.*[location 81]* [b] Elizabeth was the daughter of William Corder.*[86]* Elizabeth was born on 8 July 1812 in Fauquier County, VA*[81]* and died on 11 April 1888.

Allen B. and Elizabeth's children follow*[17, 81]*:

**151245251**, Evan Marshall (q.v., Vol. 2) b: 6 Sept. 1838 in VA,[b] d: 8 May 1922 in Grafton, Taylor County, WV, married Nancy Hustead on 14 March 1867.

**151245252**, Joshua E. b: 15 Oct. 1841 in VA,[b] d: 1918 in WV, married twice: **1M**-nfn Rigger, **2M**-nfn Hutton (no children to either marriage). Joshua was a Private in Company "A", 9th Battalion, VA Infantry in Hansbrough's Battalion.*[86]* Joshua was also reported as a Private in Company "A", Heck's Regiment.*[86]* Joshua physical description at age 25 (as of 12 May 1865) when he entered civilian life again was 5 feet 8 inches tall, fair complexion, black hair, gray eyes.*[86]* Joshua was wound at Gettysburg, PA on July 2, 1863. A shell wound reportedly fractured his fibula and he had gangreen. He was sent to Hospital Number 1 in Richmond, VA. Served as a butcher while in the army.*[86]*

**151245253**, Perry (q.v., Vol. 2) b: 15 Nov. 1843 in VA,[b] d: 14 Jan. 1919, married twice: **1M**-Eliza Woodyard on 13 Sept. 1874, **2M**-Copeland Hough.

---

a Allen B. Gawthrop is listed in the 1860 Census of Taylor County, WV.

b In 1861 when the Virginia delegates voted to secede, the delegates from the Unionist northwestern counties rebelled and set up their own restored Government of Virginia. This arrangement lasted until Congress voted to admit West Virginia into the union as the 35th state on 20 June 1863. The counties in western part of Virginia became counties in West Virginia during that same split.

c Allen B. Gawthrop is listed in the 1840 Census of Henry Co., VA, on page 17, could be the same man.

**151245254**, Thomas b: 20 April 1847,[d] d: [unmarried*[86]*] in 1927, Taylor County, WV, buried in the Gawthrop Cemetery, Taylor County, WV.

**151245255**, John Wiseman {no other information found}

**151245256**, Thelma b: in Virginia*[86]* {no other information found}

***A***llen B. had 6 brothers and 5 sisters. The 6 brothers were: **1)** James (q.v.) b: 16 Oct. 1798, married Hulda Waldo on 9 Jan. 1824, **2)** John (q.v.) b: 8 Dec. 1803, d: 25 April 1881, married twice: **1M**-Josinah Corbin on 22 May 1825, **2M**-Kathrine Radabaugh in 1871 (no children of this marriage), **3)** Thomas (q.v.) b: 7 April 1806, d: 4 Feb. 1876, married Elizabeth Wiseman on 2 Feb. 1832, **4)** Hiett (q.v.) b: 1807, d: Pruntytown, Taylor County, WV, married Mary Pool on 15 Feb. 1827, **5)** Evan H.*[H. in 81]* b: 1810 in Taylor County, WV.[b] In the research of Thomas Carr Gawthrop, there is a reference that states, ***He went West unmarried about 1838. He was near Galena, Illinois when last heard from.****[17]* **6)** Enos D. (q.v.) b: 6 March 1810, d: 27 Oct. 1843, married Ruth Wiseman on 28 Dec. 1831 (Evan H. and Enos D. may have been twins). The 5 sisters were: **1)** Sarah b: 6 Feb. 1812*[16]* (letter from David C. Gawthrop places date of birth at Nov. 1819*[112]*, d: 14 Oct. 1881 in Taylor County, WV (died unmarried at age 69 years 11 days) and is buried in the Gawthrop Cemetry, Taylor County, WV. **2)** Mary b: 6 Feb. 1815*[16]*, d: 11 Dec. 1902 in Webster, Taylor County, WV, married Wilson Boyle Brown*[16]* on 2 June 1840 in Taylor County, WV.[b]*[81]* Wilson was a tanner and a farmer. Both Wilson and Mary are buried in the Quaker Cemetery, in Webster, WV. They had 6 children: James Boyle*[16]*, Virginia Jane, Christopher Columbus, Jonathan Wilson, Elizabeth Ann, George Washington, Mary Emma and [Charles Wesley*[64]*]. **3)** Elizabeth b: 23 June 1813 in Taylor County, WV,[b] d: 19 June 1910, married John Shroyer (b: 29 Aug. 1811) on 17 Nov. 1836 in Harrison County, WV.[b] They had 6 children: Jackson, Elizabeth, Louis, Jacob B., Mary C., and [Irving*[64]*]. John Shroyer was a Gunsmith. **4)** Margaret b: 12 Oct. 1818 *[89]* in Taylor County, WV,[b] d: unmarried 27 Feb. 1888 at age 70 years, **5)** Isabella d: unmarried 8 Oct. 1863.*[89]*

REFERENCES

SOURCE [16]: A handwritten family tree, *"OUR CHILDREN'S ANCESTORS,"* compiled by Rev. Darward and Dorothy Brown for their children and grandchildren, no date was available; however, Rev Darward Belmont Brown was born on 12 January 1897. It is thought that the Brown Family Tree and the Everard C. Gawthrop Family Tree were commissioned approximately the same time.

SOURCE [17]: Genealogy work compiled by Thomas Carr Gawthrop. This manuscript was not published by a publisher; however, Thomas Carr Gawthrop was born Jan. 1938 and died Sept. 1966.

SOURCE [64]: Draft genealogy work compiled by Wm. A.A. Gawthrop, "GAWTHROP GENEALOGY," U.S. Congressional Library, CS71.G277, 1986.

---

d The 1880 census for Taylor County, WV gave the age of Thomas as 33 years.*[64]*

SOURCE [81]: Letter/package containing a draft of Gawthrop Genealogy dated 2 June 1992 from Charles (Chuck) D. Thornton, Cape Coral, Fl.

SOURCE [86]: Draft of the Descendents of Thomas Gawthrop, by Wm. A.A.Gawthrop, September 1993.

SOURCE [89]: Letter dated 7 April 1992 from David Carl Gawthrop, Charlottesville, VA.

SOURCE [112]: Letter dated 28 April 1992 from David Carl Gawthrop, Charlottesville, VA.

# Chapter 18

8th Generation

## 15124526, ENOS D. GAWTHROP ( 1810 - 1843 )

*E*nos D. Gawthrop, the sixth child and the sixth son of Thomas William Gawthrop (1776-1832) and Elizabeth Hiett (1779 - 1873), was born 6 March 1810 in Taylor County, VA[a] and died 27 Oct. 1843 in Taylor County, VA.[a] */81/* [b] Enos D. married Ruth Wiseman on 28 Dec. 1831. The marriage took place at the Gawthrop Homestead near Pruntytown, Harrison County, VA.[a] Enos D. had 83 acres in Lost Run, Harrison County, VA[a] as is recorded in 1838, Book 7, page 193 of the county land records.*/86/*

*E*nos D. and Ruth had 4 children*/17, 81/*:

**151245261** Mary Jane b: 29 Dec. 1833, married John Shrieves on 27 Sept. 1849 in Harrison County, VA.*/location 86/* [a]

**151245262** Charles Franklin b: 25 April 1836, d: 4 Aug. 1859 in Randolph County, WV.*/location 64/* [a]

**151245263** Elizabeth b: 25 Dec. 1838, married Willis Herren on 6 May 1859 in Randolph County, WV.*/location 86/* [a]

**151245264** James William*/17, 116/* (q.v., Vol. 2) b: 19 Feb.1843, married Mary Reger on 27 April 1871.

*E*nos D. had 6 brothers and 5 sisters. The 6 brothers were: **1)** James (q.v.) b: 16 Oct. 1798, married Hulda Waldo, **2)** John (q.v.) b: 8 Dec. 1803, d: 25 Apr. 1881, married twice: **1M**-Josinah Corbin on 22 May 1825, **2M**-Kathrine Radabaugh in 1871 (no children of this marriage), **3)** Thomas (q.v.) b: 7 April 1806, d: 4 Feb. 1876, married Elizabeth Wiseman on 2 Feb. 1832, **4)** Hiett (q.v.) b: 1807, married Mary Pool on 15 Feb. 1827, **5)** Allen B. (q.v.) b: 1 March 1808, d: 10 Dec. 1887, married Elizabeth H. Corder on 26 Sept. 1833, **6)** Evan (H.*/81/*) b: 1810 in Taylor County, WV [a], In the research of Thomas Carr Gawthrop there is a reference to a letter that states, ***He went West unmarried about 1838. He was near Galena, Illinois when last heard from.****/17/* The 5 sisters were: **1)** Sarah b: 6 Feb. 1812*/16/* (letter from David C. Gawthrop places date of birth at Nov.

---

a In 1861 when the Virginia delegates voted to secede, the delegates from the Unionist northwestern counties rebelled and set up their own restored Government of Virginia. This arrangement lasted until Congress voted to admit West Virginia into the union as the 35th state on 20 June 1863. Therefore, Taylor County, Virginia became Taylor County, West Virginia with the final split during the Civil War. Other counties in western part of Virginia became counties in West Virginia during that same split.

b Letter from David C. Gawthrop to Philip E. Gawthrop places the date of his death at 20 Oct. 1843.*/89/*

1819[112], d: 14 Oct. 1881 in Taylor County, WV (died unmarried at age 69 years 11 days). Sarah is buried in the Gawthrop Cemetery, Taylor County, WV. **2)** Mary b: 6 Feb. 1815[16], d: 11 Dec. 1902 in Webster, Taylor County, WV, married Wilson Boyle Brown[16] on 2 June 1840 in Taylor County, WV.[location 81][a] Wilson was a tanner and a farmer. Both Wilson and Mary are buried in the Quaker Cemetery, in Webster, WV. They had 6 children: James Boyle[16], Virginia Jane, Christopher Columbus, Jonathan Wilson, Elizabeth Ann, George Washington, Mary Emma and [Charles Wesley[64]]. **3)** Elizabeth[89] b: 23 June 1813 in Taylor County, WV,[a] d: 19 June 1910, married John Shroyer (b: 29 Aug. 1811) on 17 Nov. 1836 in Harrison County, WV.[a] They had 6 children: Jackson, Elizabeth, Louis, Jacob B., Mary C., and [Irving[64]]. John Shroyer was a Gunsmith. **4)** Margaret b: 12 Oct. 1818 [89] in Taylor County, WV,[a] d: unmarried on 27 Feb. 1888 at age 70 years. **5)** Isabella d: unmarried on 8 Oct. 1863.[89]

<u>REFERENCES</u>


SOURCE [16]: A handwritten family tree, *"OUR CHILDREN'S ANCESTORS,"* compiled by Rev. Darward and Dorothy Brown for their children and grandchildren, no date was available; however, Rev Darward Belmont Brown was born on 12 January 1897. It is thought that the Brown Family Tree and the Everard C. Gawthrop Family Tree were commissioned approximately the same time. Philip E. Gawthrop has the original work of the Everard C. Gawthrop family tree prepared by genealogist G. Cope in the early to mid 1920's.

SOURCE [17]: Genealogy work compiled by Thomas Carr Gawthrop. This manuscript was not published by a publisher; however, Thomas Carr Gawthrop was born Jan. 1938 and died Sept. 1966. This compiled work was obtained from Mary Virginia (Merrifield) Gawthrop wife of Wilbur Edmond Gawthrop (deceased) and her son, Richard Carr Gawthrop in early 1992. Thomas Carr Gawthrop was her nephew and Richard's cousin.

SOURCE [64]: Draft genealogy work compiled by Wm. A.A. Gawthrop, "GAWTHROP GENEALOGY," U.S. Congressional Library, CS71.G277, 1986.

SOURCE [81]: Letter/package containing a draft of Gawthrop Genealogy dated 2 June 1992 from Charles (Chuck) D. Thornton, Cape Coral, Fl.

SOURCE [86]: Draft of the Descendents of Thomas Gawthrop, by Wm. A.A.Gawthrop, September 1993.

SOURCE [89]: Letter dated 7 April 1992 from David Carl Gawthrop, Charlottesville, VA.

SOURCE [112]: Letter dated 28 April 1992 from David Carl Gawthrop, Charlottesville, VA.

SOURCE [116]: The History Of Barbour County, WV, published by Hu Maxwell, ACME Publishing Company, Morgantown, WV, (C) 1899, pages 387-388.

# Chapter 19

8th Generation

## 15124613, DANIEL GAWTHROP ( 1805 - 1838 )

***D**aniel Gawthrop, the third child and the first son of Thomas Gawthrop (1774-1851) and Elizabeth Thompson (1779-1864), was born on 12 July 1805 in London Grove Township, Chester County, PA*[location 91]* and died 16 March 1838 in London Grove, PA. Daniel is buried in New Garden, PA. Daniel received his education from the common school system of Chester County and became a successful farmer for his vocation in life.*[91]* He was admitted to the New Garden Monthly Meeting on the 6th day of the 6th month, 1831.*[19]* Daniel married Elizabeth Mitchell on 16 Dec. 1830 at Hockessin, DE. Elizabeth was the daughter of Joseph Mitchell[a] and Sarah Harlen of Mill Creek, New Castle County, DE. Elizabeth's father, Joseph Mitchell, was prominently identified with the agricultural interests of the state of DE.*[91]* Elizabeth was born on 25 Dec. 1810 in Mill Creek, New Castle County, DE and died on 14 April 1838.[b] Daniel and Elizabeth lived in London Grove Township, Chester County, PA. Both Daniel and his wife are buried at New Garden, PA. With the unexpected deaths of Daniel and Elizabeth, their children had to be looked after. Two of their children, Sarah M. and Emmor, were taken in by the Grandparents on their father's side, Thomas and Elizabeth (Thompson) Gawthrop. Another of their children, Lydia Ann, was taken in by the Grandparents on the mother's side, Joseph and Sarah (Harlan) Mitchell. Another of their children, Amy, was taken in by her Grandfather Thomas Gawthrop's brother and his wife, George and Amy (Chambers) Gawthrop.

***D**aniel and Elizabeth's children follow *[17, 19]*:

**151246131,** Sarah Mitchell (called Sallie) b: 20 Nov. 1831 and is recorded in the New Garden Monthly Meeting, Chester County, PA*[93]*, d: [23 Oct. 1886 in Oxford, Chester County, PA*[81]*], married William Henry Way (b: 27 March 1829*[81]*, d: 21 March 1910*[81]*) on 17 April 1862 in

---

a With the sudden death of his daughter, Elizabeth and her husband, Daniel, in 1838 somebody had to look after their 4 children. One of their children, Lydia Ann, was taken in by Elizabeth's parents, Joseph and Sarah (Harlan) Mitchell. Lydia Ann was just over 5 years old when she came to live with her Grandparents. The other three children were taken in by the Gawthrop family; Amy was taken in by George and Amy (Chambers) Gawthrop; Sarah M. and Emmor were taken in by Thomas And Elizabeth (Thompson) Gawthrop.

b Elizabeth died within a month of Daniel and apparently knew that she was going to died. Within fifteen days after the death of her husband, she signed over her property to her Uncle George Gawthrop (1784-1865).*[86]*

Avondale, Chester County, PA. Sarah and William had 4 children: James Allen, Elizabeth H. (called Lizie), Charles Henry, and Amy Anna.

**151246132,** Lydia Ann b: 27 June 1833 in New Garden, PA, d: unmarried on 26 Dec. 1907 in Hochessin, DE, buried in New Castle County, DE.

**151246133,** Amy b: 10 Dec. 1835 [in New Garden, PA*[86]*], d: unknown date in Lancaster County, PA, married Alexander N. Turner of Colerain, Lancaster County, PA on 12 April 1862 in Lancaster County, PA.

**151246134,** Emmor D. (q.v., Vol. 2) b: 31 Aug. 1837 in London Grove, PA, d: 25 Dec. 1920 in PA, married Phebe Thompson on 29 Jan. 1863.

***D***aniel had 2 brothers and 5 sisters. The 2 brothers were: **1)** Allen (q.v.) b: 22 June 1810, d: 23 June 1885, married Mary Ann Newlin on 31 July 1833, **2)** James T. b: 20 Sept. 1819 in London Grove Township, PA, d: 23 July 1889 in his home in Avondale, PA at age 69 years, married Priscilla Peirce (b: 1 Dec. 1829, d: 11 June 1860) on 24 May 1855 in the home of the bride's father. Priscilla was the daughter of Gideon and Rebecca (Lukens) Peirce of Ercild, PA. James T. and Priscilla lived in a brick house on the Gawthrop homestead near Avondale, (southern part of) Chester County, PA. James T. and Priscilla had 2 children, Lucy and Ella, but both children died young, around June 1860. James T. was buried on 26 July 1889 at New Garden Cemetery, PA. The 5 sisters were: **1)** Sarah b: 14 Sept. 1801 near Avondale in Chester County, PA*[81]*, d: 9 July 1887*[81]*, funeral at the residence of her daughter, Phebe S. Baily, buried 13 July 1887 in West Grove, PA, married Joseph Seal of Philadelphia (b: 20 Nov. 1788, d: 17 June 1842) on 13 March 1823*[93]* [c] in West Grove, PA. Joseph was the son of Benjamin and Phebe Seal of New Garden, PA. Joseph and Sarah had 9 children: Thomas G. (b: 19 April 1824), Rachel (b: 23 Jan. 1826), William b: 18 June 1828), Eliza (b: 11 April 1830), Sarah Ann (b: 11 Feb. 1833), Phebe (b: 13 March 1835), Mary Jane (b: 4 July 1837), Joel A. (b: 18 Oct. 1839), and Joseph Gilpin (b: 10 Nov. 1841).*[17]* **2)** Ann b: 9 Sept. 1803 in London Grove, PA, d: died in London Grove Township in the home of her late mother at the age of 54 years, (d: 8 Oct. 1857), unmarried, **3)** Jane b: 29 Sept. 1807 in PA, d: 9 Jan. 1837 in New Garden, PA*[location 81]*, married Hibbert Moore (b: 10 March 1806 in New Garden, PA) on 14 Oct. 1830 at New Garden, PA. Hibbert was the son David and Martha (Sharpless) Moore. Jane and Hibbert had one son: Gilpen[d] (b: 27 Oct. 1831). They moved from New Garden, PA to Rock Island, IL.[e]

---

c According to the New Garden Monthly Meeting record, NG, PA #3, ***Sarah Gawthrop married Joseph Seal, 1823, 3, 13.***

d In reference 81, Gilpen is spelled with an "i" in "pin" not an "e". However, in the Last Will and Testament of Thomas Gawthrop, his Grandfather (Chapter-9), Gilpen is spelled with an "e" in "pen" not an "i". Because Gilpen lived with his Grandparents for most of his upbringing, it is felt that the spelling of "Gilpen" is correct.

**4)** Lydia b: 12 Feb. 1913 in PA, died at age 29 years 5 months 18 days (d: 30 July 1842),

**5)** Elizabeth b: 16 July 1815 in PA, d: 20 Oct. 1819.


REFERENCES

SOURCE [16]: A handwritten family tree, *"OUR CHILDREN'S ANCESTORS,"* compiled by Rev. Darward and Dorothy Brown for their children and grandchildren, no date was available; however, Rev Darward Belmont Brown was born on 12 January 1897. It is thought that the Brown Family Tree and the Everard C. Gawthrop Family Tree were commissioned approximately the same time. Philip E. Gawthrop has the original work of the Everard C. Gawthrop family tree prepared by genealogist G. Cope in the early to mid 1920's.

SOURCE [17]: Genealogy work compiled by Thomas Carr Gawthrop. This manuscript was not published by a publisher; however, Thomas Carr Gawthrop was born Jan. 1938 and died Sept. 1966. This compiled work was obtained from Mary Virginia (Merrifield) Gawthrop wife of Wilbur Edmond Gawthrop (deceased) and her son, Richard Carr Gawthrop in early 1992. Thomas Carr Gawthrop was her nephew and Richard's cousin.

SOURCE [19]: A handwritten family tree prepared by Allen Gawthrop in 1871. Allen was the son of Thomas and Elizabeth (Thompson) Gawthrop. The son of Allen and Mary Ann (Newlin) Gawthrop, Henry Gawthrop, collected data from Allen's work along with the assistance of several family members to generate another work entitled *GEORGE GAWTHROP, The Emigrate*, by Henry Gawthrop, dated Christmas 1900. Henry's work (in typescript, not published by a publisher) is available from the Friends Historical Library, Swarthmore College, PA.

SOURCE [64]: Draft genealogy work compiled by Wm. A.A. Gawthrop, "GAWTHROP GENEALOGY," U.S. Congressional Library, CS71.G277, 1986.

SOURCE [81]: Letter/package containing a draft of Gawthrop Genealogy dated 2 June 1992 from Charles (Chuck) D. Thornton, Cape Coral, Fl.

SOURCE [86]: Draft of the Descendents of Thomas Gawthrop, by Wm. A.A.Gawthrop, September 1993.

SOURCE [91]: *Chester and Delaware Counties*, Vol 2, by Gilbert Cope and Henry Graham Ashmead, (C) 1904, page 577, obtained from the Chester County Historical Society, West Chester, PA.

SOURCE [93]: New Garden Monthly Meeting, PA records.


---

e There is conjecture that something happened to his parents in Illinois and he came back to live with his grandparents or when his parents moved to Illinois that they left him behind with his grandparents until he could be sent for (see Chapter 9, footnote d).

# Chapter 20

8th Generation

## 15124615, ALLEN GAWTHROP ( 1810 - 1885 )

**A**llen Gawthrop, the fifth child and the second son of Thomas Gawthrop (1774-1851) and Elizabeth Thompson (1779-1864), was born on 22 June 1810 in Chester County, PA and died in his home in Wilmington, DE on 23 June 1885. Allen received his education from those schools available to him in Chester County. Early in life he learned basic machinery from his father. It was in Chester County that Allen first set-up for the manufacture of the hydraulic ram. In his hydraulic shop, he also built and sold farm implements. Also, at his shop, he had another item that he did as a trade, joining.[a] Allen manufactured fine cabinets.*[117]* In 1855 he came to Wilmington, DE and established another machine shop where he successfully manufacturing hydraulic rams and farm implements.*[117]* Also, he learn and subsequencely engaged in the contractor business doing plumbing and heating. Later in life, Allen was a photographer. Allen remained a most temperate man and adherent to the Quaker faith his entire life.*[117]* He died on 23[b] June 1885 in his home in Wilmington, DE. When the news of his death was announced scores of his friends home were darkened in mourning. Throughout his 71 years he made no enemies but developed a host of friends. He is buried in Wilmington and Brandywire Cemetery, Wilmington, DE.

**F**or thirty years, Allen contributed to the development and prosperity of the Wilmington community. Seldom was there a public work afoot that lacked his quiet support. During the time he spent in Wilmington there was many worthy causes and endeavors that Allen Gawthrop supported. He served with distinction on the Board of Education and for many years he was a trustee and a member of the Wilmington Board of Health. He was a director on the Board of the National Bank of Wilmington and Brandywire of Wilmington, DE. He was well liked and had a host of sincere friends as well as relatives. Like his father, he belonged to the Society of Friends (Quakers).

**A**llen married Mary Ann Newlin (b: 10 Aug. 1811, d: 7 Nov. 1882) on 31 July 1833. Mary Ann was the daughter of Joseph and Sarah (Taggart) Newlin. They lived in West Grove,

---

a Webster's New Collegiate Dictionary, 1979 edition, defines JOINER and JOINING as: Joiner - a person whose occuption is to construct acticles by joining pieces of wood. Joining - the act or instance of joining one thing to another.

b The *History of Delaware, Past and Present*, Volume III, New York 1929, gives the date of death as 24 June 1885.

Chester County, PA until 1855 when they moved to Wilmington, DE. They lived in Wilmington for the remainder of their lifes.

*A*llen and Mary Ann had 6 children*[17, 19]*:

**151246151**, Joseph Newlin (q.v., Vol. 2) b: 23 Aug. 1835, d: 12 April 1916, married Esther Good in 1859.

**151246152**, Emma b: 29 May 1837 in West Chester, PA, d: unknown; married Evans Pennington on 24 March 1864 in Wilmington, DE. They had 3 children: Henry, Frank, and Harvey.

**151246153**, Alfred (q.v., Vol. 2) b: 19 Oct. 1839, d: 14 Oct. 1909, married Hannah J. Stroud on 4 May 1865.

**151246154**, Henry (q.v., Vol. 2) b: 7 April 1841, d: 22 July 1920, married Mary L. Thompson on 15 Feb. 1872.

**151246155**, Allen Jr. b: 9 Aug. 1843 in West Grove, PA, d: in 1919 in Wilmington, DE, buried in East Lawn Cemetery, Milmont Park, Swarthmore, PA.

**151246156**, Edith Newlin b: 27 Sept. 1851 in West Chester, PA, d: 13 Sept. 1852 in Swarthmore, PA.*[81]*

*A*llen had 2 brothers and 5 sisters. The 2 brothers were: **1)** Daniel (q.v.) b: 12 July 1805, d: 16 March 1838,[c] married Elizabeth Mitchell on 16 Dec. 1830, **2)** James T. b: 20 Sept. 1819 in London Grove Township, PA, d: 23 July 1889 in his home in Avondale, PA at age 69 years, married Priscilla Peirce (b: 1 Dec. 1829, d: 11 June 1860) on 24 May 1855 in the home of the bride's father. Priscilla was the daughter of Gideon and Rebecca (Lukens) Peirce of Ercild, PA. James T. and Priscilla lived in a brick house on the Gawthrop homestead near Avondale, (southern part of) Chester County, PA. James T. and Priscilla had 2 children, Lucy and Ella, but both children died young, around June 1860. James T. is buried at New Garden Cemetery, PA on 26 July 1889. The 5 sisters were: **1)** Sarah b: 14 Sept. 1801 near Avondale in Chester County, PA,*[81]* d: 9 July 1887.*[81]* Her funeral was at the residence of her daughter, Phebe S. Baily. She is buried at West Grove, PA on 13 July 1887. Sarah married Joseph Seal of Philadelphia (b: 20 Nov. 1788, d: 17 June 1842) on 13 March 1823*[93]* [d] in West Grove, PA. Joseph was the son of Benjamin and Phebe Seal of New Garden, PA. Joseph and Sarah had 9 children: Thomas G. (b: 19 April 1824), Rachel (b: 23

---

c When Daniel and his wife, Elizabeth, died suddenly their 4 children had to be looked after. Two of their children, Sarah M. and Emmor, were taken in by the Grandparents on their father's side, Thomas and Elizabeth (Thompson) Gawthrop. Another of their children, Lydia Ann, was taken in by the Grandparents on the mother's side, Joseph and Sarah (Harlan) Mitchell. Another of their children, Amy, was taken in by her Grandfather Thomas Gawthrop's brother and his wife, George and Amy (Chambers) Gawthrop.

d According to the New Garden Monthly Meeting record #3, ***Sarah Gawthrop married Joseph Seal, 1823, 3, 13.***

Jan. 1826), William (b: 18 June 1828), Eliza (b: 11 April 1830), Sarah Ann (b: 11 Feb. 1833), Phebe (b: 13 March 1835), Mary Jane (b: 4 July 1837), Joel A. (b: 18 Oct. 1839), and Joseph Gilpin (b: 10 Nov. 1841).*[17]* **2)** Ann b: 9 Sept. 1803 in London Grove, PA, d: died in London Grove Township in the home of her late mother at the age of 54 years, (d: 8 Oct. 1857), unmarried, **3)** Jane b: 29 Sept. 1807 in PA, d: 9 Jan. 1837 in New Garden, PA,*[81]* married Hibbert Moore (b: 10 March 1806 in New Garden, PA) on 14 Oct. 1830 at New Garden, PA. Hibbert was the son David and Martha (Sharpless) Moore. Jane and Hibbert had one son: Gilpen[e] (b: 27 Oct. 1831). They moved from New Garden, PA to Rock Island, IL.[f] **4)** Lydia b: 12 Feb. 1913 in PA, died at age 29 years 5 months 18 days (d: 30 July 1842), **5)** Elizabeth b: 16 July 1815 in PA, d: 20 Oct. 1819.


REFERENCES

SOURCE [16]: A handwritten family tree, *"OUR CHILDREN'S ANCESTORS,"* compiled by Rev. Darward and Dorothy Brown for their children and grandchildren, no date was available; however, Rev Darward Belmont Brown was born on 12 January 1897.

SOURCE [17]: Genealogy work compiled by Thomas Carr Gawthrop. This manuscript was not published by a publisher; however, Thomas Carr Gawthrop was born Jan. 1938 and died Sept. 1966. This compiled work was obtained from Mary Virginia (Merrifield) Gawthrop wife of Wilbur Edmond Gawthrop (deceased) and her son, Richard Carr Gawthrop in early 1992. Thomas Carr Gawthrop was her nephew and Richard's cousin.

SOURCE [19]: A handwritten family tree prepared by Allen Gawthrop in 1871. Allen was the son of Thomas and Elizabeth (Thompson) Gawthrop. The son of Allen and Mary Ann (Newlin) Gawthrop, Henry Gawthrop, collected data from Allen's work along with the assistance of several family members to generate another work entitled *GEORGE GAWTHROP, The Emigrate*, by Henry Gawthrop, dated Christmas 1900. Henry's work (in typescript, not published by a publisher) is available from the Friends Historical Library, Swarthmore College, PA.

SOURCE [64]: Draft genealogy work compiled by Wm. A.A. Gawthrop, "GAWTHROP GENEALOGY," U.S. Congressional Library, CS71.G277, 1986.

SOURCE [81]: Letter/package containing a draft of Gawthrop Genealogy dated 2 June 1992 from Charles (Chuck) D. Thornton, Cape Coral, Fl.

SOURCE [91]: *Chester and Delaware Counties*, Vol 2, by Gilbert Cope and Henry Graham Ashmead, (C) 1904, page 577, obtained from the Chester County Historical Society, West Chester, PA.

SOURCE [93]: New Garden Monthly Meeting, PA records.

SOURCE [117]: Wilson Lloyd Bevan PhD (editor), *History of Delaware, Past and Present*, Vol III, Lewis Historical Publishing Company, Inc., New York, copyright 1929, page 23.


---

e In reference 81, Gilpen is spelled with an "i" in "pin" not an "e". However, in the Last Will and Testament of Thomas Gawthrop, his Grandfather (Chapter-9), Gilpen is spelled with an "e" in "pen" not an "i". Because Gilpen lived with his Grandparents for most of his upbringing, it is felt that the spelling of "Gilpen" is correct.

f There is conjecture that something happened to his parents in Illinois and he came back to live with his grandparents or when his parents moved to Illinois that they left him behind with his grandparents until he could be sent for (see Chapter 9, footnote d).

# Chapter 21

8th Generation

## 15124643, GEORGE GAWTHROP ( 1815 - 1877 )

*G*eorge Gawthrop, the third child and the first son of James Gawthrop (1781-1858) and Hannah Marshall (1784-1862), was born on 29 April 1815 in Chester County, PA and died 26 Nov. 1877 (62 years 6 mth 27 days) at Marlborough, PA. George married Mary Jane Woodward. Mary Jane was the daughter of Pyle and Hannah (Reed) Woodward. Mary Jane was born about 1828 and she died at age 69 years on 3 Jan. 1897 in Kennett Square, PA.*[location 86]* George and Mary Jane lived in Marlborough, Chester County, PA. George is buried at Marlborough Cemetery, Marlborough, PA. Mary Jane is buried at Kennett Square, PA.

*G*eorge and Mary Jane's children follow *[17]*:

**151246431**, Thomas C. (q.v., Vol. 2) b: 28 May 1847, married Emma R. Pratt on 2 Oct. 1873.

**151246432**, Howard James[a] (q.v., Vol. 2) b: 2 July 1850, d: 2 May 1923, married an unknown woman.

**151246433**, William Allen (q.v., Vol. 2) b: 1 March 1858, d: 1902 in Lancaster County, PA, married Frances A. Tanguy in 1897.

*G*eorge had 1 brother and 4 sisters. The one brother was: **1)** James [Jr.[b]] (q.v.) b: 14 Jan. 1825, d: 2 March 1869, married Sarah [Sallie] C. Ridgway on 15 Feb. 1849. The four sisters were: **1)** Mary b: 9 Nov. 1809 (recorded in the Kennett Square Monthly Meeting*[recorded location 81]*), married Caleb J. Hoopes (b: 4 April 1792, d: 14 June 1865) on 12 April 1837[c] at Marlborough, Chester County, PA.*[location 81]* Caleb was the son of Abner and Sarah Hoopes of Thronbury, Delaware County, PA. Mary and Caleb had 5 children: Abner (b: 2 Feb. 1838), James G. (b: 25 Feb. 1840), Edith (b: 29 March 1843), Hannah G. (b: 20 Dec. 1847), and Sarah J. (b: 17 June 1854). **2)** Jane b: 16 Aug. 1812, married Joshua H. Moore. They had two children: John C. and George G. **3)** Rachel b: 25 Nov. 1817 in Kennett Square, Chester County, PA, d: unknown, married Thomas W.[Wistar*[81]*] Parker on 13 March 1839 (married at and recorded at Marlborough Monthly Meeting, Chester County,

---

a In a letter from Charles D. Thornton on 2 June 1992, the first two names are reversed, "James Howard."

b *Encyclopedia of American Quaker Genealogy* by Wm Wade Hinshaw, page 866.

c According to the records at the Kennett Monthly Meeting, PA as delineated by Wm Hinshaw in his notes, KP-44-2.

PA). Thomas was the son of Benjamin Parker and Sarah Passmore*[last name 86]* of East Marlborough, Chester County, PA. Thomas W. was born 4 Aug. 1814[d] and died 13 April 1869.[d] Rachel and Thomas had four children: Hannah Mary (b: 19 Jan. 1840), James G. (b: 8 April 1842, d: 2 Aug. 1845), Sarah H. (b: 21 Aug. 1844, d: 21 July 1845), and James G. (b: 12 July 1847). Rachel lived with her daughter, Hannah Mary, in Philadelphia after Thomas W. died. **4)** Hannah [Hanna *[64]*] b: 3 Nov. 1821 in Marlborough, PA,*[location 81]* d: 17 Dec. 1849 (28 yrs) at Marlborough, PA, buried at Marlborough, Chester County, PA.[e]


REFERENCES

SOURCE [17]: Genealogy work compiled by Thomas Carr Gawthrop. This manuscript was not published by a publisher; however, Thomas Carr Gawthrop was born Jan. 1938 and died Sept. 1966. This compiled work was obtained from Mary Virginia (Merrifield) Gawthrop wife of Wilbur Edmond Gawthrop (deceased) and her son, Richard Carr Gawthrop in early 1992. Thomas Carr Gawthrop was her nephew and Richard's cousin.

SOURCE [64]: Draft genealogy work compiled by Wm. A.A. Gawthrop, "GAWTHROP GENEALOGY," U.S. Congressional Library, CS71.G277, 1986.

SOURCE [81]: Letter/package containing a draft of Gawthrop Genealogy dated 2 June 1992 from Charles (Chuck) D. Thornton, Cape Coral, Fl.

SOURCE [86]: Draft of the Descendents of Thomas Gawthrop, by Wm. A.A.Gawthrop, September 1993.

SOURCE [92]: Kennett Square Monthly Meeting, PA records.


d Source - *"A Record of the Descentants of Robert Lloyd who came from Wales and Settled in the Welsh Tract at Marion Pennsylvania about 1684"* that's all one title.*[obtained from 81]*

e *According to the records at the Kennett Monthly Meeting, PA as delineated by Wm Hinshaw in his notes, KP-458-3.*

# Chapter 22

8th Generation

## 15124646, JAMES GAWTHROP [Jr.[a]] ( 1825 - 1869 )

James Gawthrop, the sixth child and the second son of James Gawthrop (1781-1858) and Hannah Marshall (1784-1862), was born on 14 Jan. 1825 in [Newlin Township*[86]*], Chester County, PA and died 2 March 1869 at Kennett Square, PA. James married Sarah [Sallie] C. Ridgway on 15 Feb. 1849 at the home of Esther Ridgway in [Kennett Square*[86]*], Chester County, PA. Sarah was the daughter of Joseph (dec.) and Esther Ridgway of Chester County, PA. Sarah was born on 19 Nov. 1826 and she died at age 69 years 4 months 13 days on 2 March 1883 at Kennett Square, PA. Sarah is buried at Union Hill Cemetery in PA. James and Sarah lived in Newlin Township, Chester County, PA. On 14 Feb. 1849, James produced a certificate from Kennett Square Monthly Meeting to marry Sarah Ridgway at her Monthly Meeting in Philadelphia (Hicksite).[a] Sarah was granted a Certificate of Removal from Philadelphia to Kennett Square Monthly Meeting.[a]

James and Sarah's children follow *[17]*:

**151246461**, Joseph Ridgway (q.v., Vol. 2) b: 16 May 1850, married twice, **1M**- Hattie Mason on 6 July 1880, **2M**- Ida E. DeVoist.

**151246462**, Hannah Mary b: 9 July 1851 at Kennett Square, Chester County, PA, d: 30 March 1885 (34 years) at Marlborough, PA, married William Way Gawthrop (q.v., a cousin) on 23 Oct. 1873 at the home of James and Sarah Gawthrop. There is no record of children.

**151246463**, Harry James (q.v., Vol. 2) b: 14 Jan. 1856, married Alice Worrall in 1880.

**151246464**, Charles G. (q.v., Vol. 2) b: 16 Jan. 1864, married Louise Hickman on 5 Dec. 1891.

James had 1 brother and 4 sisters. The one brother was: **1)** George (q.v.) b: 29 April 1815, d: 26 Nov. 1877, married Mary Jane Woodward. The 4 sisters were: **1)** Mary b: 9 Nov. 1809 (recorded in the Kennett Square Monthly Meeting*[81]*), married Caleb J. Hoopes (b: 4 April 1792, d: 14 June 1865) on 12 April 1837[b] at Marlborough, Chester County, PA.*[location 81]* Caleb was the son of Abner and Sarah Hoopes of Thronbury, Delaware County, PA. Mary and Caleb had 5 children: Abner (b: 2 Feb. 1838), James G. (b: 25 Feb.

---

a *Encyclopedia of American Quaker Genealogy, Vol.II*, by Wm Wade Hinshaw, page 866.

b According to the records at the Kennett Monthly Meeting, PA as delineated by Wm Hinshaw in his notes, KP-44-2.

1840), Edith (b: 29 March 1843), Hannah G. (b: 20 Dec. 1847), and Sarah J. (b: 17 June 1854). **2)** Jane b: 16 Aug. 1812, married Joshua H. Moore. They had two children: John C. and George G. **3)** Rachel b: 25 Nov. 1817 in Kennett Square, Chester County, PA, d: unknown, married Thomas W.[Wistar*[81]*] Parker on 13 March 1839 (married at and recorded at Marlborough Monthly Meeting, Chester County, PA). Thomas was the son of Benjamin and Sarah Parker of East Marlborough, Chester County, PA. Rachel and Thomas had four children: Hannah Mary (b: 19 Jan. 1840), James G. (b: 8 April 1842, d: 2 Aug. 1845), Sarah H. (b: 21 Aug. 1844, d: 21 July 1845), and James G. (b: 12 July 1847). Rachel lived with her daughter, Hannah, in Philadelphia after Thomas W. died. **4)** Hannah [Hanna *[64]*] b: 3 Nov. 1821 in Marlborough, PA,*[location 81]* d: 17 Dec. 1849 (28 yrs) at Marlborough, PA, buried at Marlborough, Chester County, PA.*[92]* [c]

REFERENCES


SOURCE [17]: Genealogy work compiled by Thomas Carr Gawthrop. This manuscript was not published by a publisher; however, Thomas Carr Gawthrop was born Jan. 1938 and died Sept. 1966. This compiled work was obtained from Mary Virginia (Merrifield) Gawthrop wife of Wilbur Edmond Gawthrop (deceased) and her son, Richard Carr Gawthrop in early 1992. Thomas Carr Gawthrop was her nephew and Richard's cousin.

SOURCE [64]: Draft genealogy work compiled by Wm. A.A. Gawthrop, "GAWTHROP GENEALOGY," U.S. Congressional Library, CS71.G277, 1986.

SOURCE [81]: Letter/package containing a draft of Gawthrop Genealogy dated 2 June 1992 from Charles (Chuck) D. Thornton, Cape Coral, Fl.

SOURCE [86]: Draft of the Descendents of Thomas Gawthrop, by Wm. A.A.Gawthrop, September 1993.

SOURCE [92]: Kennett Square Monthly Meeting, PA records.


---

c According to the records at the Kennett Monthly Meeting, PA as delineated by Wm Hinshaw in his notes, KP-458-3.

# Chapter 23

8th Generation

## 15124655, THOMAS GAWTHROP ( 1818 - 1864 )

Thomas Gawthrop, the fifth child and the third son of George Gawthrop (1784-1865) and Amy Chambers (1787-1851), was born on 7 Feb. 1818 at Menander Wood near Avondale, Chester County, PA and died 25 Jan. 1864 at New London, PA. Thomas is buried at New West Grove, PA. Thomas married twice: **1M**-Lydia Conard (b: 25 Jan. 1820, d: 28 Dec. 1843 at New London, PA*(location 86)*) on 13 March 1840. Lydia was the daughter of Jesse Conard (b: 11 Nov. 1778, d: 10 May 1852*(18)*) and Ann Pennington (b: 12 March 1781, d: 19 Jan. 1855*(18)*) of New London, Chester County, PA. **2M**-Susanna Conard (b: 1816, d: 28 March 1900) after the death of her sister in Dec. 1843. Susanna was the daughter of Jesse Conard (1778-1852*(18)*) and Ann Pennington (1781-1855*(18)*) of New London, Chester County, PA. Lydia and Susanna were sister. Thomas lived in West Grove, PA with both wives.

Thomas and Lydia had 2 children*(17)*:

**151246551**, Jesse b: 18 May 1842, d: 29 May 1842.

**151246552**, Lydia C. b: 22 Nov. 1843, d: unknown, married Judge of the District Court of Florida, Charles Swayne.

Thomas and Susanna had 5 children*(17)*:

**151246553**, Amy Ann b: 6 May 1847, married George L. Baker on 14 Feb. 1878 at West Grove, PA.*(location 81)* Amy Ann and George lived at the old Baker Limequarry property on the road from Avondale to Jennersville, PA.

**151246554**, Jane Susanna b: 21 July 1849 at Kennett Square, Chester County, PA,*(location 81)* married Elwood Conard on 28 Sept. 1871 at Chester County, PA.*(location 81)*

**151246555**, Mary Elizabeth b: 8 Aug. 1854, married Harvey John in 1879 in PA, Harvey's birth was in 1850.*(81)*

twin: **151246556**, George b: 10 Feb. 1857, d: 23 Feb. 1857.

twin: **151246557**, Ruth Emma b: 10 Feb. 1857, d: 1 Oct. 1857.

Thomas had 6 brothers and 3 sisters. The 6 brothers were: **1)** Joseph C. b: 29 Jan. 1815, d: 26 June 1892, unmarried. Joseph had what appeared to be polio [leg paralyzed*(17)*]. He lived with his sister, Elizabeth (Gawthrop) Hughes and her husband, William. Joseph's occupation was Tinsmith (a pot maker). **2)** one child of a set of twins without a name, b: 29 Dec. 1816, d: 30 Dec. 1816, **3)** George W. (William *(81)*) (q.v.)

b: 29 Aug. 1822, d: 23 Jan. 1892, married Louisa Way on 17 Feb. 1847, **4)** Evan b: 5 March 1824, d: 9 July 1824, **5)** William (q.v.) b: 9 Sept. 1825, d: 31 March 1882, married Sarah Brown on 12 March 1860, **6)** Jessie b: 7 April 1828 (recorded in the New Garden Monthly Meeting, Chester County, PA*(location 81)*) d: 27 Aug. 1828. The 3 sisters were: **1)** Ruth b: 11 Nov. 1813, married Isaac Moore (b: 21 March 1810 at London Grove, PA) of London Grove, PA on 18 Nov. 1841 (married at and recorded in the New Garden Monthly Meeting*(93)*). Isaac was the son of Joseph and Beulah Moore. Ruth and Isaac lived on a farm in West Grove, Chester County, PA. Isaac's mother and father operated a mill. Ruth and Isaac had 7 children: Joseph G. (b: 31 July 1843), Lindley C. (b: 26 May 1845), Hannah (b: 18 Nov. 1849, d: 31 May 1855), Thomas G. (b: 31 Dec. 1851, d: 6 Aug. 1853), Elizabeth (b: 28 Nov. 1854), twins: Channing (19 Aug. 1857, d: 12 Oct. 1857) and Darwin (19 Aug. 1857, d: 7 March 1861), **2)** the other child of a set of twins believed to be a girl (no name was found), b: 29 Dec. 1816, d: 29 Jan. 1817, and **3)** Elizabeth b: 15 Feb. 1820 (recorded in the New Garden Monthly Meeting, Chester County, PA,*(location 81)* d: 31 Dec. 1897, married William Hughes (b: 10 April 1819, d: 9 May 1894) on 20 May 1841 (married at and recorded in New Garden Monthly Meeting, Chester County, PA*(93)*). William was the son of Mark and Lydia Hughes. Elizabeth and William had 3 children: George C. (b: 21 Sept. 1843), Charles C. (b: 19 Jan. 1847) and Amy Anna (b: 20 May 1850). Elizabeth and William died at residence of Amy Anna and Dr. Milton E. Conard, their daughter and son-in-law.

REFERENCES


SOURCE [17]: Genealogy work compiled by Thomas Carr Gawthrop. This manuscript was not published by a publisher; however, Thomas Carr Gawthrop was born Jan. 1938 and died Sept. 1966. This compiled work was obtained from Mary Virginia (Merrifield) Gawthrop wife of Wilbur Edmond Gawthrop (deceased) and her son, Richard Carr Gawthrop in early 1992. Thomas Carr Gawthrop was her nephew and Richard's cousin.

SOURCE [18]: A handwritten family tree prepared for Everard Conard Gawthrop by G. Cope (Jr. ??) of Pittsburg, PA done in the mid 1920s. Philip Evan Gawthrop (Grandson of Everard) has the original work of the family tree.

SOURCE [81]: Letter/package containing a draft of Gawthrop Genealogy dated 2 June 1992 from Charles (Chuck) D. Thornton, Cape Coral, Fl.

SOURCE [86]: Draft of the Descendents of Thomas Gawthrop, by Wm. A.A.Gawthrop, September 1993.

SOURCE [93]: New Garden Monthly Meeting, PA records.

# Chapter 24

8th Generation

## 15124657, GEORGE W. GAWTHROP ( 1822 - 1892 )

***G***eorge Gawthrop, the seventh child and the fourth son of George Gawthrop (1784-1865) and Amy Chambers (1787-1851), was born on 29 August 1822 (recorded in the New Garden Monthly Meeting, Chester County, PA.*[location 93]* George lived in Oxford, Chester County, PA. George was the Director of the First National Bank of Oxford. He was well liked and universally respected by everyone in that town and county. In 1866 he bought a coal and lumber business from Captain Joseph R. McMullin in Avondale. He operated it himself for ten to twelve years when he took his eldest son into partnership. A few years later his other son, Horace, was admitted to the firm[a].*[86]* George died on heart trouble in Kennett Square, PA. The funeral services were held at the home of his son, Horace Henry, in Kennett Square, Chester County, PA on 27 Jan. 1892.[b] He is buried at Union Hill Cemetery, Kennett Square, PA. George married Louisa Way (b: 7 Nov. 1825, d: Sept. 1876) on 17 Feb. 1847 at her father's home. Louisa was the dauther of William Way.

***G***eorge and Louisa had 2 sons:*[17, 118]*

**151246571**, William Way (q.v., Vol. 2) b: 22 April 1850, d: 20 Aug.1932, married twice: **1M**-Hannah Mary Gawthrop (a 1st cousin) on 23 Oct. 1873, **2M**-Kate*[119]* Isabel May on 13 Feb. 1889.

**151246572**, Horace Henry (q.v., Vol. 2) b: 9 July 1861, d: 15 May 1953, married Phebe H.*[Harvey in 81]* Way on 11 July 1883.

***G***eorge had 6 brothers and 3 sisters. The 6 brothers were: **1)** Joseph C. b: 29 Jan. 1815, d: 26 June 1892, unmarried. Joseph had what appeared to be polio [leg paralyzed*[17]*]. He lived with his sister, Elizabeth (Gawthrop) Hughes and her husband, William. Joseph's occupation was Tinsmith (a pot maker). **2)** one child of a set of twins without a name, b: 29 Dec. 1816, d: 30 Dec. 1816. **3)** Thomas (q.v.) b: 7 Feb. 1818, d: 25 Jan. 1864, married twice: **1M**-Lydia Conard on 13 March 1840, **2M**-Susanna Conard (sisters), **4)** Evan b: 5 March 1824, d: 9 July 1824, **5)** William (q.v.) b: 9 Sept.

---

a In 1888, William and Horace Henry sold their coal/lumber yard (called WW and HH Gawthrop Oil and Lumber) to cousin Charles G. Gawthrop. William went into an early automobile dealership in Philadelphia. Horace Henry went into the Whole Sale Produce business (up and down the East coast); sold to stores like ACME and A&P, etc.*[119]*

b ***George Gawthrop died at the residence of his son, Horace H. Gawthrop, 1-29-1892, at the age of seventy years. His illness was an affliction of the heart and he was in bed little more than a week before his death.*** - Source: The Descentants of Robert and Hanna Way.*[obtained from 86]*

Picture from the collection of Dorothy L. Hipple

**George W. Gawthrop: born August 29, 1822; died January 27, 1892**

Picture from the collection of Dorothy L. Hipple

**Louisa (Way) Gawthrop: born November 7, 1825; died in September 1876**

1925, d: 31 March 1882, married Sarah Brown on 12 March 1860, **6)** Jessie b: 7 April 1828 (recorded in the New Garden Monthly Meeting, Chester County, PA,*(location 81)* d: 27 Aug. 1828. The 3 sisters were: **1)** Ruth b: 11 Nov. 1813, married Issac Moore (b: 21 March 1810 at London Grove, PA) of London Grove, PA on 18 Nov. 1841 (married at and recorded in the New Garden Monthly Meeting*(93)*). Issac was the son of Joseph and Beulah Moore. Ruth and Issac lived on a farm in West Grove, Chester County, PA. Issac's mother and father operated a mill. Ruth and Issac had 7 children: Joseph G. (b: 31 July 1843), Lindley C. (b: 26 May 1945), Hannah (b: 18 Nov. 1849, d: 31 May 1855), Thomas G. (b: 31 Dec. 1851, d: 6 Aug. 1853), Elizabeth (b: 28 Nov. 1854), twins: Channing (19 Aug. 1857, d: 12 Oct. 1857) and Darwin (19 Aug. 1857, d: 7 March 1861), **2)** the other child of a set of twins believed to be a girl (no name was found), b: 29 Dec. 1816, d: 29 Jan. 1817, and **3)** Elizabeth b: 15 Feb. 1820 (recorded in the New Garden Monthly Meeting, Chester County, PA,*(location 81)* d: 31 Dec. 1897, married William Hughes (b: 10 April 1819, d: 9 May 1894) on 20 May 1841 (married at and recorded in New Garden Monthly Meeting, Chester County, PA*(93)*). William was the son of Mark and Lydia Hughes. Elizabeth and William had 3 children: George C. (b: 21 Sept. 1843), Charles C. (b: 19 Jan. 1847), and Amy Anna (b: 20 May 1850). Elizabeth and William died at residence of Amy Anna and Dr. Milton E. Conard, their daugther and son-in-law.

REFERENCES


SOURCE [17]: Genealogy work compiled by Thomas Carr Gawthrop. This manuscript was not published by a publisher; however, Thomas Carr Gawthrop was born Jan. 1938 and died Sept. 1966. This compiled work was obtained from Mary Virginia (Merrifield) Gawthrop wife of Wilbur Edmond Gawthrop (deceased) and her son, Richard Carr Gawthrop in early 1992. Thomas Carr Gawthrop was her nephew and Richard's cousin.

SOURCE [81]: Letter/package containing a draft of Gawthrop Genealogy dated 2 June 1992 from Charles (Chuck) D. Thornton, Cape Coral, Fl.

SOURCE [86]: Draft of the Descendents of Thomas Gawthrop, by Wm. A.A.Gawthrop, September 1993.

SOURCE [93]: New Garden Monthly Meeting, PA records.

SOURCE [118]: Recollections of Dorothy L. Hipple on 3 Jan. 1990. Interviewed by Philip E. Gawthrop.

SOURCE [119]: Letter/package from John H. (Jack) Gawthrop dated 2 April 1993, Lansdale, PA.

# Chapter 25

8th Generation

## 15124659, WILLIAM GAWTHROP ( 1825 - 1882 )

William Gawthrop, the ninth child and the sixth son of George Gawthrop (1784-1865) and Amy Chambers (1787-1851), was born on 9 September 1825 (recorded in the Quaker records at New Garden Monthly Meeting, Chester County, PA)*(location 81)*; however, based on newspaper articles a different year would have to be computed for his birth.[a] William is known to have lived at several places: on a farm that overlapped the Newlin and the East Marlborough townships, Chester County, PA*(120)*[b]; Baltimore, MD; New London, PA; and West Grove in the township of London Grove, Chester County, PA. He and his wife, Sarah B., were Charter Members of the Patrons of Husbandry for New London, PA, No. 123 when they lived in New London.*(121)* However, William must have had a new calling because he apparently gave up on farming with his move to Baltimore. Early in the year 1876 he became his own Country Storekeeper.[c] The article about the store lease says that William was a merchant in New London rather than a farmer.[d] His West Grove store was looked on as being clean and modern with

---

a In the *Daily Local News*, West Grove, PA dated 4 April 1882 and the *Oxford Press*, Oxford, PA, dated 5 April 1882 (both local newspapers), there are articles that say William was 65 years of age. If that was the case, then the year of his birth would be computed as 1816 or 1817, but, if the year was transposed in these articles and the correct year being 56, then the year of 1825 is correct. The 1825 year would also relate to a statement in the memorial on William (seen later in this chapter) that says, ***...should be cut off just at a time when a young family's claims are the greatest...*** Also, the work done by Thomas Carr Gawthrop shows the birth year as 1825. It is felt that the year 1825 was the correct year of William's birth and that both articles have incorrect dates.

b In a newspaper article in the *American Republican* on 13 Nov. 1843 that says in part, ***The subscriber*** (William Gawthrop) ***having removed to the city of Baltimore, proposes selling his farm , in Newlin and East Marlborough townships, Chester County, adjoining lands of James Gawthrop, John Chambers and others, 6 miles from West Chester, 15 from Wilmington, 1 from Brandywine, and 1¼ from Marlborough meeting house, containing 170 acres of first rate limestone land. ...***

c In the *Daily Local News*, a local newspaper of West Chester, PA, an article on 31 March 1876 says, ***At West Grove Joseph Pyle has leased his store property to Wm. Gawthrop, formally a merchant of New London.***

d Maybe William was both a farmer and a merchant. A farmer belonging to the Patrons of Husbandry No. 123 when he first moved to New London and than later he became a merchant.

Picture from the collection of Ethel R. (Stalh) Gawthrop

**William Gawthrop: born 9 September 1825; died 31 March 1882**

discount prices.[e] Late in the summer of 1876 he continued toimproved his store by installing one of the first large signs on the roof of his store.[f] His country store became so well known in the county that on one occasion it was robbed. Several newspaper accounts of his store being robbed on a Thursday in March 1877.[g] Undeterred by the robbery, he continued to be a pillar of the community as is evidenced by his advertizement in the local newspaper.[h] William was well liked and respected by everyone in the town of West Grove.*[122]* [i] William died of pleurisy on 31 March 1882 [j] at his residence in West Grove, PA.*[122]* The funeral services were held at his residence in West Grove.*[123]* [k] He was buried at New West Grove Cemetery, New West Grove, PA on 4 April 1882. In the *Daily Local News* newspaper on 6 April 1882 there is a memorial to William Gawthrop that reads,*[124]*

***Communicated***

***In Memorial***

> ***This beautiful and lovely afternoon (Fourth Month 4th) witnessed the removal of one of our cherished citizens to his last resting-place. A vacancy is felt, not easily***

---

e In the *Daily Local News*, a local newspaper of West Chester, PA, an article on 2 June 1876 says, ***A Model Store – W. Gawthrop, at West Grove, has now one of the finest county stores in the county, everything is new having lately purchased a full line of goods, at the lately reduced prices. In fact almost everything the farmer and mechanic needs, is to be found at this establishment, and the ever ready and accommodating clerks will wait upon you in a giffy.***

f In the *Daily Local News* an article on the 20 September 1876 says, ***New Sign at West Grove. – W. W. Gawthrop, merchant, yesterday, put his large sign in position upon his store building. The letters are composed of genuine block letters gilded, and are of beautiful design and finely shared. A. W. Eastman has shown much taste in the ornamental work upon this large sign.***

g In the *Oxford Press* newspaper an article on 21 March 1877 says, ***Store Robbery at West Grove. – The store of William Gawthrop, at West Grove, was broken into on Thursday night last and robbed of goods and money to the amount of about $50. Suspicion rests on a party, but no arrest has yet been made. A man in sailor grab was seen at Jennerville a day or two ago. Storekeepers and others should be on their guard as there appears to be a gang of robbers going about the county.***

h In the newspaper the *Daily Local News*, William gives this advertizement, ***WM. GAWTHROP, dealer in DAY GOODS, GROCERIES, and GENERAL MERCHANDISE, West Grove, Pa. Country produce taken in exchange at highest market rates. A visit of inspection solicited. FALL STOCK JUST RECEIVED.***

i In the *Oxford Press* newspaper an article on 5 April 1882 says, ***William Gawthrop, a highly respected citizen of Southern Chester county, died at his residence at West Grove at an early hour last Saturday, of pneumonia, after an illness of only a few days. The deceased was widely known, having been engaged for many years in storekeeping, at New London, and for several years past at West Grove. The funeral took place yesterday and was largely attended.***

j The *Oxford Press* newspaper specified that he died on April 1st, 1882.

k In the *Daily Local News*, West Chester, PA an article on 10 April 1882 says, ***– The funeral of William Gawthrop was one of the largest ever witnessed in this part of the county – over 1000 people being present.***

***refilled, in the family of William Gawthrop, for it is more than sad to realize that a husband and father, in whom were blended so many of the requisite and virtues that adorn a man, should be cut off just at a time when a young family's claims are the greatest in reality, and when they most need a father's guiding care. Much that is noble in character can be noted of him. We remember him as one in whom were so many of the Christian virtues, as one of the most exemplary business men in point of integrity, for never did he make the slightest deviation from that course because of opportunity. The result of his death to the village of West Grove, with all its boasted enterprise, is a loss which, we fear, will not soon be refilled, especially in this age of grasp for accumulation. Inasmuch as we would fain have kept him here the thought comes that the crown is his, and we trust sincerely that his honest record may leave its impress as a model for imitation.***

William married Sarah Brown (b: 12 March 1835, d: 10 Nov. 1916) on 12 March 1860 in West Grove.*[125]* They were married by the Mayor of Philadelphia.[1] Sarah was the daughter of Evan and Joanna (Taylor) Brown. In an article in the *West Grove Independent* newspaper*[125]* there is a statement saying, ***She was one of the pioneer residents of the community and had spend many of her years in West Grove. Sarah was a fond and devoted mother, a firm and loyal friend, a valuable neighbor whose counsel and advice was frequently sought out.****[125]* Sarah's genial nature and royal hospitality attracted many to her home and she became admired by many both young and old.*[125]* Sarah was also buried at New West Grove Cemetery, New West Grove, PA.*[125]* She was a birthright member of the Society of Friends.*[93]* Sarah was disowned by New Garden Monthly Meeting on 5 September 1860 for marriage out of unity (MOU). Apparently William was not a Quaker in good standing when they married. MOU meant marrying a non-Quaker or marriage contrary to the rules of the Quaker society. A copy of the Last Will and Testament of William Gawthrop has been transcribe at the end of this chapter.*[126]*

William and Sarah had two sons and two daughters:*[17, 122, 125]*

**151246591**, Evan Brown (q.v., Vol. 2) b: 3 June 1861, d: 31 July 1925, married Bertha M. Conard.

**151246592**, Ernest b: 25 Oct. 1866 in West Grove, PA, d: unknown, married Bessie nln a Pittsburg (sic) Lady.*[91]*

**151246593**, Mary b: 26 April 1868 at West Grove, PA, d: unknown, did not marry. She lived at home with her mother for most of her mother's life*[125]* and after the death of her mother, she lived with her sister, Joanna B.

**151246594**, Joanna B. b: 31 Oct. 1873 at West Grove, PA, d: unknown, did not marry, performed very skillfully on the violin. She lived at home with her mother for most of her mother's life*[125]* and after the death of her mother, she lived with her sister, Mary.

---

1 This marriage by the Mayor of Philadelphia is not according to the Quaker religion (considered marriage out of unity (MOU)).

Picture from the collection of Josephine S. Gawthrop

Left to right, standing:

Evan B. Gawthrop,

b: 3 June 1861, d: 31 July 1925 (the son),

Everard Conard Gawthrop,

b: 3 April 1886, d: 15 Dec. 1955 (the grandson).

Sitting:

Sarah (Brown) Gawthrop,

b: 12 March 1835, d: 10 November 1916 (the wife of William).

On Sarah's lap:

Herman Everard Gawthrop,

b: 3 July 1909, d: 3 October 1918 of Flu (the great grandson).

William had 6 brothers and 3 sisters. The 6 brothers were: **1)** Joseph C. b: 29 Jan. 1815, d: 26 June 1892, unmarried. Joseph had what appeared to be polio [leg paralyzed*[17]*]. He lived with his sister, Elizabeth (Gawthrop) Hughes and her husband,William. Joseph's occupation was Tinsmith (a pot maker). **2)** one child of a set of twins without a name, b: 29 Dec. 1816, d: 30 Dec. 1816, **3)** Thomas (q.v.) b: 7 Feb. 1818, d: 25 Jan. 1864, married twice: **1M**-Lydia Conard on 13 March 1840, **2M**-Susanna Conard (sisters), **4)** George W. (q.v.) b: 29 Aug. 1822, d: 23 Jan. 1892, married Louisa Way **5)** Evan b: 5 March 1824, d: 9 July 1824, **6)** Jessie b: 7 April 1828 (recorded in the New Garden Monthly Meeting, Chester County, PA,*[location 81]* d: 27 Aug. 1828. The 3 sisters were: **1)** Ruth b: 11 Nov. 1813, married Issac Moore (b: 21 March 1810 at London Grove, PA) of London Grove, PA on 18 Nov. 1841 (married at and recorded in the New Garden Monthly Meeting*[93]*). Issac was the son of Joseph and Beulah Moore. Ruth and Issac lived on a farm in West Grove, Chester County, PA. Issac's mother and father operated a mill. Ruth and Issac had 7 children: Joseph G. (b: 31 July 1843), Lindley C. (b: 26 May 1945), Hannah (b: 18 Nov. 1849, d: 31 May 1855), Thomas G. (b: 31 Dec. 1851, d: 6 Aug. 1853), Elizabeth (b: 28 Nov. 1854), twins: Channing (19 Aug. 1857, d: 12 Oct. 1857) and Darwin (19 Aug. 1857, d: 7 March 1861). **2)** the other child of a set of twins believed to be a girl (no name was found), b: 29 Dec. 1816, d: 29 Jan. 1817, and **3)** Elizabeth b: 15 Feb. 1820 (recorded in the New Garden Monthly Meeting, Chester County, PA,*[location 81]* d: 31 Dec. 1897, married William Hughes (b: 10 April 1819, d: 9 May 1894) on 20 May 1841 (married at and recorded in New Garden Monthly Meeting, Chester County, PA). William was the son of Mark and Lydia Hughes. Elizabeth and William had 3 children: George C. (b: 21 Sept. 1843), Charles C. (b: 19 Jan. 1847) and Amy Anna (b: 20 May 1850). Elizabeth and William died at residence of Amy Anna and Dr. Milton E. Conard, their daughter and son-in-law.

## *WILL OF WILLIAM GAWTHROP, LONDON GROVE, PA[126]*

***Be it Remembered, That I, WILLIAM GAWTHROP, of the township of London Grove in the county of Chester, and state of Pennsylvania do make and publish this my last Will and Testament, in manner following, that is to say:***

***1. I will and direct that all my just debts and funeral expenses be paid as soon as possible.***

***2. I give and devise unto my beloved wife, SARAH B. GAWTHROP, her heirs and assigns forever all that my house and lot where we now reside situate in the village of West Grove in said township of London Grove being ____ feet in front on ____ street and extending therefrom ____ feet, with the appurtenances. I further give and bequeath unto my said wife all the household goods and furniture, books and ornaments which now are in said residence or its appurtenances with such articles or implements as belong thereto or which may be therein at the time of my decease, also the stock, carriages & thereon.***

*3. As for and concerning the rest, residue and remainder of my estate, real and personal, whatsoever and wheresoever the same may be, not herein specifically disposed of, which I may die seized and possessed of, after the payment of my debts and expenses and discharge of my mortgage or judgement debts, if any there be, on the real estate hereinbefore specifically devised, I do hereby give devise and bequeath the same and every part thereof unto my wife and children their heirs and representatives or to such person or persons for such estate or estates and in such shares and proportions as would by the intestate laws of this commonwealth be entitled to the same if I had died intestate.*

*And lastly. I hereby nominate and appoint my said wife, SARAH B. GAWTHROP executrix of this my will and testament and I do hereby authorize and empower my said executrix, whenever she, upon consultation with my other heirs, may deem it expedient to sell at public or private sale any or all of my real estate and execute a proper deed or deeds for the same; the proceeds of such sales to be distributed among my heirs as real estate and the purchaser or purchasers not to be liable for the appropriation of the purchase money thereof.*

*In witness whereof, I the said WILLIAM GAWTHROP, have to this, my last will and testament, set my hand and seal, this Nineteenth of August - A.D. One thousand eight hundred and eighty one (1881).* *signed WILLIAM GAWTHROP (Seal)*

*Signed, Sealed, Published, and Declared by WILLIAM GAWTHROP, the testator above named, as and for his last will and testament, in the presence, who in the presence of each other in his presence and at his request, have hereunto set our hands as witnesses thereto.* *signed GEORGE B. JOHNSON and JOSEPH PYLE.*

*West Chester, April 8th 1882. Then personally appeared GEORGE B. JOHNSON and JOSEPH PYLE who on their solemn affirmation, did say that they were present, and did see and hear WILLIAM GAWTHROP the testator in the foregoing instrument of writing named, sign, seal, publish pronounce and declare the same as and for his last Will and Testament, and at the time of so doing he was of sound and well disposing mind and memory, to the best of their knowledge and belief.*
*Affirmed before me.* *Register name is unreadable.*


REFERENCES

SOURCE [17]: Genealogy work compiled by Thomas Carr Gawthrop. This manuscript was not published by a publisher; however, Thomas Carr Gawthrop was born Jan. 1938 and died Sept. 1966. This compiled work was obtained from Mary Virginia (Merrifield) Gawthrop wife of Wilbur Edmond Gawthrop (deceased) and her son, Richard Carr Gawthrop in early 1992. Thomas Carr Gawthrop was her nephew and Richard's cousin.

SOURCE [81]: Letter/package containing a draft of Gawthrop Genealogy dated 2 June 1992 from Charles (Chuck) D. Thornton, Cape Coral, Fl.

SOURCE [91]: *Chester and Delaware Counties*, Vol 2, by Gilbert Cope and Henry Graham Ashmead, (C) 1904, page 577, obtained from Chester County Historical Society, West Chester, PA.

SOURCE [93]: New Garden Monthly Meeting, PA records.

SOURCE [120]: Package dated May 24, 1990 mailed from the Chester County Historical Society, West Chester, PA, contains a newspaper article from the *American Republican* someplace in PA, dated 13 November 1843 on a farm for sale due to William Gawthrop (1825-1882) moving to Baltimore, MD.

SOURCE [121]: Package dated May 24, 1990 mailed from the Chester County Historical Society, West Chester, PA, contains a copy of Patrons Of Husbandry from the book on *History of Chester County, Pennsylvania*, by G. Cope and J.S. Futhey, I. Everts (ed), Philadelphia Publishing Co., 1881.

SOURCE [122]: Package dated May 24, 1990 mailed from the Chester County Historical Society, West Chester, PA, contains a newspaper articles, *Daily Local News*, dated 3 April 1882 and 4 April 1882, and the Oxford Press dated 5 April 1882 on the death of William Gawthrop (1825 - 1882).

SOURCE [123]: Package dated May 24, 1990 mailed from the Chester County Historical Society, West Chester, PA, contains a newspaper article, *Daily Local News*, dated 10 April 1882, on the funeral services of William Gawthrop (1825-1882).

SOURCE [124]: Package dated May 24, 1990 mailed from the Chester County Historical Society, West Chester, PA, contains a newspaper article, *Daily Local News*, West Grove, PA, dated 6 April 1882 on the memorial about William Gawthrop (1825-1882).

SOURCE [125]: Package dated May 24, 1990 mailed from the Chester County Historical Society, West Chester, PA, contains a newspaper article, *West Grove Independent*, West Grove, PA, dated 16 Nov. 1916, and several articles from the *Daily Local News*, dated 10 Nov., 11 Nov., and 14 Nov. 1916 on the death of Sarah B. Gawthrop (1835-1916).

SOURCE [126]: Package dated May 24, 1990 mailed from the Chester County Historical Society, West Chester, PA, contains a copy of a handwritten Last Will and Testament of William Gawthrop (1825 - 1882).

## INDEX

## INDEX (continued)

## INDEX (continued)

**Volume: Chapter-Page**

## INDEX (continued)

## INDEX (continued)

**Volume: Chapter-Page**

## INDEX (continued)

**INDEX (continued)**

## INDEX (continued)

**Volume: Chapter-Page**

**INDEX (continued)**

**Volume: Chapter-Page**

**INDEX (continued)**

# Appendix A

## Thomas Gawthrop's Letters

This appendix contains letters of the times dating from July 3, 1747 to April 30, 1779. The majority of these letters were from Thomas Gawthrop to individuals in America. These letter may be found in different volumes of the *Pemberton Papers*, Historical Society of Pennsylvania, 1300 Locust Street, Philadelphia, PA. The contents of this appendix:

Letter from Thomas Gawthrop in NY to Israel Pemberton, Jr., dated July 3, 1747. Concerning Thomas' afflictions--physical and otherwise.

Letter from Thomas Gawthrop on-board ship to Israel Pemberton, Jr., dated Dec. 1, 1747. Concerning the cheerful nature of everyone and that he will send another letter soon.

Agreement between Isaac Greenleaf and Thomas Gawthrop on-board ship, dated Dec. 2, 1747. Promise to deliver to Thomas Gawthrop a deed for certain tract in New Jersey.

Letter from Thomas Gawthrop on-board ship to Israel Pemberton, Jr., dated Dec. 4, 1747. Purchased land in New Jersey.

Letter from Thomas Gawthrop London, Eng. to Israel Pemberton, dated 2 mo. (Apr) 8, 1748.

Letter from Thomas Gawthrop Warrington, Eng. to Israel Pemberton, dated 2 mo. (Apr) 19, 1748.

Letter from Thomas Gawthrop in Stainton, Eng. to Israel Pemberton, dated May 20, 1748.

Letter from Thomas Gawthrop to Israel Pemberton, dated 5 mo. (July) 29, 1748.

Letter from Thomas Gawthrop to Israel Pemberton, dated 6 mo. (Aug.) 25, 1748.

Letter from Thomas Gawthrop in Stainton, Eng. to Israel Pemberton Jr., dated 11 mo. (Jan.) 12, 1748.

Letter from Thomas Gawthrop to Israel Pemberton Jr., dated 7 mo. (Sept.) 6, 1749.

Letter from Thomas Gawthrop in Kendal, Eng. to Israel Pemberton Jr., Philadelphia, dated Nov. 24, 1752.

Letter from Thomas Gawthrop in London, Eng. to Israel Pemberton, dated 6 mo. (June) 17, 1753.

Letter from Thomas Gawthrop in Eustatia to Israel Pemberton Jr., Philadelphia, dated Jan. 25, 1756.

Letter from Thomas Gawthrop in Rhoade Island to Israel Pemberton Jr., Philadelphia, dated April 26, 1756.

Letter from Thomas Gawthrop in Buckingham to John Pemberton in Philadelphia, dated Sept. 2, 1756.

Letter from Thomas Gawthrop in Rich Land to Israel Pemberton Jr. in Philadelphia, dated Oct. 22, 1756.

Letter from Thomas Gawthrop going down the Bay to Israel Pemberton Jr. in Philadelphia, dated June 12, 1756.

Letter from Thomas Gawthrop bound for Barbatos to Israel Pemberton Jr. in Philadelphia, dated 6 mo. (June) 25, 1757.

Letter from Thomas Gawthrop in Ye Capes to Israel Pemberton Jr. in Philadelphia, dated Oct. 24, 1757.

Letter from Thomas Gawthrop in the Ely in Scotland to Israel Pemberton Jr. in Philadelphia, dated Nov. 13, 1757.

Letter from Thomas Gawthrop in Ye Isle of Ely West of Scotland to John Pemberton in Philadelphia, dated Nov. 19, 1757.

Letter from Thomas Gawthrop in Kendal to Israel Pemberton Jr. in Philadelphia, dated July 30, 1758.

Letter from Thomas Gawthrop near Kendal, Eng. to Israel Pemberton Jr. in Philadelphia, dated April 10, 1762. Of friendship in affliction. Of Thomas' young son who lost his mind. Of Thomas' thought to settle in PA.

Letter from Thomas Gawthrop to Israel Pemberton Jr. in Philadelphia, dated Jan. 5, 1765.

Letter from Thomas Gawthrop in Nantuckett to Israel Pemberton Jr. in Philadelphia, dated June 25, 1766.

Letter from Thomas Gawthrop in Barbados to Mary Pemberton in Philadelphia, dated March 1, 1766.

Letter from Thomas Gawthrop in Munolan to Israel Pemberton Jr. in Philadelphia, dated Oct. 24, 1766.

Letter from Thomas Gawthrop in Carolina to Israel Pemberton Jr. in Philadelphia, dated Nov. 24, 1766.

Letter from Thomas Gawthrop in London to Israel Pemberton in Philadelphia, dated June 27, 1767.

Letter from Thomas Gawthrop in Gate Beck to John Pemberton in Philadelphia, dated April 22, 1768.

Letter from John Griffith in Chelmsford to John Pemberton in Philadelphia, dated June 30, 1767.

Letter from Thomas Gawthrop in Preston Patrick to John Pemberton in Philadelphia, dated Dec. 30, 1769.

Letter from Thomas Gawthrop in Preston Patrick to Israel Pemberton Jr. in Philadelphia, dated July 6, 1774.

Letter from Thomas Gawthrop in New York to Israel Pemberton Jr. in Philadelphia, dated Oct. 10, 1774.

Letter from Thomas Gawthrop in Preston Patrick to Israel Pemberton Jr. in Philadelphia, dated March 14, 1775.

The substance of what Thomas Gawthrop said upon leaving Philadelphia on Dec. 1, 1777.

Letter from Mary Pemberton to Israel Pemberton Jr. near Virginia, dated April 3, 1778.

The substance of a draft by J. Pemberton of a Testimony from the Philadelphia Monthly Meeting for Thomas Gawthrop to Friends in Kendal, Eng., dated April 30, 1779.

An unidentified letter from Thomas Gawthrop (more than likely it came from the PEMBERTON PAPAERS, Vol.??, p.??), dated xxxx x, 17xx.

July 3, 1747; in NY, from Thomas Gawthrop to Israel Pemberton, Jr.
Concerning Thomas' afflictions -- physical and otherwise.
(PEMBERTON Papers, Vol 4, p.70)

Israel Pemberton Jun
Mert In Philadelfia

New York 5mo. 3. 17[illegible]
From Thomas Gawthrop

Newyork ye 3d of 5mo 1747

Estemed Friend

having this opertunaty Makes use of It to Inform thee, Much of an Inward Deth atends my Speret and Stupadaty my mind yeat tis Some Comfort to my Drooping Soul to find In my Brest Love to'th Brethren and Some times to ye hole Creation of God Desiering that ye Depths below May not Swallo up my Life But If So, he that Comands ye Sea to Give up his ded yea Deth and hell obeys his all Ruling Voice I of him may be Remembred and In his time place and way may Shine forth to his Glory

oft have I had pleasure unutterable In ye Land vales of Humillaty and probation and oft have had to Say It was Good for me that I was Afflicted wounded and Bruised By ye foul feind tha Sued ~~to be~~ [illegible] him which Is ye Husband of my Soul oh that he may be ye Covering of my Eys at all times, Dwells he within a Cottage Shall I Despise his Bed oh nay, the Gall and vinniger be my ~~Daly~~ food

one Complaint would fallow another But Let them Stop my Love Is to thee and M. J. plese to Let hir Read my Scrible and Shall be Glad to Reseve and Suck Sum ~~Soots~~ Sweets from Ether of you pe
Thyn Tho Gawthrop

my Love Is to Father Brother with other Friends in them have had but poor helth since I left your Town am going to making hear [illegible] towards Rhode Island

Dec. 1, 1747; on-board ship from Thomas Gawthrop to Israel Pemberton, Jr. Concerning the cheerful nature of everyone was and that he will send another letter soon. (PEMBERTON Papers, Vol 4, p.82)

Respected Friend — aboard ye Ship Widow ye 1st 10 mo

I hoped thyn shall take an oportunaty with J Greenleaf on ye afare and send thee an account from ye Capes we are all chearfull and well I salute thee in a degree of that Love that first cemented us together and Bids farewell

Tho Gawthrop

J Green his Love Is Remembered to thee please Give mine to father Mother and M Jordon Grace Loyde and that Famaly

From abd. the Ship Widow
1st 10 mo. 1747
From Thos. Gawthrop

query for a ... some of ye old settlers in Jersey — a warrant for 1750 Acres to him in Jos: Coopers hands dated 28th Feb. 1712

To
Isr. Pemberton Junr
at Chester
or Philadelphia

From aboard the Ship Widow 1st 10 mo 1747
Thos. Gawthrop

Dec. 2, 1747; on-board ship, agreement between Isaac Greenleaf and Thomas Gawthrop. Promise to deliver to Thomas Gawthrop a deed for certain tract in New Jersey. (PEMBERTON Papers, Vol 4, p.83)

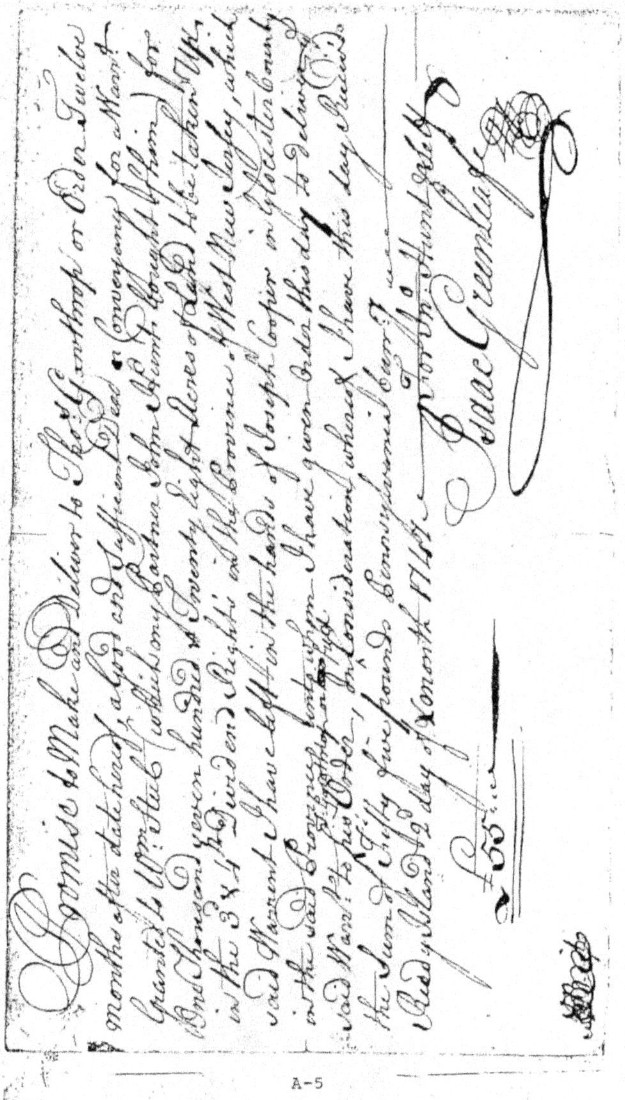

Promise to Make and Deliver to Thos. Gawthrop or Order Twelve months after date hereof, a Good and Sufficient Deed or Conveyance for a Warrt. Granted to Wm. Steel (which my Partner John Hunt bought of him) for One Thousand seven hundred & Twenty Eight Acres of Land to be taken Up in the 3 & 4th Dividend Rights in the Province of West New Jersey, which said Warrent I have left in the hands of Joseph Cooper in Glocester County in the said Province, unto whom I have given Order this day to deliver ye said Warrt. to his Order, in Consideration whereof I have this day Recd. the Sum of Fifty five pounds Pennsylvania Curr.y

Ready Island 2d day of 10 month 1747

For Jno. Hunt & Self

Isaac Greenleaf

£55..

**Dec. 4, 1747; on-board ship, from Thomas Gawthrop to Israel Pemberton, Jr.**
**Purchased land in New Jersey. (PEMBERTON Papers, Vol 4, p.83)**

Israel Pemberton Jun
In Philadelfia

4 of 10 mo 1747 at Kedysfield [illegible]

Esteemed Friend

According to thy Dyrection have Bought y^e Warrant and Pade him for It Fifty Five pounds your Coveance have hearwith Sent y^e Resete [illegible] I Should have thought of a Bond for y^e mony But as thou only mentiond a Resete and Considering thee Honnor and Intrest with thee I thought It may Suffice If thou think proper Shall take Half of y^e Grant and Desier thee [illegible] write to J Hunt to make us Two Seperate deeds to y^e same purport hear is Jos: order to J Cooper for y^e Deliverance of y^e Warrant y^e Care of taking y^e Lands up I Shall Leave to thee and y^e Expence Arising from Such Surveys Shall be willing to Defray when I Reflect on thy Repeated Kindness towards poor me I Cannot But Look on them as Singular Blessings of providence may we be Kept humble Dependants on him that hath Called us with So high and Heavenly Calling In a Sence of whose Goodness which Bows my mind I Salute y^e Dear friend and Bids Farewell Tho Gawthrop

to Give my Love to H. Jordan to all thy Children Father & mother and Brothers

Ps as to thy Letter to J Hunt I think to Shew It to Brother which I hope may Serve for I have So Much In debt to thee that I thought to have Sent y^e Letter Back to thee for when I tould thee of my Sircomstan[ces] I had no [struck through] vews of Such a kindnes

5 Days [illegible] their a [illegible] of y^e Papers [illegible] found out [illegible] we are [illegible] Baucly [illegible] to [illegible] me to Richard Smith [illegible] [illegible] taking up y^e Land [illegible] Bought y^e Warrant [illegible] to me [illegible] trouble and I Shall take [illegible]

2 mo. (Apr.), 8, 1748; London Eng., from Thomas Gawthrop to Israel Pemberton. Of being a prisoner in France and now being in England, and of the title to land in NJ (PEMBERTON Papers, Vol 4, p.97)

Ever esteemed Fr[illegible] 1748

London ye 8 of 2 Month

I writ to thee by way of Lisbon and Gave
thee Acount of our being Carred Into France have now to
Salute thee hear not Douting But thou'll be Gratefull to
hear of our Safe arival In England where things and
places Looks with another Aspect may my Soul be thankfull
for all favors and Deliverances Recived from him that
works and who Dare Say what Dos then ye Darkness and
Superstition of our own Nation I have oft thought was
Great and ye [illegible] buried Law but oh ye Dothe we went
thro Tongue nor pen Cant Set it forth In these Barbarous
Cuntry's Is. G— hath had Some Good opertunatis and tho' I
I have Been much Shut up yet have had to Rejoyce
on his Account for we have Been So Nearly united
In this our outward and Inward Affliction that I have
had to Drink of those Streams which Refresh ye Brother
hood oh may thay Ever Run oh may thay Increase
and Cover Nations Kindreds Tongues and all People
that ye Earth may again Injoy her Sabaths and men
be heald of those Breaches Rents and Devitions So
that all may with one Eye, and with one hart wate
for Gods Salvation that thay may Lift up ye
voice togather and praise him that Lives for
Ever may we be as ye first fruits Cultivated
by ye Great husband man and Brought forward
yea I, to Bear, as ye worlds which Is in such Confu
-tion May behold admire and Give Glory to
our father which Is In heaven that ye Sons
of God may Sing for joy and ye Nations may
Clap there hands togather Blesing him that Cums
in ye name of ye Lord I salute thee Dear frend as
one which wates for ye Consalation of Israel and Bids
thee with thyn Dealy farewell Thos Gawthrop

Is plese to Give my Love to thy Kind father and
Mother whose many favors I Cant But Gratfully
acknowledg also to Ansel Lightfoot or any other Inquiring [illegible]

2 mo. (Apr.), 8, 1748; London Eng., from Thomas Gawthrop to Israel Pemberton. Of being a prisoner in France and now being in England, and of the title to land in NJ (PEMBERTON Papers, Vol 4, p.97)

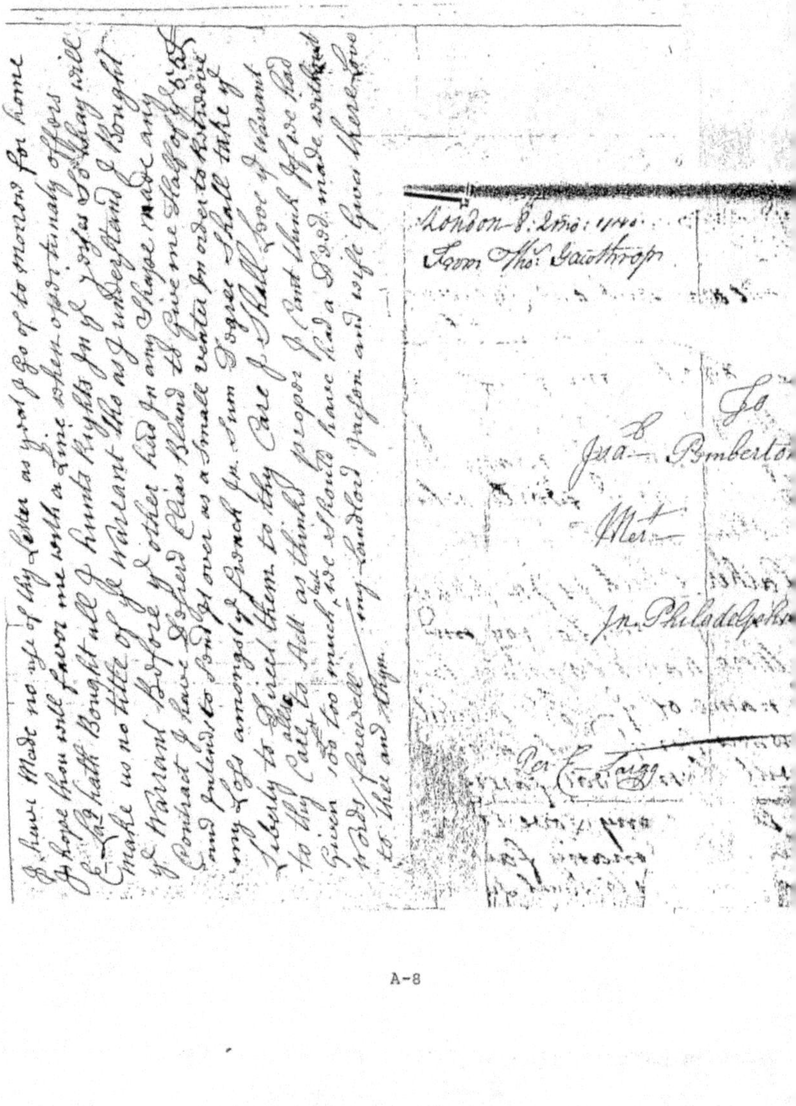

I have Made no use of thy Letter as yet I Go of to morrow for home I hope thou will favor me with a Line when opertunaty offers E. Lat hath Bought all J hunts Rights In ye [illegible] So they will make us no title of ye warrant tho as I understand I Bought ye Warrant Before ye other had In any Shape made any Contract I have Desired Elias Bland to Give me Half of ye [illegible] and Intends to Send It over as a Small venter In order to Retreeve my Loss amongst ye French In Sum Degree Shall take ye Liberty to Direct them to thy Care I Shall Leve ye warrant to thy Care also to Act as thinks proper I Cant think If we had Given 100 too much but we Should have had a Deed made without words farewell my Landlord Jacson and wife Give there Love to thee and thyn

London 8: 2mo: 1748
From Thos Gawthrop

To
Isa Pemberton
Mert
In Philadelphia

Per [illegible]

2 mo. (Apr.), 19, 1748; Warrington Eng., from Thomas Gawthrop to Israel Pemberton. (PEMBERTON Papers, Vol 4, p.100)

[illegible] Jackson [illegible]
Devonshire Square
London
To
Isra. Pemberton
In Philadelphia

Warrington 2 mo 19 48
From Thomas Gawthrop

Warr. 2d 19 of 2d mo 1748

Esteemed Friend

these May Serve to Inform
thee I am now within Little more than
a days journal of home and tho in our passage I have Gon thro many Dificultys
yet was in degree Resigned to that overrul-
-ing Providence which is over his Children
we had very hard Gales most of ye way
and very Contrary Some days before was
taken one day above all we was in Emin[ent]
Danger Capt was Surprised and Said he
never Se ye Sea run So high before and
Severall of them thought if thee had not be[en]
allmost an uncomon Bote we must have [illegible]
I may Acknowledg that for Some time [illegible]
I was under Great heaviness and Before [illegible]
never knew Such fears of judgment and
how it would be with mee whether this was
on my own account or not I dont know.
But may I never forget his Dealings which
often shaks his his Rod and the [illegible] Sea
and not tremble.
Give my kind Love to thy wife I hope
your kindnesses will not be forgot by mee
or other by him who hath Made a Cup of
water Rewardable may you Live to ful[fil] [illegible]
[illegible] and your Crowns meet you when [illegible]

In ye English wishes of your Friend Tho Gawthrop
my Love to all your Children and Enquiring Friends

A-9

May 20, 1748; in Stainton Eng., from Thomas Gawthrop to Israel Pemberton Sr. (PEMBERTON Papers, Vol 4, p.116)

Dear friend Stenton ye 20 of ye 3 1748

I Recevd Thyne which was verry Grafull to me to be Remembred by thee for I have you often In mind and was never nearer In Spirit than Since I Came home, Being often Ingaged for your wellfare Everry manner of way, which I Doubt not But ye Blesing of providence will Attend your Colany, may there be Sutable Returns of Honor and Obedience to So Great a LORD, and So Good a ffather Long before this I presume you have heard ~~of our being~~ Caried Into france, and allso what of moment befell us In our pasage, and alltho Some may think Straing at our hard hap, yeat It was no Great Surprise to me, and tho our Sufferings was Considerable, Both In Body and Mind I have had often to Kiss that hand and Worship Before him which Is ye preserver of men, and tho he Leads down In his own time After he hath plunged again and again he Bringeth up to prase him which Lives and Rules In ye habitable parts of ye Earth, whose works Is his own and who Dare Say to him what dost thou, It Is about five weeks ago I Got home found my Wife But poorly In helth and had Been for Some time and Is Still weakly Childer was and Is well, Rouland Willson Is Ded as allso please to Inform Hannah Cooper her father Is Ded her Brother Robart was at our hous this Day weak and I Sent her mother that Shee ordred by J Greenleaf we are In Great Expectation of a General peace Artiles being allredy Signed by Several ~~(?)~~ of ye ministers of ye Powers Concerned wherein Each Is to Give up there Several Conquests

May 20, 1748; in Stainton Eng., from Thomas Gawthrop to Israel Pemberton Sr. (PEMBERTON Papers, Vol 4, p.116)

wherein Each Is to Give up there Several Conquests
Some thinks ye King of Pra— hath no Small h[illegible]
In ye afare and thay Say he Is to be well pade for
It I oft think tis pitty that Misanersy vows Should be
Cloud ye minds of princes and unfill them to Act for
him by hose providence thay Rule and to home
thay are Accountable ye King we hear Is Gon over
O Dear friend may these Find thee In ye Fellowship
of ye Gospel of peace with all thyn as tho named I Rest thy
Affectionate Fr Tho Gawthrop

I have Sent a few Sticks to Eli Bland to Get forward
for Phila one of which plese to Accept of thy Son Is—
ye [illegible] Rofs thy other three Sons Each one and If
ye Sixe Got Safe to hand plese to Give Jos Crosby one
I would have Sent more But not knowing how thay would
take for am [illegible] to many But hops youl Resive them
as Tokens of Frdship farewell

Stainton 20th 3mo 1748
From Thomas Gawthrop

To
Isr Pemberton
In
Philadelphia
America

[illegible] By thy Friend [illegible] Bland

5 mo. (July) 29, 1748; from Israel Pemberton to Thomas Gawthrop.
(PEMBERTON Papers, Vol 4, p.129)

Dr ffd
Thos. Gawthorpe 29. 5mo: 1748

I am sorry to here of thy and the rest of our fds ~~[illegible]~~ falling into our Enimeys hands, and that we have not yet had any accots of your being released, but am in hopes ~~[illegible]~~ thou art got ~~[illegible]~~ home ~~[illegible]~~ to thy family & fds long before this time, of an account of wch I hope we shall have by the next vessell from Brittaine, there being one dayly expected from London My Son Charles was in but a poore State of health when thou left us and he Continued in a wasting State without much Sickness untill the 21st day last, and ~~[illegible]~~ there being worse to a more Sensible he Departed this life without Sigh or groan and very Sensible to the last Of his way. a youth of an inoffensive life and ~~[illegible]~~ from Some Conversation I had with him Some days before his Death Respecting his future State

5 mo. (July) 29, 1748; from Israel Pemberton to Thomas Gawthrop.
(PEMBERTON Papers, Vol 4, p.129)

found him in a very tender frame of mind, I told him that I had not for some time
expected his recovery and that I hoped he had in his sickness been mindful
to prepare for his Change, he told me that not a day had past passed without Consi-
-deration of it and that his earnest desire had been to the Lord that
he might be prepared for his Dissolution, but said he had desired life that
he might be further serviceable to me, for he knew I should want his assistance
I told him his parents affections were great towards him yet as it so appears
it was the Lords pleasure to take him from us and it was our Duty to
Submit to his Devine Will for he knew what was best for us, and as he had
passed his time here in a good Degree of Innocency I doubted not but if the
Lord should remove him from us it would be a happy Change to him, for
he could not be insensible how prone youth were to fall into things that
were hurtfull to them & displeasing to God, and that if it was gods
pleasure to take him hence in his Innocency he would escape those things
that he might if he lived longer be liable to fall into, he said he was
very sensible of it & desired my prayers for him & hope he should be resigned

resigned to the Lords will, the weather being very hot we
had for the benefit of the aire taken him to my Plantation some
days before his death, the Day before he dyed, Hester White found
a Concern on her to go there to visit him which she did, [illegible]
[illegible] and after some time of prayer by them he
expressed his great Satisfaction with her visit, and told her she came
with a right Commission to him, the loss of so hopefull a youth whose
affection & Duty was very great to his parents, was a heavy tryal to us but
as it was the Lords pleasure to deprive us of him we freely resigned to his holy
will believing it to be his great Gaine, I shall be glad of a few lines from thee
when thy leisure will permitt, our worthy fd. Saml Nottingham
[illegible] has been gon hence for Barbados some time in ord.r to visit
from thence hither, his visit was very acceptable here our fd. Danl
Stanton is gon with him and after they have performed their visit at
Barbados he intends to pay you a visit in Brittaine, fd. are generally
well here, my loving Dear Love is to thee and thine with the salutation
-tion of sincere Conclude this from

Thy affectionate fd. I P

Sophia Hume has been some time
here she came from Carolina by land
and intends to return for London by
the first vessell w.ch will be some time
the latter

6 mo. (Aug.) 25, 1748; from Thomas Gawthrop to Israel Pemberton, (PEMBERTON Papers, Vol 4, p.130)

Respected Friend

I presume Before this Cums to hand thou will have heard of our Being Taken by a ffrench privateer of Beyon we fell Into there hands ye 30 of 10 month about 125 Leg from ye Lyzard and about 80 from Cape Clear on ye 26 we was Caried Into portpasage a Leage from hence ye Capt. of ye prise had Been In Jerland Spoke oure Tounge ffluently he alowd us our Beds and provitions tho ye Last was Short anuff Ere we Got In for when thay Came abord thay Spared nothing this was a new Seen of Life to us whilest we were out at Sea we were often promisd we Should have all our Monis and Cloths But when we Came near to Land we was Given to understand otherwise we made a purs or Sum of 100 Sterling or upwards of ye Monis we Gave up to ye Capt. of ye prise who Seemingly was well Content nay promised to Return Two Thirds of our Coyn again But ye morning we went of for Beyon our Irish harted Capt. tould us we were all to Go on Bord ye privateer to Be Searched I Gave him a Smal purss with about 12 pounds Ster poor P. Davis Gave Every farthing John Grifeth Lost Considerable of his own Besids 100 Belonging to Some In your Contry I Cwll had Received Betwixt 30 and 40 pystolls of his Contry men ye Dutch to Lave But 10 went 29. we Arivd at Beyon was put In ye Chatto In nasty Louse Beds and very poor provisions 4 of 11th we Got Leave to Go to Dax with 14 other Prisoners where we Stade till ye 24 when ye Cartteel was Come to pasage we Returnd to Byon and So for this place we hope to Imbark for England to morrow If ye Wind prs fare thus Dear ffriend I have Given a hint of our outward afflictions which hath Been permited to fall to our Lots, ye which hath Been But Trifeling In Cumparison of those Troubles of ye Mind

6 mo. (Aug.) 25, 1748; from Thomas Gawthrop to Israel Pemberton, (PEMBERTON Papers, Vol 4, p.130)

these words Can't Declare nor Letters Convay ye Idea of
But now ye Storm Seems to Be a Little over and within this
Day or tow that Good hand I think Is underneath, ye Clouds Bea[illegible]
ye Stons Bastes out In a Sence of which I Salute thee and thyn
and Concludes thy — Effectionate Friend Thos Gawthrop

Give my kind Love to father and mother with Brothers
and all Inquiring friends I think to Rite a gain as Soon
as I Get to London Remember me to J Armitt and wife
To Jo Crosby have Saved Soveral of his papers Some for ye
Champions of Bry as Is power of atornay with other some Lette[illegible]
allso to J Smith to all thy Childer as tho named Dearfr[illegible]
Just now we are Informd of Ad Warrin farewell
taking three ffrench men of wars one 80 Gun the[illegible]
ye french trade Seems allmost Ruend and many
of them fells Senciably ye Effect of wars our peasable
princapel was highly Aploded when before ye Commi-
-ssary Many Can See ye Boutys thats In ye truth But
ye way Seems tow narrow tho thay own Its ye most
Christean and most Glorious we had tow or three ours
Discours with Some of ye fryers wherein truth was
Brought over them Soveral of our Cuntry men was
Glad to See these Learnd Rabiss Princepls or Erro
So portrade thanks Be to him ye Majestie of
and Erth which tho his may Ly amongst ye s
at times his Quickning power Is Experanced Even
to Rase ye Dead and to Speak to his prase who a Lone
Is worthy as to our Sufferings for End thay are I know
not nather dare I Say what dost thou this Leson oft have
I thought It my Duty to prispose to others But Little
thought Such was So near my own door

6 mo. (Aug.) 25, 1748; from Thomas Gawthrop to Israel Pemberto
(PEMBERTON Papers, Vol 4, p.130)

To
Israel Pemberton Junr
Philadelphia
Pensilvania
America

From Thos. Gawthrop
at St. Sebastians

recd abt 25 Octo 1748
via Lisbon

11 mo. (Jan.) 12, 1748; in Stainton Eng., from Thomas Gawthrop to Israel Pemberton Jr. (PEMBERTON Papers, Vol 5, p.18)

Respected Friend
Isr.ll Pemberton Jr.

Stainton [illegible] 11 mo. [illegible]

After Saluting thee Wife and Children In that Love
that Makes all Its votaries as one flock and family I may Inform thee
I Rec.d thyn. Bearing Date ye 28 of 8 mo. was Glad to hear of your wellfare
for I have oft to Remember you and tho Distant In Body yet present
In Spirit frequently, Being Ever Glad when favoured with Life's
flowing to Converse with my friends Both those that are present
and allso absent ye fountain Being at times unsealed ye weary is
Refreshed Being Admitted to Drink Into ye one Spirit which Is ye very
orignal of Being this hath Been our first Call of friend Drink oh
well beloved may he worke all our works for us and In us of his
own Good plesure Both to will and to do [illegible] of his own preparing
Let our Baptisme be Bearing his fann till ye floor be purged then
ye wheat hel Gather Into his Garnel that we may there meet
when these tossings Is over are my Ernest Breathings —
petter Davis hath Been hear as allso Jo Griffith Sometime Since
ye Latter I hear haith Been unwell and Lade By for Some
time at Jona. Rains In Lancashire John Hesham was
hear a few Days ago whose Respect for America Is
very obvious he Spoke much In ye Comendation of J. G.
But thaught he was very Law yeat with hopes he would
Rise with Greater Luster, and according to my Sence of
ye State of ye Church and Churches thay that visit ye
Living Seed In these parts Must often go Into ye Deeps
and Ly amongst ye Slain Beneath ye alter where no Help
or Admittance Scarce can be to ye Table of ye Lord
But I am weary of Complaining Rather Breathing after Resig
nation to that Hand that Rules ye Times and ye Seasons —
I was Glad to hear of thy Bro James Safe Arrival as yeat
have not Seen him But hopes on his way Into ye North he'l
Call at my poor Cottage. as to my Coming Into Amer.a Must
Suspend for ye present. my wife Being not free to Such a
Removall She haith had her helth very poorly Since I got
home

11 mo. (Jan.) 12, 1748; in Stainton Eng., from Thomas Gawthrop to Israel Pemberton Jr. (PEMBERTON Papers, Vol 5, p.18)

[illegible] hath pade me ye Mony I pade him abou
ye [illegible] for ye Land, Desiers thou would Deliver ye Wa-
[illegible] [illegible] hath not [illegible] Likely he hath made no Great
Bargen for his Second purchis [illegible] promesdh [illegible]
[illegible] Extraordinary For Relinquishing ye Bargon and
[illegible] they have Sold it [illegible] So well we may Reson-
ably Expect Something for our part which I hear
of any thing for us But promises shall Give thee
Intelygence for Intends there Shall [illegible] with me
[illegible] ye profits I [illegible] to Remind [illegible] what he offered [illegible]
whole [illegible] tho he had no Right to Sell it
plese to Remember my Love to thy father and mother
I can oft think of Philadelphia Friends with pleasure
as at this time my Love flows to many of you whose
dwelings is in ye Light. Remember me to [illegible]
Thos Brown [illegible] and wife to [illegible] [illegible]
John [illegible] and wife Bro John [illegible] Cooper and
wife John Smith and wife Hannah as a proof of
my friendship and freedom I Give ye this trobl of Reme
mbring me to my friends many more Both in Town
and Cuntry I would ask how thay fared If I had
opertunety But this may go where I cannot Let
it [illegible] to inform [illegible] in this [illegible]
of Clay and place of probation and If any wants to
know how I fare I find it a hard But profitable Lesson
to Be Resigned to what hath and falleth to my Lot
Since I Saw thee may thy prayers be for my preserv
ation thes all times that in a Blesed [illegible] we
may meet to join in Selebrating High praises to
ye Shepherd of Israel who Leads his in paths untrod
to wean theire minds from visables to Lean on him
till he Brings them to ye Still watters of Life and
to Shilohs Streams which make up all ye [illegible]
[illegible] ye whol City of God as a fellow Sitteson with
thy Son wife and [Sisters] flock I Salute thee and Bid thee
Dearly farewell

Tho Gawthrop

11 mo. (Jan.) 12, 1748; in Stainton Eng., from Thomas Gawthrop to Israel Pemberton Jr. (PEMBERTON Papers, Vol 5, p.18)

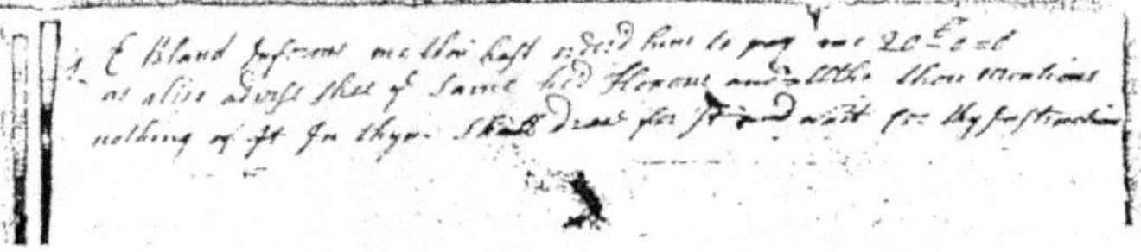

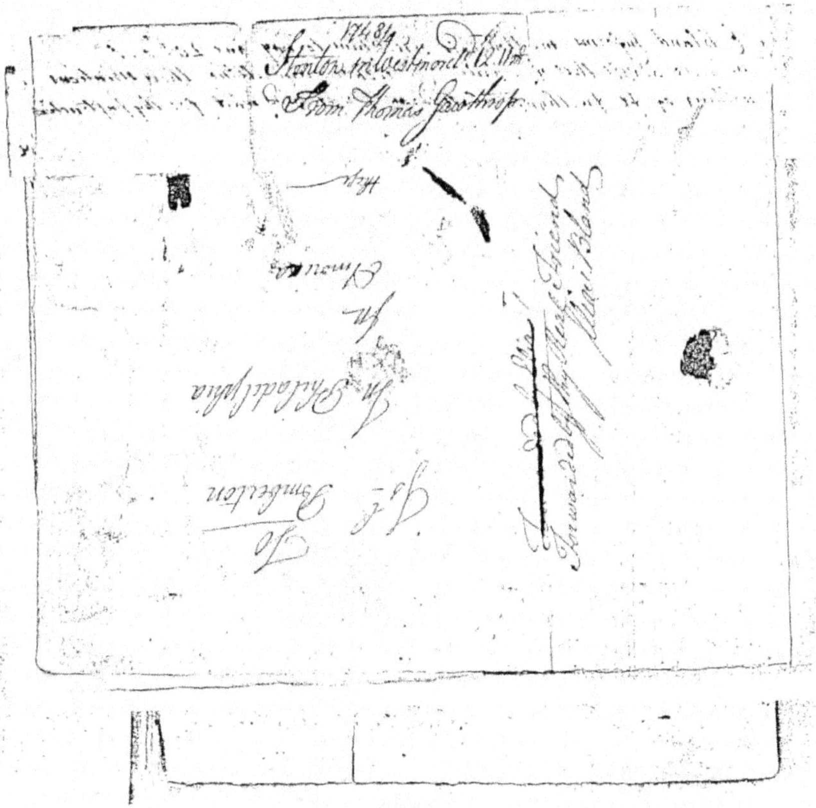

7 mo. (Sept.) 6, 1749, from Thomas Gawthrop to Israel Pemberton Jr.

Stanton 6. 7 mo. 1749
From Thomas Gawthrop

For Isr Pemberton Jr
in Philadelphia

## 7 mo. (Sept.) 6, 1749, from Thomas Gawthrop to Israel Pemberton Jr.

Esteemed Friend                    Stenton ye 6 of 7m 1749
Isr Pemberton Jr

having this opertunaty I Could not But
Send thee a few Lines that If posable ye Tys of Love
and Friendships which hath Subsisted from ye time of
our first acquaintance might Still Live and Remain unshaken
The yearly Meeting for ye Northern Countys was at Kendal
where I had ye pleasure of Seeing thy Bro James whose
prudent Conduct Rendered him Agreeable to ye Sencable
part Friends not only those that had Been at fathers hous
who most naturally must be Indeared to him But others
allso Spoke much In his Commondation and as he had
a full opertunaty to See most of what we Call America
Friends and ye Meetings Being atended with a Good Degree
of that hart melting Power I hope he would Reaps
Some Satisfaction we had ye Company of our Fd J Griffeth
who had Severall full oppertunatis to ye Mutual Comfort
of ye Sencable part of Friends After Sade meeting he
and Willm Backhous went for Ireland Is of Late Returned
and Gon Southward, Jane Hoskins and Companion have
Been thus farr North ye Latter Is Gon for Scotland Jane
and Danl Stanton Is to Be at Kendall to Day so far
as knows thay are all well I Hume Is Coming North-
wards May ye Labours of Love Bestowed upon us have
ye Desired End that ye North may Give up and ye Sides
thereof be Beautified and filld with ye Glory of ye Highest
as to my own fare, my fears are many and Doubtings
Heavier than a Millstone ye floods have over whelmed
me Form Tyed down as In ye midst of ye Sea or as one
Buried under ye Mountains or Lodged In a Dark Lonson
Prison hous hose Gates Is made of Iron and Walls of ada-
ment where I have to mourn without Bread or Watter hear
I have to Remember times thats by past when my Soull
was Like a Vessall pelunged Into ye Eternall fountain and
Girt with Bands as Strong as Iron Rased By ye Devine
hand to ye Refreshing of ye Weary Strengthening of them
that was Redy to faint But now I am fixt as on a poub
where an Invisable hand keeps me In ye wind and Sun

7 mo. (Sept.) 6, 1749, from Thomas Gawthrop to Israel Pemberton Jr.

till ye Bar I Shall be Quit Desolvd If a Little watter falls from ye Clouds my Bands Is so Loos I Soon Loos It again ye heat of temtations Is Such I oft think I Can or Dare Live thro them. I oun I See there Is need to Come under again ye Devine hand and Some times Secret hops warms my frozen Soul that he that first Choos will not Cast of forever But when he hath Tryed his Children he will then Resceve them and tho he Takes ye vesel all to peses yeat he will not Break them that are pasive In his hand (for not one of his Bones Did he Sufer to Be Broken) But will joynt More Close and Make ye Bands of Love more Strong and So more fitt for ye Masters use But these hops oft take wing and fly Like a fantom or Idle dream But Let me Stop and Sease to Repine he Lives whose Life I Desire may Increas tho with ye Loss of mine Even he who first purchased myn with ye Loss of his own by which our Friendship Came to have Its Birth In a Sence of which I a fresh ye Salute his Life In thee and thyn and Bids farewell Thos Gawthrop

Ps. plese to Remember my Dear Love to Father Mother and Brother J as allso to thy Dear wife and all your Childer to J Armit and wife J Smith and wife he was Sr kind to Send me I H Book ye which I Reseved and Cannot But think It a Choise pese and Love ye Author for his works Sake there Is Many more Is fresh In my thoughts as J Cooper and wife H Morris S morris But must not Be too tedious farewell

I Gave thee Account In my Last of thy kind favor I Reseved of E.B. as to J Hunt Makeing any Gratuaty for Giving up I warrant there Is nothing Done as J.G. Is Coming to Town Soon thou may have an oportunaty to Speak to him about it

Nov. 24, 1752 letter from Thomas Gawthrop in Kendal to Israel Pemberton Jr., in Philadelphia (PEMBERTON PAPERS, Vol.8, p.96)

Rec'd 24. 11 mo. 1752
From Thomas Gawthrop

Israel Pemberton Jun^r
in Philadelphia
To y^e Care of
John Hunt London

**Nov. 24, 1752,** letter from Thomas Gawthrop in Kendal to Israel Pemberton Jr., in Philadelphia (PEMBERTON PAPERS, Vol.8, p.96)

Esteemed Fd
Is Pemberton

haveing this opeturnaty Could not wells omit Sending a Line Sumtimes I think thou'l want to hear what Coms of me and If So may Inform thee I have had a hard Leson to Learn. Since I Came from Phyladelfia which hath Sore puseld me that is to Rejoyce In Suffering, when Suffering Is to be or permited by ye Great master It hath often Caus'd me to Blur my Book of Concience and at times throw It by as Impossable to atain But In these times Master was versy kind and tells, with him all things Is posable thus my poor Drooping Spirits being Rased a Little trys again and Keeping Low In thought of Self makes this much Esier for If our perterbations Is from without we being Like a snug tite well Laden vesal Lives thro Every Storm or gust of wind or Is It from within we are tryed by Desertions and Great poverty of Spiritt being Like a snug Ship Careing Little Sale Is not Easaly overset what Heghts have this Soul of mine Seen with you which was unworthy of ye Least vition and now again What Depths as If Hell from beneath and ye powers above had Distined my Ruin. In these Agonis I had Steang Acusers Both within and without a Long Long parly or tryal there hath been May I Com of Clear thus farr I have Learnt It was and Is Good for me that I was aflicted had I not met with Storms I had never Struck my top Gallant masts So might have Been over sett Since no Gally with ores nor Gallant Ship will Ever Be permited to trade and Carry ye Choice wares of ye Gospell In and on ye pure River of Life.

I shall be Glad to have a Line from thee If thou [illegible] my [illegible] at Various times [illegible] thee wife and Children and Sumtimes as I think favoured with ye Spirit of Prayer for your wellbeing Both [illegible] and [illegible] at this time [illegible] [illegible] [illegible] [illegible] [illegible] my Love to thy wife [illegible] [illegible] [illegible] [illegible] to ye [illegible] [illegible] [illegible] [illegible] [illegible] Gawthrop [illegible] [illegible] [illegible]

6 mo. (June) 17, 1753; in London Eng., from Thomas Gawthrop to Israel Pemberton, (PEMBERTON Papers, Vol.9, p.20)

To Isr. Pemberton Jun.r

Merchant

in

Philadelphia

p. Capt. Shirley } forwarded by thy friend John [illegible]

London 17. 6mo. 1753
from Thomas Gawthrop

6 mo. (June) 17, 1753; in London Eng., from Thomas Gawthrop to Israel Pemberton, (PEMBERTON Papers, Vol.9, p.20)

1753

Endeared Fd London ye 17th of 6mo

In that Love which Distance
Cannot Race nor time wearout I Dearly Salute
thee this meeting may inform thee I hope
will not Esaly be forgot by many ye Good presance
of our God Being Emenently felt to Sement ye
Harts of ye faithfull and to ty them togather
In ye Bundall of Love and Life so that ye
Great Cause was near and Dear to a many of
us two propositions was Lade before this
which ye Sencable thought would be of Great
Sirvis to this Nation But carried in ye Negative
ye one was for a yearly meeting of Women friends
ye other for Ministers and Elders which at present
we have not ye want of which has Rendred ye
Good order of Disapline Lame and Inafectuall
thay are Left to Be Reconsiderd next yearly M
and Dear Fd Being for Going out of town
I must Bid ye farewell with Dear Love to Self
wife Childer thy Honourd Father and mother
and Rests thy Afued Fd Tho Gawthrop

P.S. May just Give thee ye hint Last Night
I Spoke with J Hunt Consurning ye Warrant
thou advised to buy he Sade he would Give
me 20 Gunies for Releasing ye Bargain ye
which will in full Satisfy me when pade
as Half of ye prophets Belong thee when it Coms
to my hands shall Give thee Advise
thereof to Draw for ye Same But E Lagg
J Hunt saith Dispoutes ye paying for ye Lands
allthoe he hath Given his Bond for ye mony, Dont Blame my Long
postscript

Jan. 25, 1756, letter from Thomas Gawthrop in Eustatia to Israel Pemberton Jr., in Philadelphia (PEMBERTON PAPERS, Vol.11, p.69)

From Thomas Gawthrop at Eustatia Rec.d by
25 1756
To Isr.l Pemberton Jun.r Philadelphia

Jan. 25, 1756, letter from Thomas Gawthrop in Eustatia to Israel Pemberton Jr., in Philadelphia (PEMBERTON PAPERS, Vol.11, p.69)

Respected Frd
Is. Pemberton
I Writ to thee from Liverpool
am now at Statia Road having Inclosed a Large
Scrall which I writt a few days a Go and hearing
of this oportunaty I thought to venter to Inclose
It may Serve to Give thee a Little amusement
over a Sorrow pipe with thy Dear Spous I oft
thought when my fingers was using ye Shuttle
at home If I had ye Like oportunaty as former
-ly I Should be a Little Chearfull and Indeed
I know no Body has more Reson So to be than
we Strouling folks how Ever ye paper thou
May use to Light thy pipe with tho Sullied with
my nonsence for I Sometimes think ye older I Grow
and ye Madder But thou knows Beggers are Some
times this and Sum times that I writ thee
Last under ye Tytle of a Scavanger Now of a
Begger I know not what ye Next Change will
bee; and no wonder If we are to Becum allthings
to all men that So Some may be Ganed
our Capn has Great markits hear for provistion
Its Likly we must Stay hear 2 or 3 days I have
not Been a Shore but thinks to Go by permyssion
am with unfeyned Love to Self and wife mother famaly

thy Real Frd Tho Gawthrop

plese to Give my Dear Love to our Worthy English
Frds John Hunt & wife thy Bro: John James & Saml
Fothergill If with you I was at his hous his
wife and He was pritty well and was very kind
in Aquiping Mee for ye Sea and I Shall be very
Glad to See him, Should Like to Go to Barbados
before I See you But understands twill be very
Deficult Geting a pasage there from these parts

April 26, 1756, letter from Thomas Gawthrop in Rhoade Island to Israel Pemberton Jr., in Philadelphia

April 26, 1756, letter from Thomas Gawthrop in Rhoade Island to Israel Pemberton Jr., in Philadelphia

Esteemed Fd
Is - Pemberton

Road Island ye 26 4mo 1756

yesterday I Landed at this place thinks to go towards Boston this week and If can be Clear of them parts by ye yearly meeting here If any Letters Come to thy hand [Correct] plese to forward them to this Town have Been at Tortola and If I had thought our English Friends had not Been Gon home Should have Been Glad to have Seen or at Least writ to them and I think Should have Lade Before them ye Afflicted Case of ye Virgin Islands and yeat worthy of a visit from them Beliving If master Sent them thay would have Been a Blessing In his Hand and would have tended to ye mutual Comfort of ye Visitters and visited If thay Should be on ye Continant plese to give my Dear Love to them with J.H. perhaps for It hath Been [Source of hart] to me to think of there Return and not by way of ye Islands for there names allredy Is planted In there Harts may thay Live thay flourish tell them thay are worthy though west Indians and that not only Amongst friends But others there Is an open Door to preach ye Gospel of Jesus I Left Tortola near four weeks ago Came to Estatiah where I Stade Several days But Could meet with no pasage to Barbados nor yeat to Antegue So Shipt my Self for this place you have oft Been ye Subject of my poor thoughts with Strong Desires to ye father of all our mercies he may Guide you by his wisdom Into ye Secret of his Pavilion and hide you under ye Hollow of his hand till his wrath Be over past the It be In Silence for It Is an Evel Day a Day of Darkness when ye Deeds of Darkness Is Brought and Brought upunto Remembrance before him a Day In which he Is weary with forbearing ye Indignaty of men that thay are Puting on his Son In Bosome

plese to give my Dear Love to thy wife & Children & thy worthy Mother & a line to thy Brother may my Love Pass to all my Frds If any Letters for me Come to hand plese to Dispose of them as thinke proper and Send Forget to write often and very free and largely since our arrival [illegible]

Sept 2, 1756, letter from Thomas Gawthrop in Buckingham to John Pemberton, in Philadelphia (PEMBERTON PAPERS, Vol.11, p.117)

To

John Pemberton

In

Philadelphia

Buckingham 9 mo 2d 1756

Thos Gawthrop

**Sept. 2, 1756,** letter from Thomas Gawthrop in Buckingham to John Pemberton, in Philadelphia (PEMBERTON PAPERS, Vol.11, p.117)

John Pemberton                Buckingham 9mo 2d 1756
Loving Friend

Sorry we Should Miss So
of Seeing Each other After thou had Rid So
farr to meet me But takes thy Care and pain
In as much Love as If I had ye pleasure
of Seeing thee I Came thro ye Back Contry
was at ye Great Medows Last firstday hear
yesterday Intends ye falls meeting on first
day Second day Midletown 3 at Byberry
4 at Abington 5 Franckford 6 at Gorman-
town I Desier If thou hast heard of any
Letters for me In Town thou would be so
kind to Send me them to ye falls I am thy
Affectionate Fd                Thos Gawthrop

pleise to Give my Dear Love to
thy Aged mother Brothers
and Sisters have Sum
thoughts If thy Mother
be a Houskeeper to try
If Shee will Give a poor
Beggar Like mee a Lodg
In her Hous for with
Scrubing and Scratshing
In ye woods I am Ragged
& Ruff Inwardly and outwardly

Oct. 22, 1756, letter from Thomas Gawthrop in Rich Land to Israel Pemberton Jr., in Philadelphia (PEMBERTON PAPERS, Vol. 11, p. 135)

Esteemed Fr.

Is. Pemberton. I thought a Line
would be agreeable to thee as now I got a Long
am full as well in health as when in town
thinks to be at Gohany to day am not Resolved
of Going to Maden Creek But Rather
towards Trenttown or Bristol If thy Br. John
Be Come Back Desires he would Send me
that Letter from Tho Jackson to Bristoll
in hast Concludes with Dear Love to thee Self
Thy Affectionate Fd Tho Gawthrop

Rich Land ye 22 of 10 mo: 1756.

To
Isa. Pemberton
In
Philadelphia

June 12, 1757, letter from Thomas Gawthrop going down the Bay to Israel Pemberton Jr., in Philadelphia (PEMBERTON PAPERS, Vol.12, p.31)

From Thos: Gawthrop going down the Bay 12: 6mo: 1757 in ye Ship ... Dunbar bound for Barbadoes

To Isa- Pemberton Merct Jr. Philadelfia

ye Bay 12 of 6 mo: 1757

Esteemed Frd
Isa- Pemberton

I thought a Line would ~~would~~ be agreable, to hear from me this Is writ a bout ye midel of ye Bay we have had a pritty Good time Down, we were a Gainst Newcastle yeasterday morning a bout 9 a Clock, have Got Some Could and hath a paine In my Brest, hath allso a Degree of peace to Boy up and keep from sinking, I Expect thou will favor me with A Line when ye vessels sails Should be Glad to be Remembeed by thee, with Dear Love to thy Self I Conclud thyn In ye Fellowship of Gospell Suffering In Pacience In hope

Thos Gawthrop

6 mo., 25, 1757, letter from Thomas Gawthrop bound for Barbatos to Israel Pemberton Jr., in Philadelphia (PEMBERTON PAPERS, Vol.12, p.31)

ye Bay 12 of 6 mo: 1757

Esteemed Fr

Isa. Pemberton

I thought a Line would ~~would~~ be agreable, to hear from me this is writ a bout ye midel of ye Bay we have had a pretty Good time down, we were a gainst New castle yesterday morning a bout 9 a Clock, have got some Could and hath a pane in my Brest, hath also a degree of peace to Boy up and keep from sinking I Expect thou will favor me with A Line when ye vessels sails should be glad to be Remembred by thee, with dear Love to thie Self I Conclude thyne in ye Fellowship of Gospell Suffring in Pacience in hope

Thos Gawthrop

From Thos Gawthrop ye Bay 12: 6 mo 1757 bound for Barbadoes

To Isa Pemberton Junr in Philadelphia

Oct. 24, 1757, letter from Thomas Gawthrop Ye Capes to Israel Pemberton Jr., in Philadelphia (PEMBERTON PAPERS, Vol.12, p.77)

Capes 25: 10mo: 1757
From Thomas Gawthrop
onboard the Philadelphia
Capt Stewart bound for Liverpool.

To
Isr. Pemberton
In
Philadelphia

Oct. 24, 1757, letter from Thomas Gawthrop Ye Capes to Israel Pemberton Jr., in Philadelphia (PEMBERTON PAPERS, Vol.12, p.77)

Ye Capes, ye 24 of 10 m 1757

Esteemed Fd

I Receivd thy Kind Epistle as
also my Bags by ye Pilot Boat was at Castle
on firstday was Indeared favord with a Sence
of fresh Extendings of Aughtfull Goodness
ye which Remains as on my mind Both
Humbling and Refreshing may It Ever Continue Espeatialy ye Humbling Quallaty for
It may well be Calld ye Balsum of Life
ye Restorative of helth, ye School of wisdom
ye place of Safty and Hiding of ye Righteous
this Humbling hand my worthy Brethren
ha known. Oh may we be presered as
In ye Hollow of It thro all Storms
and fire tryals we may have to go thro
I know not But I Leave ye Continant
Clear a Quiat Serenaty attends my mind
and Sumtimes Cannot But Begg that
ye Evill Days may be Shortened for ye
Elects Sake and that ye Son of Righteous
ness may Break forth Like a morning
without Clouds or as ye Sun In his Strength
with Bright Shining After Rain that ye
Shepherd of Is. may be known by all
his flock and his voice understood from
ye voice of ye Strangee ye way of Life Know
from all Fals ways and Crooked paths of
mens Contriving and Casting up which when thay
have Smoothd and Routd their Jo piced Stons wound
ye tender feet and for all the Lines of judgment thay all
Lead into ye wilderness and not to ye fold of Rest

But have Exceeded myn Entention when I look up my pen.
In a warmanner I salute thee and thyn as tho named
and once more Bids you all farewell Tho Gawthrop

Ps I Like our Capn thus far well I Desier my Dear
Love thou wouldst Remember to all Inquiering
Fds I Cannot But Gratfully Acknowledg my Friends
Kindness to be far more than Ever I Expected
and Let others think and say what thay plese I must
Conclude you are a people Both Generous and Kind
to Strangers willingly Condesending to those of Low
Degree
I hope thou wilt not fail to give me a Line after
If I Live to get home Shall want to hear How
you fair

Nov. 13, 1757, letter from Thomas Gawthrop the Ely In Scotland to Israel Pemberton Jr., in Philadelphia (PEMBERTON PAPERS, Vol.12, p.79)

Esteemed Fd — The Ely In Scotland ye 13 of 11 m 1757

My Last to thee was from ye Capes May In form thee of a Short Safe Blowing pasage Especially for Eight Days past often Running 8 or 9 knots under a forsail and some times Skuding with Bare pols yesterday we made ye C[illegible] of Ierland Got below fair head then ye wind came Contrary and at Last Shelter here with Great Difficulty we are at ancor I have some thoughts If I can Get to Go over from this to ye mainland and so home by Land ye bulky papers I think to Let Go In ye Ship to Hillary and Scots Care for I know not which will be most safe or way to Get to hand thus far as to ye Body

my mind In Degree at times have Been favord with free Extendings of Love which words Cant Express nor Lines Draw or set forth But not allways no no often In Depths of Desponding and Like other worms of ye Grave have to go thro vales and shadows of Doth as to ye which my soul Longs for to be In ye full and free posession of and some times I am Led not to think Strange at these my fire tryals for I have oft had to tell others that ye Lord will have a tryed proved fine people such a seed Both Elect and precious my Lot hath Been amongst whare we were fed Even to ye full togather of what not allways of ye Bread of plesure and Reigning Bowls of ye kingdom But sumtimes ye Bread of adversaty and wine of sore amasements Deep sorrows of Bitter seaty ye waters of Afliction poverty and wretchedness and with this Cry on ye feast day Is any ones sorrow Like unto mine [illegible] Burning Instead of Beauty Instead of a Stomicher a Girding on Sackcloth &c.

Nov. 13, 1757, letter from Thomas Gawthrop the Ely In Scotland to Israel Pemberton Jr., in Philadelphia (PEMBERTON PAPERS, Vol.12, p.79)

Jnstead of [illegible] Jn ye presence of ye Great King
and praising his name Jn ye Courts of his Holliness as on a
ten Stringed Jnstruments our harps have Been
Hung upon ye willows as by ye Strange waters of Babylon
where some have [illegible] and others wanting have Cryed
Jn ye Ears of ye Soul Cum Let us hear of your Hebrew song
and of ye victories of Syons King But a Las how Shall
we sing Jn a Strange Land a Land of Horror a Land
of famine a Land of Darkness and of ye Shadowing
with Deth, Deth which may be felt where ye Strong
and marrow Bones Lyeth Jn this Land of pits snares and
Graves as wood Cut up for ye fire no Jt Js ye Living
whome he Raiseth Jn Life that Can prase him and
those he Brings out of ye Troubled waters of Affliction
that Can sing ye Song of moses on ye Banks of Salvation
these Can See him which Js there Rock and sing to Jt for Jt
Braseth them thay See his Glory as with Eye to Eye thay
Lift up ye voyce togather Each Jn there orb and Station
and tho thay may Differ one from another Jn Glory
yet ye Least Js agem a Star to his prase as ye Greatest
Stone tho as a pyller or post of ye Gate of ye Cetty Celesti-
-al or as a morning Star Jn ye [illegible] Created heavens
for thay have no one of them any thing But what
thay have Reseved from him and therefore being before
him which Js but thay worship him Jn him Self that Js
true Jn his own Spirit

according to ye mesure Reseved hear Elders Casts down
there Crowns before him yet Ere not as naked as ye
Least Child having Loft all pride and Selfishness Jn
ye grave where thay than have Been with these Lord

in his sufferings
and have known him and ye power of his Re-
surrection [illegible] that thy soul and mind may
[illegible] to [illegible] to my Dear friend & [illegible]
Beloved Brother In ye Covenant of Love and Life
Is my Strongest Cry      Tho Lowthrop

Dear fr— Excuse this my Rambling pen
If thou shouldst think I am by my self of a mind I am not
with none [illegible] for it I know [illegible]
temperance and patience [illegible] ye Holy Ghost
waiting [for him] to [illegible] forth and go before us ye
way to ye Crowne of Life and will give it to
us if we are not [illegible] with [illegible]
to [illegible] up [illegible] my dear Love [illegible]
to thy [illegible] and kind friendly & thy
[illegible] Children and [illegible]
Mary [illegible] and wife with
many others [illegible] to [illegible] long
to hear of your [illegible] for the [illegible] may
be on this side of ye Sea [illegible] will
not be a [illegible] of winds or Rocks but [illegible]
be with you [illegible] now [illegible] to bid
farewell

Nov. 19, 1757, letter from Thomas Gawthrop ye Isle of Ely West of Scotland to John Pemberton, in Philadelphia (PEMBERTON PAPERS, Vol.12, p.75)

Esteemed Jn Pemberton ye Isle of Ely west of Scotland ye 19 of 11 m 1757

In much oneness of Brotherly Affection I salute thee may Inform thee It was Caus of Joy to me when thou was without worthy fr J C In England to see thy tender hart so deeply Bowed and Baptised for Sions Sake and that of her sympathy Extending to ye afflicted In our parts as also that dear Affection for thy dear Companyon these were Signs of a well grounded hope sure and stedfast Both Rooted and grounded In ye Truth But now In this my visit to you all my Bowels burns [illegible] comforted to possess our selfs I think) Early thy [illegible] Perseverance In ye Day of [illegible] Bearing of my [illegible] Dear friend and favorite of Heaven keep [illegible] in [illegible] for It is this that cuts up all sin by ye Roots In ye hart. It keeps ye mind and spirit pure and such see God [illegible] seeth ye King In his glory [illegible] with thousands and tens of thousands of his Saints and Cunning to set In Judgment on [illegible] and truth over a guilty world In Righteousness and truth which sight doth not afford matter for a vain mind to feed on with nice Distinctions and Curious Speculations all which is But Chaff making [illegible] Bulke But Light But Rather as these advance the Large and favor they grow In Saving knowledg of ye him which is there Lord and Saviour Jesus Christ thro ye Blessed operation of his God those are not Busie Bodys nor high minded But God's which as to them as a [illegible] of life [illegible] -ing from ye snares of [illegible] doth thus Living In his presence ye are kept humble and teach -able Like Children [illegible] weak and foolish as In ye Day when they first Beheld and as they [illegible]

ye Lord will Rais to ye praise of his Glorious name Both [illegible] and other parts of his Earth my hart fills with Love to ye Seed of ye world over which are now held down as By Chain and my soul Being Bound Can Salute ye Same In that Love more Boundless than ye ocean and more free than [illegible] and Subtler than ye are Superior to ye Rage of Satan [illegible] than Death and Deeper than ye Grave [illegible]

Nov. 19, 1757, letter from Thomas Gawthrop ye Isle of Ely West of Scotland to John Pemberton, in Philadelphia (PEMBERTON PAPERS, Vol.12, p.75)

Lord will [illegible]
& other parts of his Earth my [illegible] fills with Love to ye Suffering
seed of world over which are now held down as by Chains of Deth
and my Soul Being Bound Can Salute ye Same In that Love thats

more Boundles than ye ocean and more free than outward Light
and Subtler than ye air Superior to ye Rage of Satan Stronger
than Deth and Deeper than ye Grave Higher than ye Elliments
and farr farr more Lasting than Sun Moon or Stars

we have had 23½ days passage from Land to Land yeasterday
we made ye north of Irland and made a Great Run a Long side
Coast But at night ye wind heded us and In ye morning was
obliged to Stand for this or Some other place we Got In hear well
But not without ye apearance of ye Greatest Danger many of ye
men saith thay Ever was In to Scape Being wreet our
Capn and mate Behaved wisely ye former being as farr as I
Can judg prefirable to any I Ever was under before my mind
was kept Quiat In a Degree of Confidence In ye Distressing
moments which was no small favor may I be truly thankfull
to matchles Bounty for his Deliverances and mirces to this poor
worms and unworthy Cretures before I Left your parts had
thoughts yf we Should be put Into any part of Scotland to Go home
by Land yf I Could have some thoughts to morrow or as soon
as Can to Go on Shore to Inquire yf It Is practicable to Got
from hear to ye mainland which yf It be, have freedom
I think to Leave ye vesel and to make Such an Etemt
so that yf this Cums to thy hand without other Remark
ye Land way ~~[illegible]~~ Is my Intended Root please to Give my
Dear Love to thy mother whose Kindness to mee Lies
forcably on my mind and I hope I Cannot But Greatfully
Remmember please to tell hir ye token Shee Gave will
be seasonable to help to purchas a Hiland pony allso Give
my Love to thy Bro. James and wife Dan. Stanton & Daulter with [illegible]

July 30, 1758 — letter from Thomas Gawthrop in Kendal to Israel Pemberton Jr., in Philadelphia (PEMBERTON PAPERS, Vol.12, p.135)

Esteemed Fr.d Near Kendall y.e 30 of 7 m. 1758
Is.l Pemberton

I have oft thought of thee and famaly since I got home with strong desires that y.e Lord may bless you all with all goodness and fitt you for his services hear and for his riches and glory hearafter that when a few fleeting moments is over eternal habitations in his glorious relms of light may be adminesterd where all tears will be wiped away and where y.e weary is at rest seeing of y.e traval of y.e soul and is sattisfied with y.e pure streames of love and life which freely flows to y.e hole famaly and cyty of God y.e ernest of y.e purchast inheritance oh how it comforts us hear and revives y.e drooping mind induing with corage and strength life and grace yea favor boath with God and good men so that we can say all our springs o Lord is in thee a life oh well of salvation and we will sing unto thee of thy life we'l drink in thy banquting hous rejoyce under thy banner of surprising love we will be glad and ever worship thee thou king of saints allthe like poor worms we have to grope our way from stage to stage and from one period to an other y.e Father's eye sees and knoweth his where ever thay are and will be found of all that seeks and feels after him a stay to y.e youth and a staff to lean on to y.e advanced before him in years being loaded with y.e cares of y.e Church of God for which Christ dyed and which y.e Holy Gost hath made you overseers he is near you feel after him and he will be found of you to fill and furnish to every word and work to his glory y.e good of his people to your present comfort and eternal peace in a fresh sence that he is good I salute you all my dear friends and bids

you dearly farewell
Tho Gawthrop

April 10, 1762, near Kendal, Eng., from Thomas Gawthrop to Israel Pemberton Jr.. Of friendship in affliction. Of Thomas' young son who lost his mind. Of Thomas' thought to settle in PA. (PEMBERTON PAPERS, Vol.15, p.133)

Esteemd Frd

I once was In hops
to have had a Comfortable Little
peace In your woods to have
Spent ye Latter part of Life fre
from ye Cares of a Bustleing
World which I thought I had free
Dom of mind to Leave a Little
Mony with thee to Ingage for
me a Little Land thou favored
me with a Draft of It Some
time ago But I never knew
Whether thou had pade for It
all or onely for ye warrant
I Desier thou would Let me know
how It Is by first oportunaty
my Sircumstance Is such by one
Cross ocurance and Another that
It will be much better for me
to Dispose of ye Land If It will
Give any thing all of my famaly
Seeming Avers to America to Settle
In at present

I am with Affection not to be Exprest In
Words thy ~~Fr~~ Afflicted Frd Tho Gawthrop

near Kendal 10. 4mo
1762
From Thos Gawthrop
Recd in the begg of 8mo 1763
via New York.
answerd immediately after rec'd
it, but neglected sending this...

To
Israel Pemberton
In Philadelphia
America

April 10, 1762, near Kendal, Eng., from Thomas Gawthrop to Israel Pemberton Jr.. Of friendship in affliction. Of Thomas' young son who lost his mind. Of Thomas' thought to settle in PA. (PEMBERTON PAPERS, Vol.15, p.133)

Esteemed Fr Near Kendall 4th 1762 10th

I Received thyn with much Sattisfaction for I am much Strypt of Any to Simpathize with In ye Path I have to walk In It being Lonesum and muinfull So that to hear from a Fr or So one Is truly Refreshing Sometimes as If It were an Angel In ye valy of Affliction whole thee and thy Dear wife I am well assured Is no Strangers my minde hath been Led to Sink Deep Into your Late hard trobles and a Little to Consider them and to Compare with mine that have of Late Befallen me and tho thay fall far Short of yours yeat I have freedom to Impart Some of them to you as a traveller meeting a nother or overtaking one Rehearseth to his fellow what he hath met with— my Second Son After I Came home was verry Sober and well Inclined of whome I flattered my Self with having much Comfort In being Like a tree promising for much Good fruite But alas Is now Like one pluct up by ye Roots having Lost his understanding In a Great mesure and at times Even much Lunatick he had ye mesals verry Sore and we thought he would have fallen Into a Decline or Consumtion but what shall we Say Save this ye Lord hath permited or done It how marvellous and Afflicting So Ever It may be, many fears Distresseth me Conserning him as allso what he may do to a younger Brother thats Dayly and Nightly with him but Some times I Cannot but Confide In him that Sets Bounds to ye Rageing Seas and to ye Proud waves Come thus far and hear Let them be Stade ye Prayers and Tears for his Recovery Seems to be fruteless In a Great mesure alltho I sometimes thynk thy Crys proseed -eth not out of feigned Lips but alas Its Like -ly thay are not Clean anuf to Aproch that Holy Ear and obtain ye Blessing of a Crumb for him that falls from ye Child -rens table oh that he which Granted ye Cannanites Request would In his abundant Goodnes favour mine

Jan. 5, 1765, from Thomas Gawthrop to Israel Pemberton Jr., Philadelphia, (PEMBERTON PAPERS, Vol.17, p.124)

1mo: 5. 1765
from Thomas Gawthrop

from Thomas Gawthrop
1mo: 5. 1765

To
Israel Pemberton
Jr
Philadelphia

**Jan. 5, 1765,** from Thomas Gawthrop to Israel Pemberton Jr., Philadelphia, (PEMBERTON PAPERS, Vol. 17, p.124)

1 m^o 5^th 1765

Dear Fr^d
Israil Pemberton

I have often purposed to write But have hitherto been Let by one thing or another often having to vew mine own Infirmatis with Secrett Crys who Is so poor and weak as I yeat Can Sumtimes Remember wherein theres Strength and suffi-tience I have oft had to take a vew of my very Steps In your Contry and tho I Cannot Charg my Self with Cappitall Crimes yeat Can Sit down as an unprofitable Servant as with my mouth In y^e Silent Dust In this Tryed Situation of Late I have found Sum warmth of Love to Rise afresh for y^e Seed Royal In your Parts Like Smal Sparcks of fire and I Cannot Say But I have turnd a Side to See as one did In former times a wonderfull Sight y^e Burning of y^e Bush without being Consumed may I hear Distinktly as he did to know my furder work and Servis and may be Inabled to Labower to our Great Masters Honhour which hath Called us to Glory and virtu whether at home or Insent Give up to follow him In Different Climets
Pleas to Give my Dear Love to thy wife and famaly to thy mother and Brothers with y^e Same to thy Self
I Conclude thy Fr^d

Tho Gawthrop

P.S.
I Recevd thy Letter was much pleased to be Remembred by thee and thy near Simpathy with poor unworthy mee thou Gave me account thou had not Disposed of y^e [illegible] But had Sum mony of mine In thy hand If [illegible] Sould It is well If It is not may Lef. It a Long till thou Hears furder from me
But Desiers thou would Remit me y^e mony by first oportunaty y^e Sooner and y^e Better for If my [illegible] thoughts Should grow a Burden two heave to bear and [illegible]

[left margin, written sideways:] Should open I Shall be at a ward for his end I Cannot But Look on thee as [illegible] that thy Love Egged with thee all thy while thy poor Son Is still a Dear [illegible]
Thy Fr^d Friend

A-47

June 25, 1766, from Thomas Gawthrop in Nantuckett to Israel Pemberton Jr., Philadelphia, (PEMBERTON PAPERS, Vol.18, p.144)

Esteemed Fr.d Nantucket ye 25 of 6 m. 1766

I Came hear yasterday as allso J Griffith and J Ross we were togather at Newport yearly m-ing have since been at Several meetings towards Sandwich I Cannot See I Shall be with you till your yearly meeting have Been favoerd with Helth so as to Get a Long as fast as It Is Common for friends to do tho I find our age Is not Like youth I Receved ye Letters thou Sent If any Cum to hand In time for me may Send them to flushing I hope to be on Long Island In a Months time If well and nothing unforseen prevent my Dear Love Is to thy Self wife and famaly with Desiers your prayers may be for your poor weak Sinceer friend

Tho Gawthrop

March 1, 1766, from Thomas Gawthrop in Barbados to Mary Pemberton, Philadelphia, (PEMBERTON PAPERS, Vol.18, p.104)

Barbadoes I. 1 of 3 m. 1766

Esteemed Fd

Mary Pemberton.

May Inform thee I came
hear Last third day tis uncertain when
I Shall Leave this place I could Like to
See Tortola If any opertunaty offer to Get
there In a few weeks But If non Such offer
thinks To Ship my Self for ye Continant
Should be pleased It might be to your place
and to Renew Revive ye Coals of former Friendship
Invite my Self to thine and Husbans Care
alltho I own when I Consider ye Short Space
of time It is Since I was to you no small
trouble and Expence I am Ready to vent a
Shamefull Blush and was It not that Sumthing
what Shall I Call It But that one thing needfull
I Should be a Shamed In your Citty to Show my
head I find hear things Is at a verry Low Ebb
and But few Left In this place that bears
our name have had one meeting of which
I Dare not Complain oh may ye Strength
of Israel Guide me In all ye Little Servises
he may Call for at my hands
plese to Remember poor me In your
prayers that Guidence and utterance may be
given with help In ye needfull time of trouble
the which will much oblidg thy Effetionate
Fd

Tho Gawthrop

plese to give dear Love to
thy Husband Brother James and John youamy
Love flowethe to all friends

Oct. 24, 1766, from Thomas Gawthrop in Munolan to Israel Pemberton Jr., Philadelphia, (PEMBERTON PAPERS, Vol.19, p.12)

Munalan ye 24 of 10m

Dear Fd

having this opertunaty may just Inform thee we Got Hear to day I am But very weakly as yeat ye Could I Bear Bun Badly But hops as I Grow Stronger may Indue It Better to My great Comfort I find allsuffitien Help or Dar to asist In Labower oh may I Ev Look for and wate for It. pleise to Give my Dear Love to thy wife In much Afection I Conclude thy

Fd Tho Gawthrop

Carolina
Hico County 9 24th
1766

Esteemed fr

having this opportunity
May inform we got pretty well here
this morning hoping to reach Cro
to eright Cannot see as great here
fore we shall go nocthard all the
of State of of travel (and in in
places yeat have not Complent
if allsufilient Have being clat
te minister help to y Comforting y
Weary Traveller being in hast y
Conclude thy Affesmate fd

Tho Gawth...

**June 27, 1767,** from Thomas Gawthrop in London to Israel Pemberton, Philadelphia, (PEMBERTON PAPAERS, Vol. 19, p. 95)

London y^e 27 of 6m 1767

Loving Fr.
Is. Pemberton

I Sent thee a few Lines by way of New york of my Safe Arival on my native Land much to my Sattisfaction, after I Came hear as y^e vessels was not Cume hear I went Down to Colchester yearly meeting where I met with our worthy ffriends John Griffith & William Reckitt to my Comfort this morning my things is Got a Shore thinks to Leave this place to morrow Night for home, I understand our Dear Fr. Alice Alderson is Ded yearsterday Called to See David Barclay which he Informs he had pade J willson 25 L for me on thy Account which Sum 15 L 10 =0=0 I Repade to his Clark and took there Reccete for thy use I Earnestly Desire thou would be So kind as Settle y^e afare of y^e track of Land with y^e Propriator as Soon as posable and Send me thee Charg that If the mony thou hast will not answer y^e Expence may I Remit thee what will for as I have Severall Children Sume of them may Incline to Cum and Settle It when thay See It is mine Being halfe with Dear Love to thy Self and ffamaly I Remain thy Affectionate

Fr. Tho Gawthrop

P.S. I have not Seen Susanah Hatton nor J Davis Since I Left them at Falmouth Sush I hear is poorly may Direct for me to J. Row Spittle Field London to forward

To
Is.^c Pemberton
Merch.^t at
Philadelphia
p Capt. Cambers Pensylvania

Lond. 27 6mo 1767
from Tho.^s Gawthrop

April 22, 1768, from Thomas Gawthrop in Gate Beck to John Pemberton, Philadelphia, (PEMBERTON PAPAERS, Vol.20, p.19)

April 22, 1768, from Thomas Gawthrop in Gate Beck to John Pemberton, Philadelphia, (PEMBERTON PAPAERS, Vol.20, p.19)

Esteemed Frd. Gate beck ye 22d of 4 mo 1768

John Pemberton

Inclosed Is a Letter I thought to have sent thee some time ago but was Disapointed of that oportunaty It now cums by a young Lad thats Recummend to ye Care of J Fisher by our worthy Friend Isaac Willson Severall of thy welwishing friends would be much obliged to thee for a Compassionate Eye towards him as an object of pitty and allso to asist In Geting him a good place

my minde Is truly Affected ~~with~~ for your fresh troubles which threaten you yeat a secret hope atendeth that all protecting providence will be a safe hideing place to his Children that put there In him and Cannot have any Dependance on ye Arm of flesh In some of my Distressed moments since I came home Reflecting on my situation It Rose In my minde thy Tryals Is not yeat over nor ye winter past therefore Live Law Live Humble for I will never Leave nor forsake worm Jacob But my name shall be as a Covert for thee as a Stone Is to ye worm Both from ye Devourer and ye pinching frosts as allso from ye Sumers scorching heat as beneath this Holy powerfull Name Let my Spirit Salute thee and thyn and Remain thy Affectionate Brother worm

Tho Gawthrop

June 30, 1767, from John Griffith in Chelmsford to John Pemberton, Philadelphia, (PEMBERTON PAPAERS, Vol.19, p.97)

To
John Pemberton Merch<sup></sup>t
in
Philadelphia

Chelmsford 6mo 30 1767
From John Griffith

June 30, 1767, from John Griffith in Chelmsford to John Pemberton, Philadelphia, (PEMBERTON PAPAERS, Vol.19, p.97)

Chelmsford 31st 6mo 1767 —

Dear Friend

I recd thy acceptable letter by Thos Gowthorp, who meeting Conterary winds in the Chopps of our Channel, were obliged to put into Falmouth, & from thence Come by land with young Fisher to London a few days after our Yearly meeting there, Came down with Jos Row his wife & Sukey to our Yearly meetg at Colchester & Spent a little time at our house, but hearing at Colchester that the vessel was arrived at London, was in haste to return that he might get his things on shore & set out homward; he appeard to be in usual health, with a good degree of cheirfulness, & had some good service at Colchester — our Yearly meeting for largeness, I think was much as usual & in the main a Solemn good meeting, there was not much besides the usual business, a few propositions but none that occationd much debate except one, relating to a minute made (I think) in 1744, requiring frds to deal with those who go out in marriage, after they have done it, notwithstanding mo meetings may have cleard themselves before, they have gone out, wch some of us think, a great hardship on frds & the way to reinstate them again at any rate, however few observe it as it now stands, & we think it a pitty any minute shod remain, that frds are under a necessity to act conterary to — It seemd not like to be easily ended & so, to put it of, it is refferd to the meeting for sufferings to give their sense of it next year — We had acct of the Decease of divers publick frds, among the rest Alice Alderson, Mary Glover, Mary Waring & Joseph Milthorp. I understand Edmund Peckover is yet living, but very feeble & like a child as to his faculties — Jonah Thompson, S Hotting, W Shapples, Saml Spavauld, J Storer, C Payton & T Dodson & a pretty many other publick frds attended, C Payton was at ours, and is gone to the other eastern Yearly meeting, honest Abra Shackleton, Jos Inman, Isaac Jackson, & two or three other frds attend from Ireland — I was very glad to find that my Choice Horse was found, & like to receive good usage again, & think it a noble kind act of thy Bro Israel, to take him in that Condition & not suffer me to be a looser by him, I hope he is not so hurt, but that in a while he may recover

June 30, 1767, from John Griffith in Chelmsford to John Pemberton, Philadelphia. (PEMBERTON PAPAERS, Vol.19, p.97)

recover so as that he will not loose by him. I also observe thy account of his remarkable benevolence in making my Daughter Amy a present of £10 towards house keeping, I hope & desire she may have & retain a gratefull sense of his great kindness herein; remember my dear love to him & return my sincere & hearty acknowledgments to him for his kind regard to us both — I had the fore part of this month wrote a letter to his wife & sundry others which I took to the yearly meeting, intending to write thee from London, & send all per first opportunity, but, towards the later end of the meeting, I took an extream cold; the weather for the time being remarkably cold. that I was obliged to leave London in a poor condition. & am not yet wholly recovered, but hope I am in the way for it — — as to what thou says of dividing the money my house sold for among my children — I wrote in answer to thine of 2d mo last, my tho$^{ts}$ of Amys pre-cipitate proceedings, & have much disapproved of the manner however the thing it self may turn out — and that I did not see I co'd make any alteration at present in the settling of things relating to my children — that I know of no way to supply Amys present necessity but by borrowing of £50 — & that her share of the rent w$^{ch}$ W$^{m}$ Horne is to pay, might pay the interest of that £50 untill the land is sold. thou says thou has helpt her to some money, if thou & thy father Jeanes, are willing & think it best to advance that much for her, & and have the rent coming in for interest, and all in your own hands, my case that am now growing in years, & infirm shod be a little tho$^{t}$ of, as well as my children's & how much I necessarily spend, & have spent in the service, I have been now settled in England above 16 years have had but very little from my estate over there all that time; Hannah has had upwards of £50 to begin with of mine, & there will be pretty hansome when the land is sold. so that I am not willing at present to do any other than as I have settled before.

June 30, 1767, from John Griffith in Chelmsford to John Pemberton, Philadelphia, (PEMBERTON PAPAERS, Vol.19, p.97)

before, but expect if thou has not distributed the money
as thou mentions, before this Comes to hand, that thou will
remitt it to me either, by it Self, or, with the years
rent payable next Spring, by Josiah Bunting & Silas
Jones & the race rent by Lloyd, w^ch will be £5.10
without any deduction -- but if thou has given it
the Children before this Comes to thy hand I shall
Desire thee to remitt me as much, out of the money
arising from the Land, when that is Sold -- I know
my Children are like others, they want to get all they
Can, but am well Sattisfied, If they and others were
to Consider things Impartially, they would think Consid-
-ering every thing I have done as well by them as I ought
at present -- I am very sensible of thy great &
repeated regard & kindness to me and them, hope ever
to retain a gratefull sense of the same, & so Conclude
with much love to self & wife thy truely affectionate
in w^ch my d^r wife Joins me
& much obliged friend

I think a little strange I have
not had a line from my children
nor my Sister since I came away
tho had from a pretty many other

John Griffith

Dec. 30, 1769, from Thomas Gawthrop in Preston Patrick to John Pemberton, Philadelphia, (PEMBERTON PAPAERS, Vol.21, p.96)

Preston y<sup></sup> 30 of 12 m 1769

Dear and much
Esteemed Fr John Pemberton

I Received thyn was Comforted In y^e Read-
-ing of it by our Fr Rachel Wilson which
got home this day two weeks I see her yesterday shee and famaly well In helth as we can
thro mercy these I send by my two youngest
sons which Intend to settle amongst Friends In Nottingham [illegible] which I have given to them
If any thing hapen to them as want of helth
that thay Should Incline to return home and
wants mony I Desire on there Aplication
thou would Advance and Lend them ten pounds
towards paying there pasage Back thy Cordial
Advice to them I hope will be of great Servis
to them and Abundantly gratefull to mee
Shal [illegible] take Care to Repay thee y^e mony
Intended a Longer Letter but time will not
permit [illegible] with y^e Salutation of Love unfeigned
to thyn and I Conclude thy Fr Tho Gawthrop

John Pemberton
in
Philadelphia

July 6, 1774, from Thomas Gawthrop in Preston Patrick to Israel Pemberton Jr., Philadelphia, (PEMBERTON PAPAERS, Vol.26, p.117)

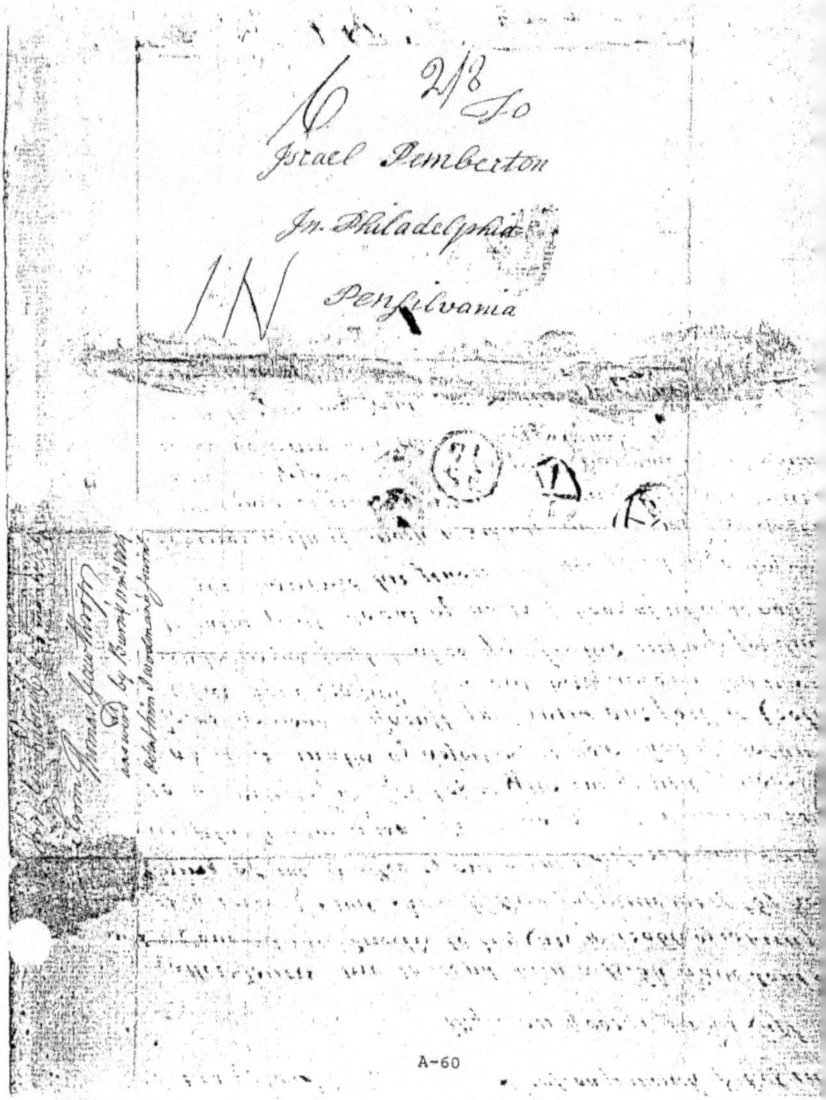

6 2/8

To

Israel Pemberton

Jn. Philadelphia

1N Pensilvania

July 6, 1774, from Thomas Gawthrop in Preston Patrick to Israel Pemberton Jr., Philadelphia, (PEMBERTON PAPAERS, Vol.26, p.117)

1774

Much Esteemed Frd — Preston patterick ye 6 of 7 m

My Son George In his Last
Letter Desires me to Send him a Bible have sent one
with a Concordance Directed to thy Care ye troble of which I hope
thou will Excuse Ra- Willson Informd me of thy Remem-
-bering of me as allso of our Sons wellfare which was verry
Acceptable was allso Glad to hear that ye Indians Is likely
to be visited with ye Light of ye Glorious Gospell power
and it is matter of Rejoising to hear that ye Testimony
Gains Grownd a Gainst Inslaving our fellow Creators
Sister Jane Crossfield hath been verry unwell this winter
and Spring past But is Got Better my wife for Sum
months past So out of helth I thought Shee would not
have Survived her Illness ould age I find as to my Self
Brings with it much weakness and Sunderry Infirmaties
I am much Afflicted with ye Rumatisam Ernestly Desiering
thou will favor me with a few Lines once more which
will be verry Grattfull to thy Affectionate Frd
plese to Give my kind Love to thy Wife Tho Gawthrop
and farmaly

Oct. 10, 1774, from Thomas Gawthrop in New York to Israel Pemberton Jr., Philadelphia, (PEMBERTON PAPAERS, Vol.28, p.80)

Newyork ye 10 of 10 mo

Much Esteemed Friend

May Inform I came hear yeasterday I find traveling to be very hard for an ould man as I am. I have thought to Stay hear to morrows meeting after which thinks to Leave this place. thy horse performs well: my Companyon hath been very kind and Agreable as it is not a time to boast So neither dare I much Complain, there is wages for Honest Laborers Let that be to poor me, Ever anough please to Give my Dear Love to thy wife and family In much nearness of Affection I Concludi thy Loving Frd

Thos Gawthrop

March 14, 1775, from Thomas Gawthrop in Preston Patrick to Israel Pemberton Jr., Philadelphia, (PEMBERTON PAPAERS, Vol.27, p.96)

Preston patrick 14. 3mo. 1775
from Thomas Gawthrop

To Israel Pemberton
In Philadelphia
Pensylvania
America

March 14, 1775, from Thomas Gawthrop in Preston Patrick to Israel Pemberton Jr., Philadelphia, (PEMBERTON PAPAERS, Vol.27, p.96)

Preston pattrick ye 14 of 3d mo 1775

Much Esteemed Friend

Israel Pemberton

I Resived thyn of ye 1 of 4 m 1774 which was truely Acceptable as allso thy kind Gift of John Woolmans jurnall as yeat have not Got ye Epistless But have Got one of J Willson. I am Glad to find friends In these troblesum times preserved Stedfast in ye paths of peace tho' Suffering Should be there Lot. Sister Jane Crossfield hath been but poorly this Winter but is now Got Better. Rachel Willson is at London and Dangerous Ill. My Dear wife was taken from me about 2 weeks since by Death and my Self but verry poorly I hope thy favor will Excuse my not Inlarging at presant with Dear Love to thy wife I Conclude thy

Affectionate Frd

Tho Gawthrop

Dec. 1, 1777, The substance of what Thomas Gawthrop said upon leaving Philadelphia (PEMBERTON PAPAERS, Vol.31, p.49b)

The substance of a few Expressions dropt by our beloved Friend Thomas Gawthrop, on his departure from Philadelphia the first of the 12th mo 1777

Master said, Thou came poor among them, & has been in much Poverty: be content to leave them so. I have taken their Crown from off their Heads: let them wear Dust & Ashes the appointed time; then shall their Sun break forth as brightness & my Glory be their Crown and Diadem. —, I am glad I have been a=mongst you. — I have seen his protecting Providence over this City; but the People do not see it, neither are they humble & gratefull for his Mercy. —

April 3, 1778, from Mary Pemberton to Israel Pemberton Jr., near Virginia, (PEMBERTON PAPAERS, Vol.32, p.15)

Philada Apr. 3. 1778
From my Dear Wife
Mary at [illegible]

[illegible]

Israel Pemberton
New Winchester
Virginia
Favoured by Cousin
Charles Logan

April 3, 1778, from Mary Pemberton to Israel Pemberton Jr., near Virginia, (PEMBERTON PAPAERS, Vol.32, p.15)

Philad.a the 4 Month 3: 1778

My Dearest

The 31st of last Month I received thy very affecting Letter dated the 6th and 7th of the same With a circumstantial account of the Illness and Decease of our Friend Thomas Gilpin, and of the Alarming State of our Worthy and beloved Friend John Hunt; soon after I had read it, a Person who Came to Market from over Schuylkill, brought us the sorrowful Intelligence of his Death, which he said was in a Letter from Thomas Wharton to his Wife, which they did not think proper for him to take, lest it should be taken from him, on this I thought it necessary in some degree to prepare his Wife for the melancholy tidings, and communicated thy Letter to her, which she read several times over, and seem'd from thence apprehensive that she should hear of his Decease, which before was quite unexpected to her, having flatter'd herself with an expectation of a Personal interview with him In a short time, She is deeply affected with a sense of the Loss she sustains, as many others I believe will be with that of a Publick one in our Religious society, which seems greatly stript of valuable members; I wrote thee the latter end of last Month by the Frds who went from the Half years Meeting Viz.t George Churchman and Mary Cox, these Letters were to go by a Friend whose name is Jeremiah Brown which I hope thee hast received, since then I have received a Letter from our Friend and old acquaintance Thomas Gawthrop dated Falmouth the 7th of the 1st mo Signifying he arrived there the 5th, after a Passage of 27 Days and a few hours, mostly fair Winds and moderate Weather, and though their Company in the steerage was disagreeable, yet the Passage was render'd in some degree Comfortable, General Wilson, with whom he went, being exceedingly kind Paying much regard to his Age and Infirmities, and that he was kindly received by his Friends in his native Land much to his satisfaction, of this he desired me to Inform thee with his Love to thee and the rest of the Friends in Banishment as if named; in which George Napper Joins, of his son James would be advertized of this no doubt it would be acceptable. I observe thy directions respecting the Carriage, but have very little expectation of disposing of it in that Way, James Ogilbe has Just now been here, he by the advice of John Vanderen, has employ'd a Man to fence in the two Lots in which the Grain is Sow'd being each twelve Acres of Rye and Barley, and says there are Posts and Rails near enough to do it, and intends to assist in spliting the Rails &c, and then

**April 3, 1778,** **from Mary Pemberton to Israel Pemberton Jr., near Virginia, (PEMBERTON PAPAERS, Vol.32, p.15)**

Thee thinks of leaving the Widdow, as there is fifty Pounds Due to him for Wages but he has
secured himself by seling their Barley being an hundred and fifty seven Bushels at 8/ wch
Reuben Haines bought, and gave him a note to Pay on demand, Mary insists she has a
right to the whole sum, I however desired Reuben to keep half the Money in his hands
till thy return, and James assures me that he does not intend to take it, but was afraid
that she would receive it, and that he was at a Loss how he should be Paid, it seems she
intends to stay on the Place, but the Person she had in view to assist her is not wiling to come
and, the other having bought a Plough and two Horses, intends to farm for one half the Profit
which he thinks safer these precarious times, than to take a Place, and is wiling to do it
for thee, and then would make his home at Marys. thus much I thought best to Inform thee
My Dearest respecting thy Bolton Farm, as to Evergreen the acc.t inclosed by Vincent
Gilpin he was not easey to take, but I understood by Jamey Rhoads that he had given thee
Information in his Letter about it, I think myself unequal to the cares and concerns of this
troublesome and uncertain World, yet am a Wonder to myself that I am enabled to hold up
through my deep tryals and excercises, and can but ascribe reverent thankfulness to the
Almighty preserver that I am in a capacity as thou observes to write to thee my beloved
and should rejoyce it were in my Power to communicate any thing that would tend to thy
strength and incouragement under thy seperation and suffering, my earnest desire is that
the same divine support that has hitherto been with us may be continued, which will
be sufficient for each of us, and our dear Friends who are deprived of their beloved Husbands
very unexpectedly to them both, they are Properly sensible of the Loss of these valuable
and near Connections and behave with becoming Prudence on the malancholy ocation.
This comes by a son of Edward Penington and Cousin Charles Logan to whom we must
refer for Particulars not mentioned, the Later will be able to give an acc.t of our Families
ours, through Mercy are well all but Pollys youngest Child who me think is on the mending
hand my Little Molly very hearty, we all Joins in the salutation of Dear Love to thee wth
the rest of our Dear connections and Friends, from whom to hear soon will greatly rejoyce
thy affectionate and deeply concerned Wife

Mary Pemberton

April 3, 1778, from Mary Pemberton to Israel Pemberton Jr., near Virginia, (PEMBERTON PAPAERS, Vol.32, p.15)

My Dearest after sealing my Letter and Just sending it to Cousin Charles a Lad came in
with the Packet in which was thy acceptable Letter of the 24th. from David Brown, con-
tradicting the acct. of our Dear Friend John Hunts Decease, but of undergoing the Painfull
Opperation of the taking of his Leg, which for a Person of his age I think must be very
Dangerous his Poor Wife hearing of the Letter sent for it. upon which I sent for her Sister
to read the Letter and then sent it over, I think tho' her Life may be spared this must be to her
a very Affecting Case, I shall be exceeding glad to hear thou art releived from thy Painfull
Disorder and that thy Change of Habitation may be to thy satisfaction, but nothing so agreable
as the Inteligence of thy return home to thy anxiously concern'd and truly Affectionate

M. P.

My Dear Love to our Relations and Frds

Particularly our Dear Fr. J Hunt, if Living.

April 30, 1779, The substance of a draft by J. Pemberton of a Testimony from the Philadelphia Monthly Meeting for Thomas Gawthrop to Friends in Kendal, Eng. (PEMBERTON PAPAERS, Vol.33, p.15)

To the Quarterly and Monthly Meetings of Friends
at Kendal in Westmorland Great Britain

Dear Friends

Our Antient friend & brother Thomas Gawthrop, after he had [illegible] visited many of the Meetings of friends on this Continent, and apprehended himself clear & easy to return home, being detained a considerable time among us; Our love & fellowship with him, engage us to testify to you, the benefit & Comfort we had by his company, and innocent instructive conversation, and the near Sympathy he manifested with us in various close exercises & [illegible] which through Infinite Wisdom [illegible] during his stay in this City; his Reverent humble waiting in deep Silent worship in our Publick Assemblies being truly edifying, and when favoured in ministry his counsel [illegible] with the virtue of Truth, and his concern [illegible] for our preservation, in Stability & faithfulness to our Christian Testimony, and [illegible] union with us in the exercise of the Discipline of the Church helpful & encouraging, and his resignation & Patience under his long detention [illegible] Examplary becoming a minister of the Gospel.

It has been comfortable to us to hear of his preservation through the dangers of the Seas, & arrival among you, and we sincerely desire that the same Divine Arm of Power, which hath been his Guide and Stay in his younger years, may continue to be his Staff

April 30, 1779, The substance of a draft by J. Pemberton of a Testimony from the Philadelphia Monthly Meeting for Thomas Gawthrop to Friends in Kendal, Eng. (PEMBERTON PAPAERS, Vol.33, p.15)

Staff and Sure Support in his declining Age, and when
it may please the Lord to remove him from the Church
militant, that he may be mercifully favoured with the
joyous Sentence of "Well Done" Enter into thy masters Rest.

Signed in and on behalf of our Monthly Meeting of Philadelphia held the 30th day of the fourth month 1779 — by

We Salute you with brotherly affection & are Your Loving friends —

Dear Friend

Philad: 5mo 5 1779 —

This is Intended to convey to thee a Certificate from our
monthly meeting which I hope
may come safe to thy hands and altho' I might write thee
a long letter respecting the State of things here without enter
ing on matters of a political nature
yet for fear of an unkind construction to give offence to any thro whose hands it may happen I choose to
forbear and may therefore only inform thee of the fresh
affliction which in the course of Divine Providence has
attended us by the decease of my dear brother Israel
on the 22 of the last month after a long weak state not being perfectly restored his health since his
illness in Virginia, his virtues & qualifica
tions being well known to thee thou'l be sensible his removal is a
great loss to us, added to that of his valuable wife who also dyed
in the tenth month last —
many Occasions for the exercise of Faith & patience in this day of singular tryal still continue
but we have grounds to hope that the favour of Divine Providence
remains for the Strength & Support of those whose trust & confidence is placed ... [illegible] ... Kingdoms of this world
in my wife & family join Thy Affectionate fr. J.P.

To Thomas Gawthrop

xxxx x, 17xx, An unidentified letter from Thomas Gawthrop (more than likely it came from the PEMBERTON PAPAERS, Vol.??, p.??)

Respected Fr

Beeing at Sea not farr from ye Island of Tortola
and thinking I was far from home I began to look
over myn Instructions to Inform mee In Soom part
of Busenss for my owner as allso ye Bills of Lade-
ing that So I might Loos no time when I came
to market In this over hall of Everything I find
this writ In Larg Capitals just over a gainst my
masters Seall thou art to be on ye Island A Rear
Common Begger and Go About from Hous to Hous
Craving Alms for Christ Sake thou must know when
I Read ye Above I Remembred my Beeing In France
and Spain where I See many of that Fraternaty
Called Beging Fryers and I Dispised them In my
very Soul for those Misarable Creatures had ye
Impudence to Begg of us who were Strangers
prisoners Hiraticks as thay Called us yeat If we would
Giv them allms thay'd pray for us So- Just that time
a Day could Scarce See them with patience and
I Dare Say to my Cuntrymen that Could understan
me I Did not Spare throing out Reflections on
this their Disolute way of Life for I Lookt on them
as So many Idle Loobbers and ye plow or Some
Honest Imployment would have Been much
Better for them and ye Common welth and what
Galld me most thay Coverd themselves with ye San-
-taty of Religon too But who knows what thay may
Come to themselfs I also find In mine Instructions
to be very Importuning to Call on ye poor as well
as ye Rich ye Stranger and ye home Born ye Charit-
able and them that are without Bowels as this Is to
be my trade I am to Inform them that thay that Giv
to ye poor Lends to ye Lord who will Surtanly Repay
them them that are truly Hospitable to ye Son
and poor me It Looks Likely I Shall have Great
need of patience that when I Com to their Door
(Espeshaly ye Rich) and with A pittious moane Sets
forth our Real need as allso ye Child I- for my Instructions Runs So I must Carry him with me and that for
him only I am to be Imployd who Is By Birth a Great King

xxxx x, 17xx, An unidentified letter from Thomas Gawthrop (more than likely it came from the PEMBERTON PAPAERS, Vol.??, p.??)

Son and that I Should bring all those Alms to him
without Repine and that he would in that House tell me
ye particulars what to Say as allso provide nesesarys to
presarve Life I find allso I must not Expect Great things
for ye Begging trade Is Grown very Bad and tho with
tears in thy Eys may Begg for ye Prince of Both la-
nay tho he himself hath Bore harts as hard as Adamant
with his tender voice yea I'me Informd by a Line
~~[illegible]~~ I'me not to think It Strang If thay Abuse me
and Evilly Intreat me If thay Send me from there Dor
Empty If thay take me up Carry me be fore ye powers
of ye Earth there Judg me as I did ye fryars of France
nay If thay Should Beat and Stone me and him
and Send us to prison and Sentance to Deth ~~[illegible]~~
my orders Runs I must then Rejoyse thi Dear friend
for So Ile Call thee for I know thy hart Abounds
with Charaty ~~[illegible]~~ yea Simpathy for Honist Beggers
for I Expect when my master and his Reatel Coms
to thy Door thou'l rather keep us out nor order
master to be Lodged where ye Beast Eats his provin-
dgs to me an hard Lesson I have Been Learning
~~[illegible]~~ betimes Ever Since I Last So thee and am
but Like one Learning his A.B.C. Its So Contrary
to Reason to use Beggers Ill If thay'l Give us
nothing thay might pitty one and Let us Go A-
-bout our business If thay would not Lodg my
Prince in ye Gift Chamber or ye Best Room
in ye House thou knows ~~[illegible]~~ he Is worthy tho
it were A pallas, to his Honour Let It be Spoke
his Delight Is in ye Humble Cot. thay need not
treat us as there Enymies with Insolence and pride
nay Some will use all ye machinations of
wickedness to Root us out of ye Earth by Laying
field to field as Some Did formerly till there
Is no Room for an Honest Begger thus these
Searchings Crows thay Croke on the High twigs
of Bows on there Emagination and at other times
Struts in ye fircoats far Like Demy Gods in there
own Eys picking up ye presious Seed of ye whose
Barran maws Is Like ye Grave nay worse than.

xxxx x, 17xx, An unidentified letter from Thomas Gawthrop (more than likely it came from the PEMBERTON PAPAERS, Vol.??, p.??)

So Likes Gahona where there Is nether Sun Due nor
rain nor Ever will be whom thay tent ~~to~~ Afflec this
manner I am Like to tell them But dare not Ex-
-cept my ~~Lo~~ Bid me thay are but Beggers orday
worse than Such that ~~that~~ there Baggs Is moth
Eaten there Gould Is Rusted and there houses
will be Disolate that ye Grornd Is near to
be Cursed for there Sakes and It would have
Been much to there Eternall profit thay had
all there tresures filled with Charaty oh that
I Could Delight my Self In ye will of my Lord
and Sitt Down In ye unprofitable Servants place
Like a Begger on ye Grownd weaping ye Garment
Given ~~tho~~ under ye juniper tree In ye Lonesom
Wilderness without Bread and without water tho
with a Holy Zeal pleaded my masters Cause
According to Direction and In Abillaty Given
thes Seems by ye hints In mine Instructions
I Shall have hard treatment to meet with
from that wicked Painting Proud Mulder
ing Spirit of Jesabell I am feard turn
Begger for once to him whose I Scans
and hears ye Bowd Soul that he would
preserve So poor a Wretch as I am from
ye Hands of unresonable men for all men
hath not faith or not ye Least Grain these are
Like vesels at Sea without Helm Driven
a bout with fferse winds So that Its Danger
ous Coming nigh them thare Like Simeon
& Levi as Jacob Sade So Saith my Soul o Come
not thou into there Secrit, to there Assembly
mine Honnor the A beger Be not thou united
for In there Angar thay Slue a man and In there
Self will thay Diged Down a Wall oh this Self
will) Cursed Bee there Anger for It was feirs
and there wrath for It was Cruel I will Devide
them In Jacob and Scatter them In Israel Ito here
thay Carry top and top Gala to thay ply ye oars
whe it thay Chance In fact to Swim In there Lodg Doth

unother part of mine, orders, Dovfeth Closly to often Call on ye poor Let them know that If thay are so and know It and are willing to Entertane Strangers that Journ with my master ~~and~~ Sufficient to take up our Aboad with them. and that tho Beggers by trade yeat, we were willing to work for them In there plan-tation or at Least that thay had Called there own. for If I Durst tell them my master Is Haire of all thay have and that his father who hath A Right to Bestow hath ~~had~~ Given him ye heathon for his Inheritance and ye utmost parts of ye Erth for his possition for Acts of Love he hath performd But oh how ye Rich worldlings and prowd pharasis will Snear at A Beggers Discours on these things how will thay Sneak a way Displeased But ye poor In-sin to Inform them we are well Acquainted for laying ye Axe to ye Rook of ye Strongest tree that ye barran Grownd may be made fruitfull ye wilderness may be made as Eden and ye Desert as ye Garden of God pray that my masters Going forth Shall be prepared as ye morning and his Coming In as ye Early and Latter ~~Rain~~ Rane In One Season. and that all Sorrow and Sith Shall flee away that there Bread Shall be Sure and there watter Shall never fail and that my master will help Redig ye fountains makeing ye Earth to Reel and ye Rocks to Rend and find ye or Other Springs which flows Like a River from under ye threshhold of ye hous of God this Should be to Drink at to Bath In to watter ye Garden ~~or~~ or plantation with, After which It Should Devide or Rather Spread to wards ye four Corners of ye ~~Earth~~ Creation ye first Incumpasing ye hole Land of Havilla (or family of God Boath In heaven and on Earth) In which Land there Is Goold and ye Gold is Good for It will never Rust nor moulder nother In time nor In an Endless Eternaty for It Is still ye most Bright and weighty which In ye Holiest fire tis on this ye Great King prints his Image Coat of Arms and Royal motto holynes unto ~~the~~ there is allso ye Bdellium and ye Onixs Stone ye Second Incumpaseth ye hole Land of Ethiopia what ye Blacks and Blackest Cumpass all what ye foolish and ye wicked ye other two Denotes not Incumpasing

But Going thro America a Land of Enimis ye next Its name Euphrates and no more one would think If there not all over Grown with Earth Some of ye Poor may be perswaded to Let us In, and Believe So Great a Guest In my Vessel may Give thee an Account what Success I have had In my Outward ~~I~~ See there Is Rest for It and Ropineers [illegible] But oh I am foolish as Such Rosts thyn T Gawthrop

## APPENDIX B

### Who's Who In Your Family

This Who's Who in your family was from an unidentified magazine article. This article was sent to Philip E. Gawthrop by Richard & Linda Gawthrop on January 2, 1991. Items 1 through 4 and items 8 through 17 were extracted from that article. Items 5 through 7 have been added to enhance the reader enjoyment of this material.

•1. Your **first cousin** is your parent's brother's (or sister's) child. However, the first cousin's child is **not** your second cousin, as is sometimes thought to be the case, but your **first cousin once removed**. The child of the first cousin once removed is your **first cousin twice removed**. The child of the first cousin twice removed is your **first cousin three times removed**, etc.

•2. Your **second cousin** is your *grand*parent's brother's (or sister's) *grand*child. That second cousin's child is your **second cousin once removed**. That second cousin once removed child is your **second cousin twice removed**, and so on.

•3. Your **third cousin** is your *great grand*parent's brother's (or sister's) *great grand*child. That third cousin's child is your **third cousin once removed**. That third cousin once removed child is your **third cousin twice removed**, and so on.

•4. Your **fourth cousin** is your *great, great grand*parent's brother's (or sister's) *great, great grand*child. That fourth cousin's child is your **fourth cousin once removed**. That fourth cousin once removed child is your **fourth cousin twice removed**, and so on.

•5. Your **fifth cousin** is your *great, great, great grand*parent's brother's (or sister's) *great, great, great grand*child. That fifth cousin's child is your **fifth cousin once removed**. That fifth cousin once removed child is your **fifth cousin twice removed**, and so on.

•6. Your **sixth cousin** is your *great, great, great, great grand*parent's brother's (or sister's) *great, great, great, great grand*child. That sixth cousin's child is your **sixth cousin once removed**. That sixth cousin once removed child is your **sixth cousin twice removed**, and so on.

•7. Your **seventh cousin** is your *great, great, great, great, great grand*parent's brother's (or sister's) *great, great, great, great, great grand*child. That seventh cousin's child is your **seventh cousin once removed**. That seventh cousin once removed child is your **seventh cousin twice removed**, and so on.

•8. **Sibling** have parents in common. Brothers and sisters are siblings.

•9. **Grandnephew (or Grandniece)** -- the *grand*child of your brother or sister.

•10. **Great uncle (or Great aunt)** -- the brother (or sister) of your *grand*parents.

•11. **Great-*grand*uncle (or Great-*grand*aunt)** --the brother or sister of your *great grand*parents.

•12. **Stepfather (or stepmother)** -- the husband of your mother (or the wife of your father) by a subsequent marriage.

•13. **Stepchild** -- the child of your husband (or wife) by a former marriage.

•14. **Stepbrother (or stepsister)** -- the child of your stepfather (or stepmother).

•15. **Half brother (or half sister)** -- the child of your mother and stepfather or the child of your father and stepmother.

•16. **Lineal** relations -- those in the **"direct"** line of ascent or descent, such as *grand*father or *grand*daughter.

•17. **Collateral** relations -- those relatives who are "linked" by a common ancestor, such as uncles, aunts and cousins.

The remaining pages of this appendix show examples of how different persons are related. The item on page B-3 shows the relationship between the author and Charles (Chuck) D. Thornton Jr. The item on page B – 4 the relationship between the author and Helen Jean Gawthrop. The item on page B – 5 shows the relationship between the author and Rebecca Gawthrop Garrett as well as the relationship between the author and Harold Gene Gawthrop. The item on page B – 6 shows the relationship between the author and John H. Gawthrop and George Gawthrop Jr.

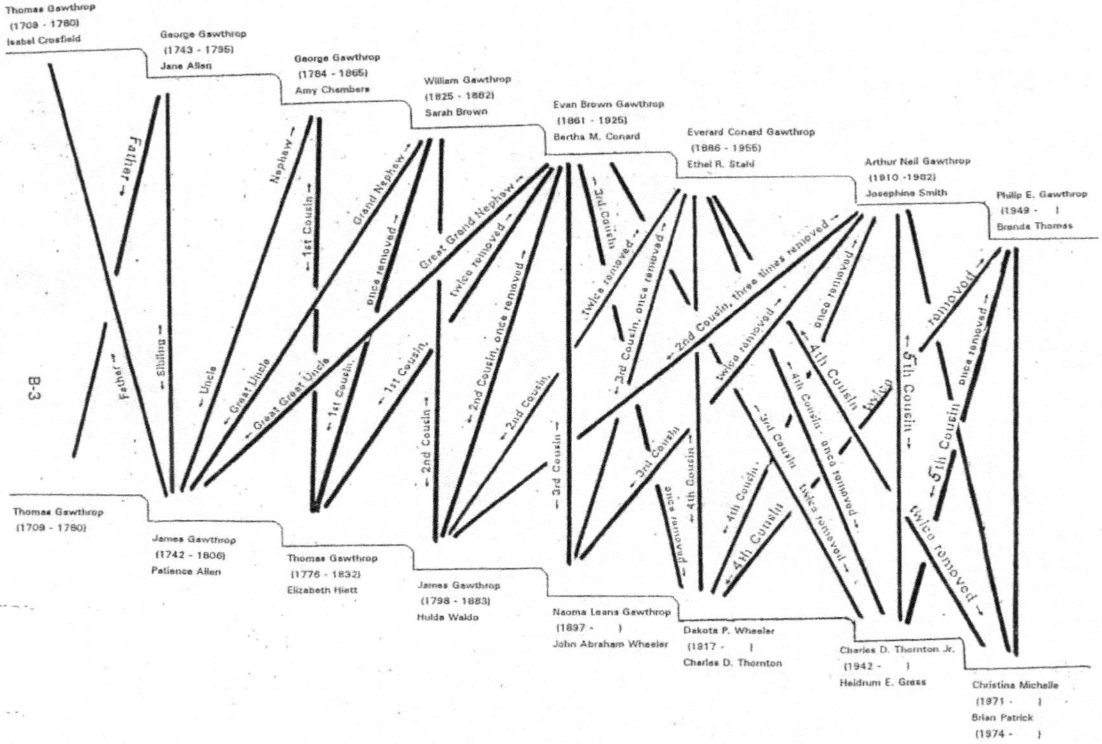
Thomas Gawthrop
(1709 - 1780)
Isabel Crosfield
George Gawthrop
(1743 - 1795)
Jane Allen
George Gawthrop
(1784 - 1865)
Amy Chambers
William Gawthrop
(1825 - 1882)
Sarah Brown
Evan Brown Gawthrop
(1861 - 1925)
Bertha M. Conard
Everard Conard Gawthrop
(1886 - 1955)
Ethel R. Stahl
Arthur Neil Gawthrop
(1910 - 1982)
Josephine Smith
Philip E. Gawthrop
(1949 - )
Brenda Thomas
Thomas Gawthrop
(1709 - 1780)
James Gawthrop
(1742 - 1806)
Patience Allen
Thomas Gawthrop
(1776 - 1832)
Elizabeth Hiett
James Gawthrop
(1798 - 1883)
Hulda Waldo
Naoma Leana Gawthrop
(1897 - )
John Abraham Wheeler
Dakota P. Wheeler
(1917 - )
Charles D. Thornton
Charles D. Thornton Jr.
(1942 - )
Heldrum E. Gress
Christina Michelle
(1971 - )
Brian Patrick
(1974 - )
Father
Father
Sibling
Uncle
Nephew
Great Uncle
Great Great Uncle
1st Cousin
Grand Nephew
1st Cousin
1st Cousin, once removed
1st Cousin
Great Grand Nephew
twice removed
2nd Cousin
2nd Cousin, once removed
2nd Cousin
3rd Cousin
3rd Cousin
twice removed
3rd Cousin, once removed
2nd Cousin, three times removed
twice removed
3rd Cousin
once removed
4th Cousin
3rd Cousin
4th Cousin
4th Cousin
4th Cousin
once removed
4th Cousin - once removed
3rd Cousin twice removed
twice
5th Cousin
removed
once removed
5th Cousin
twice removed

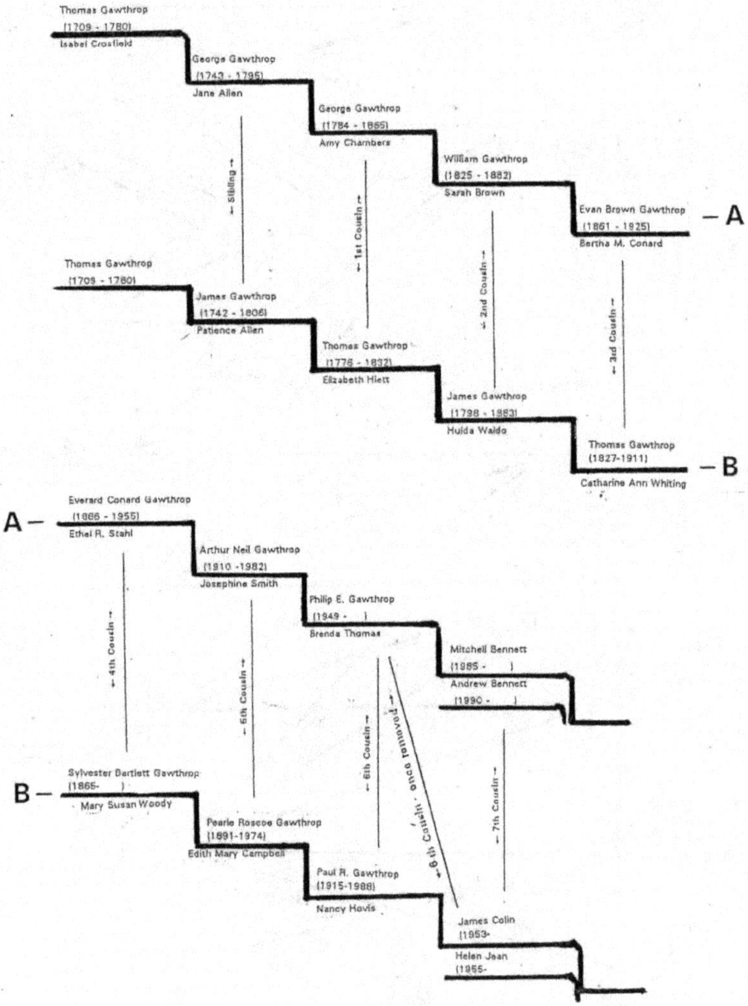
Thomas Gawthrop
(1709 - 1780)
Isabel Crosfield
George Gawthrop
(1743 - 1795)
Jane Allen
George Gawthrop
(1784 - 1865)
Amy Chambers
William Gawthrop
(1825 - 1882)
Sarah Brown
Evan Brown Gawthrop
(1861 - 1925)
Bertha M. Conard
— A
← Sibling →
← 1st Cousin →
← 2nd Cousin →
← 3rd Cousin →
Thomas Gawthrop
(1709 - 1780)
James Gawthrop
(1742 - 1806)
Patience Allen
Thomas Gawthrop
(1776 - 1837)
Elizabeth Hiett
James Gawthrop
(1798 - 1883)
Hulda Waldo
Thomas Gawthrop
(1827-1911)
Catharine Ann Whiting
— B
A —
Everard Conard Gawthrop
(1866 - 1955)
Ethel R. Stahl
Arthur Neil Gawthrop
(1910 -1982)
Josephine Smith
Philip E. Gawthrop
(1949 - )
Brenda Thomas
Mitchell Bennett
(1985 - )
Andrew Bennett
(1990 - )
← 4th Cousin →
← 5th Cousin →
← 6th Cousin →
← 6 th Cousin - once removed →
← 7th Cousin →
B —
Sylvester Bartlett Gawthrop
(1865- )
Mary Susan Woody
Pearle Roscoe Gawthrop
(1891-1974)
Edith Mary Campbell
Paul R. Gawthrop
(1915-1988)
Nancy Hovis
James Colin
(1953-
Helen Jean
(1955-

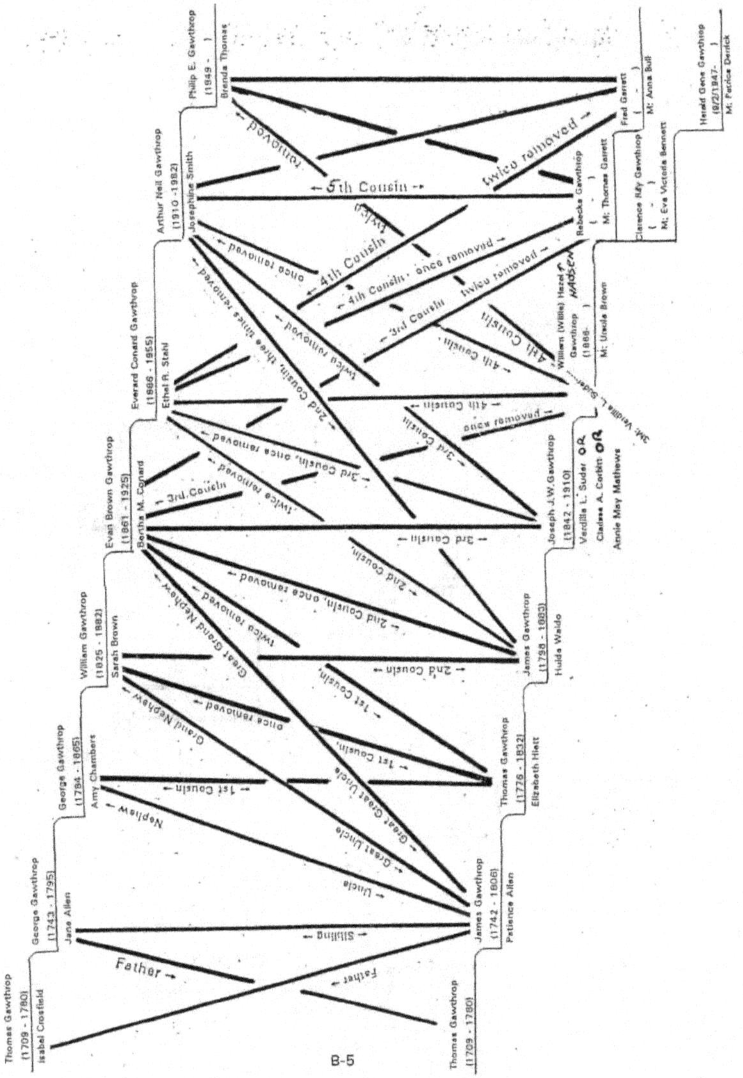
Thomas Gawthrop
(1709 - 1780)
Isabel Crosfield
George Gawthrop
(1743 - 1795)
Jane Allen
George Gawthrop
(1784 - 1865)
Amy Chambers
William Gawthrop
(1825 - 1882)
Sarah Brown
Evan Brown Gawthrop
(1861 - 1925)
Bertha M. Conard
Everard Conard Gawthrop
(1886 - 1955)
Ethel R. Stahl
Arthur Neil Gawthrop
(1910 - 1982)
Josephine Smith
Philip E. Gawthrop
(1949 - )
Brenda Thomas
Thomas Gawthrop
(1709 - 1780)
James Gawthrop
(1742 - 1806)
Patience Allen
Thomas Gawthrop
(1776 - 1832)
Elizabeth Hiett
James Gawthrop
(1798 - 1883)
Hulda Waldo
Joseph J.W. Gawthrop
(1842 - 1910)
Verdilla L. Suder OR
Clarissa A. Corbitt OR
Annie May Mathews
3M. Verdilla L. Suder
William (Willie) Hazel Gawthrop
(1866- )
HANSEN
M: Ursula Brown
Rebecka Gawthrop
( - )
M: Thomas Garrett
Clarence Ray Gawthrop
( - )
M: Eva Victoria Bennett
Fred Garrett
( - )
M: Anna Bull
Harold Gene Gawthrop
(9/2/1947- )
M: Patrice Derrick
Father →
← Father
← Sibling →
← Nephew
← Uncle
← Great Uncle
← Great Great Uncle
← Grand Nephew
← Great Grand Nephew
← 1st Cousin →
← 1st Cousin,
once removed
← 1st Cousin,
← 2nd Cousin →
← 2nd Cousin,
← 2nd Cousin, once removed
← twice removed
← 3rd Cousin →
← 3rd Cousin
← 3rd Cousin, once removed
twice removed
← 2nd Cousin, three times removed
← twice removed
← 4th Cousin →
← 4th Cousin
← 4th Cousin, once removed →
once removed
← 3rd Cousin twice removed →
← 4th Cousin
← 3rd Cousin
once removed
← 5th Cousin →
twice removed →
← removed

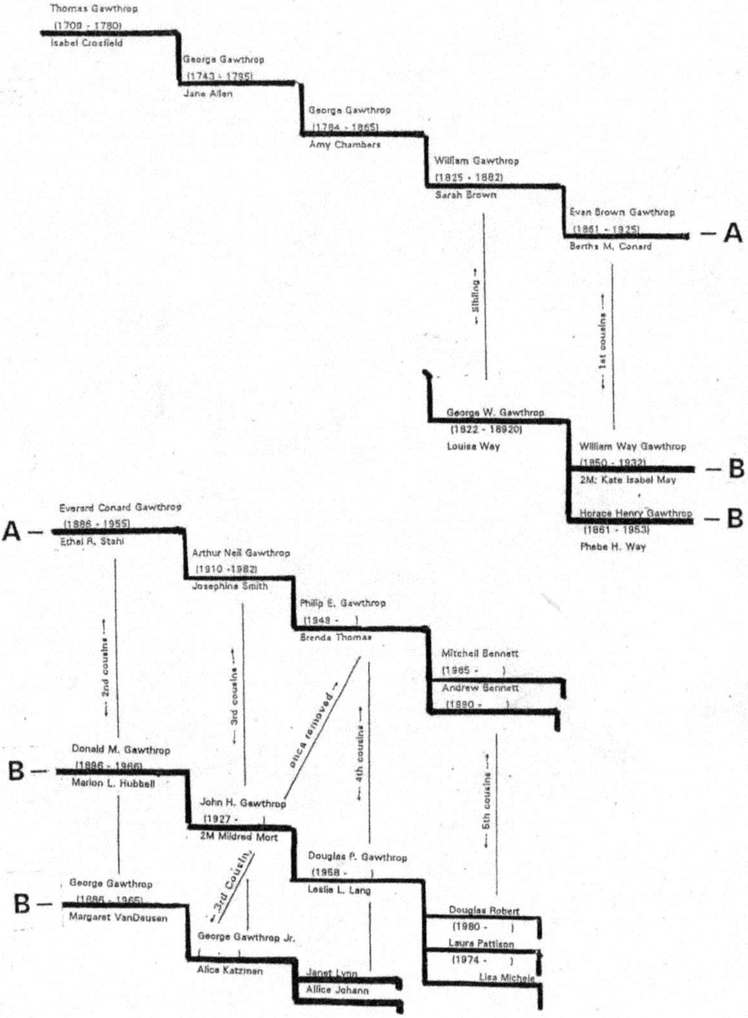

Thomas Gawthrop
(1709 - 1780)
Isabel Crosfield
George Gawthrop
(1743 - 1795)
Jane Allen
George Gawthrop
(1784 - 1865)
Amy Chambers
William Gawthrop
(1825 - 1882)
Sarah Brown
Evan Brown Gawthrop
(1861 - 1925)
Bertha M. Conard
— A
Sibling
1st cousins
George W. Gawthrop
(1822 - 18920)
Louisa Way
William Way Gawthrop
(1850 - 1932)
2M: Kate Isabel May
— B
Horace Henry Gawthrop
(1861 - 1953)
Phebe H. Way
— B
A —
Everard Conard Gawthrop
(1886 - 1955)
Ethel R. Stahl
Arthur Neil Gawthrop
(1910 -1982)
Josephine Smith
Philip E. Gawthrop
(1949 - )
Brenda Thomas
Mitchell Bennett
(1985 - )
Andrew Bennett
(1990 - )
2nd cousins
3rd cousins
once removed
4th cousins
5th cousins
B —
Donald M. Gawthrop
(1896 - 1966)
Marion L. Hubbell
John H. Gawthrop
(1927 - )
2M Mildred Mort
Douglas P. Gawthrop
(1958 - )
Leslie L. Lang
Douglas Robert
(1980 - )
Laura Pattison
(1974 - )
Lisa Michele
B —
George Gawthrop
(1886 - 1965)
Margaret VanDeusen
3rd Cousin
George Gawthrop Jr.
( - )
Alice Katzman
Janet Lynn
Allice Johann

## Appendix C

## James Gawthrop's Family

This appendix contains the James Gawthrop Family Chart (these pages are numbered so that they could be put together in a foldout type chart). The 6th Generation on this chart shows Ann, Thomas, Ruth, Hugh, James, and George Gawthrop, the children of Thomas Gawthrop and Isabel Crosfield. The 7th Generation shows only James Gawthrop and Patience Allen's children: Ester, Thomas, Isabella, James, Edith, Hannah, Rachel, Ruth.

The 8th Generation shows 3 families: **1)** Thomas Gawthrop and Elizabeth Hiett's children: James, Hiett, Evan, John, Thomas, Allen B., Enos D., Sarah, Mary, Elizabeth, Margaret, and Isabella, **2)** Isabella Gathrop and Daniel Wade's children: Daniel, William, James, and Robert, and **3)** Hannah Gawthrop and Jacob Jenkins' children; Jonathan, John, Rachel, Israel, Ruth, Mary, Ann, Asa, Edith, and Hannah.

The 9th Generation shows 9 families: **1)** James Gawthrop and Hulda Waldo's children: Lucinda Ann, Thomas, William G., Elizabeth Peace, Susanna W., Henriette Goff, Sarah Jane, Joseph James Wrightsman, Harrett Tartar, Mary Frances, and Emeline, **2)** Hiett Gawthrop and Mary Pool's children: Richard Hambleton, Hulda, Luina, Phebe, and Sarah Matilde, **3)** John Gawthrop and Josinah Corbin's children: Elizabeth, Henry Haines, Sarah, Thomas Franklin, Salina, Edith Hellen Mary, Oline Arena, and Asa Garnett, **4)** Thomas Gawthrop and Elizabeth Wiseman's children: John Allen, and James Henry, **5)** Allen B. Gawthrop and Elizabeth H. Corder's children: Evan Marshal, Joshua E., Perry, and Thomas, **6)** Enos D. Gawthrop and Ruth Wiseman's children: Mary Jane, Charles F. Elizabeth, and James William, **7)** Mary Gawthrop and Wilson Boyle Brown's children: James Boyle, Virginia Jane, Christopher Columbus, Jonathan Wilson, Elizabeth Ann, George Washington, Mary Bmma, Charles Wesley, **8)** Elizabeth Gawthrop and John Shroyer's children: Jackson, Elizabeth, Louise, C., Irving, Minerva, and John, and **9)** Edith Jenkins and Isaac S. Moore's children: Mariana, Nellie, and John W.

The 10th, 11th, 12th, 13th and 14th Generations show numerious families. Appendix-C \ pages C – 2 through C – 7 can be attached together making up a large pull-out chart. These pages make up the entire James Family as I know it to be.

Thomas Gawthrop (1706-1780) M: Isabel Crosfield

6th Generation | 7th Generation | 8th Generation | 9th Generation | 10th Generation | 11th Generation | 12th Generation | 13th Generation | 14th Generation

- 1. Ann Gawthrop
- 2. Thomas Gawthrop
- 3. Ruth Gawthrop
- 4. Hugh Gawthrop
  - 1. Ester Gawthrop
  - 2. Thomas Gawthrop (1776-1832) M: Elizabeth Hiett (1779-1873)
    - 1. James Gawthrop (1798-1883) M: Hulda Waldo (1804-1894)
      - 1. Lucinda Ann Gawthrop (1825-1915) M: Alpheus Zinn (1818-1876)
        - 1. William Davidson Zinn (BTH: 16 May 1857) M: Florence Swearingen
          - 1. Dorrance Zinn
          - 2. Gay Zinn M: Robert B. Dustman
            - 1. Robert B. Dustman, Jr.
            - 2. Mary Jean Dustman
        - 2. Silvanus Waldo Zinn (BTH: 21 April 1859) M: Lorena H. Harris + + 2M: Mertie Horne
          - 1. Aubrey L. Zinn
          - 2. Rosetta Zinn
          - 3. L. Glen Zinn
          - 4. Bertha Zinn
          - 5. Gladys Zinn
          - 6. Hurley E. Zinn
          - 7. Curtis C. Zinn
          - 8. Carl Zinn
        - 3. Luella Zinn (BTH: 31 March 1861)
        - 4. Claudius Alpheus Zinn (BTH: 15 Feb. 1872)
      - 2. Thomas Gawthrop (1827-1911) 1M: Catharine Whiting (1823-1869)
        - 1. Almira Catharine Gawthrop
        - 2. Adoriam Judson Gawthrop (1852-1912) 1M: unknown 2M: Minerva A. Cooper
          - 1. John Hilbert Gawthrop (1870- )
          - 2. Sylverter Gawthrop (1870s- )
          - 3. Charles Gawthrop (1880- )
        - 3. Mary Frances Gawthrop M: unknown
          - 10 children 5 boys & 5 girls
        - 4. Tammazine Elzine Gawthrop
        - 5. Susannah Peace Gawthrop M: unknown
          - 6 children 3 boys & 3 girls
        - 6. John Albert Gawthrop (1898-1943) 1M: Katie Radabusch 2M: Ida Ervin
          - 1. Rhoda Gawthrop
          - twins
          - 2. Joe Ford Gawthrop (1893- ) M: Iris Clenzing
            - 1. Catherine Gawthrop
            - 2. Helen Gawthrop
            - 3. Lucy Gawthrop
            - 4. Lois Gawthrop
          - 3. John Frank Gawthrop (1893-1964) M: Anna Mary Kessler (1896-1986)
            - 1. Mary Louise Gawthrop M: Gault
            - 2. Martha Jean Gawthrop 1M: Milam 2M: Wilson
            - 3. John Frank Gawthrop Jr. (1922 - )
            - 4. Marjory Lee Gawthrop M: Young
            - 5. Joanne Gawthrop M: Harrison
            - 6. John Daniel Gawthrop (1932 - )
        - 7. Sylvester Bartlett Gawthrop (1865- ) M: Mary Susan Woody
          - 1. Silvanus Edwin Gawthrop (1887- ) M: Mamie McClain
          - 2. Worthy Clay Gawthrop (1889-1890)
          - 3. Edward Gawthrop
          - 4. Pearle Roscoe Gawthrop (1891-1974) M: Edith M. Campbell
            - 1. Paul R. Gawthrop (1915-1988) M: Nancy Harris
              - 1. James Colin Gawthrop (1953-
              - 2. Helen Jean Gawthrop (1955-
          - 5. Hertzel Thomas Gawthrop (1906- )
          - 6. Opal Gawthrop M: Simmons
            - 1. Clarence Simmons M: unknown
              - 1. Mary Margaret Simmons
        - 8.[1.] James Ferell Gawthrop (1871-1881)
        - 2M: Mary C. Chandler (1833-1905)
        - 9.[2.] Elizabeth Tryphane Gawthrop M: unknown
          - 1. girl
          - 2. boy (boy died)
        - 10.[3.] sister, died young
        - 11.[4.] sister, died young
      - 3. William Gifford Gawthrop (1826-1851) M: Mary Whiting
        - two children died as infants
        - 1. Wirt Bartlett
- 5. James Gawthrop (1742-1807) M: Patience Allen (1746- )

- M: J. Edward Law

- 4. Elizabeth Peace Gawthrop (1830-1921)
  - 1M: John W. Bartlett (1821-1865)
    - 3. Elsie Bartlett
    - 4. Florida Bartlett
    - 5. Henry Clay Bartlett (1860- )
    - 6. Rus Bartlett
  - 2M: Pendleton Drummond (1829-1902)
    - 1. (twin) Lee Drummond (1871- )
    - 2. (twin) Cora Drummond (1871- )
      - M: Floyd Frame
    - 3. Arthur Drummond (1873- )
- 5. Susanna W. Gawthrop (1833- )
  - M: Hamsdell Bartlett
- 6. Henrietta Goff Gawthrop (1833-1873)
  - M: Elias Martin Sapp
    - 1. Sophroia Ellen Sapp (1853- )
    - 2. DeBlanca Sapp (1863- )
- 7. Sarah Jane Gawthrop (1836-1838)
- 8. Joseph James Wrightsman Gawthrop (1842-1910)
  - 1M: Clarissa A. Corbitt (1845-1867)
    - 1. Joseph Waldo Antoine Elias Gawthrop (1862-1870)
    - 2. William (Willie) Hazel Hadsen Gawthrop (1866- )
      - M: Ursula Brown (1882-1955)
        - 1. Clarence Ray Gawthrop (1911-1993)
          - 2M: Eva Victoria Bennett (1913-
            - 1. Herald Gene Gawthrop (BTH: 2 Sept.1947-
              - M: Patrica Derrick (1948-
                - 1. Amy Victoria Gawthrop (BTH: 31 Jan.1877-
                - 2. Samuel Reese Gawthrop (BTH: 8 May 1982-
            - 2. Gerald Dean Gawthrop (BTH: 2 Sept.1947-
              - M: Betty V. Wray (1940-
            - 3. Rita Kaye Gawthrop (BTH: 25 Oct.1948-
              - 1M: Fred Ammon Fry
                - 1. Melanie Fry (Evans)
              - 2M: Kenneth Gail Evans
                - 1. Lena Gail Evans
                  - M: George Forest Hill
                    - 1. Heather Lyn Hill
                - 2. Margaret Ann Evans
                - 3. Mary Alice Evans
                  - M: Eric Dean Cook
            - 4. Allen Ray Gawthrop (2 Jan.1954-
              - M: Cathy Hackworth
                - 1. Allison Gawthrop
                - 2. Alex Gawthrop (1986 - )
                - 3. Jennifer Gawthrop
        - 2. Rebecka Gawthrop (1916-
          - M: Thomas F. Garrett (1914-1986)
            - 1. Thomas Frederick Garrett (1938-
              - M: Anna Bull (1936-
                - 1. Terri R. Garrett
                  - 1M: Kenneth Bridges
                    - 1. Garrett Ray Bridges
                    - 2. Justin Bridges
                  - 2M: Rob Aikman
                    - 3. Jordan Brooke Aikman
            - 1st Foster child: Gaye (Jones) Lucas
              - M: Delmus R. Lucas
                - 1. Branden J. Lucas
                - 2. Heather Lynn Lucas
            - 2nd Foster child: Sandra Reeder
              - M: 2 times—5 boys, 3 Grandchildren
  - 2M: Annie May Mathews (1848-1888)
    - 1. Hulda Mary Gawthrop (1869- )
    - 2. Annie Lonia Gawthrop (1872- )
    - 3. Hattie Theodocia Emistan Gawthrop (1873-1877)
    - 4. Myrtis Annetta Gawthrop (1877-1877)
    - 5. Thomas Eddie Gawthrop (1880- )
  - 3M: Verdilla L. Suder (1860-1951)
    - 1. Ida Florence Gawthrop (1888-1970)
      - M: John McCray (1876-1954)
    - 2. Minnie Loretta Gawthrop (1891-1953)
      - M: Emory Moore Anderson
        - 1. Jackson Moore Andreson (1913- )
          - 1M: Frances Williams
            - 1. Richard W. Anderson
              - M: Carole (n/n)
                - 1. Bradley Jackson Anderson
                - 2. Daniel Jason Anderson
                - 3. David Joseph Anderson
            - 2. David Anderson
            - 3. Linda Anderson
          - 2M: Dorothy Mae Allan
        - 2. Mary Margaret Anderson
        - 3. Joseph Gawthrop Anderson
          - 1M: Yovonne Bennett
          - 2M: Maris (n/n)
            - 1. Dennis Anderson
    - 3. Oliver Cordelia Gawthrop (1894-1975)
      - M: John William Carr (1874-1962)
        - 1. John William Carr Jr. (1915- )
          - M: Virginia Dean
            - 1. Betty May Carr
            - 2. John William Carr III
    - 4. Naoma Leana Gawthrop (1897-1993)
      - M: John Abraham Wheeler (1890-1979)
        - 1. Dakota Pead Wheeler (1917- )
          - M: Charles D. Thornton (1913-1983)
            - 1. Dakota D. Thornton
              - 1M: David F. Sutter
                - 1. Monica Jenean Sutter
                  - M: Frederick Hoeffler
                - 2. Jon Paul Sutter
                - 3. Kevin Richard Sutter
              - 2M: Richard W. Watkins
            - 2. Charles D. Thornton Jr. (1942- )
              - M: Heidrum E. Gress
                - 1. Christina Michelle Thornton (1971- )
                - 2. Brian Patrick Thornton (1974- )
            - 3. Constance D. Thornton
              - M: Edward J. Frautschi
                - 1. Heather K. Frautschi
                - 2. Christopher E. Frautschi
                - 3. Stephanie L. Frautschi
            - 4. Janice C. Thornton
              - M: Richard K. Olsen
                - 1. Kristen L. Olsen
            - 5. Holly V. Thornton
    - 5. Joseph James Waldo Gawthrop

(1899-1919) | 1M: Richard J. Shapiro | 1. Amanda L. Altieri
Died in train yard/was crushed | 2M: Arthur J. Altieri
2. Richel N. Altieri
1. John David Wheeler
2. John Abraham Wheeler Jr. | 3M: Sue Ann | 1. Shane Wheeler
M: Doris M. Evans
2. Mary Jene Wheeler
9. Harrett Tarar Gawthrop | M: Kenneth Husby | 1. Kenneth John Husby
(1844-1863) | 1. Lily Sears
M: Israel Sears | (1861-1871)
(1835-1900) | (trampled by horse) | 1. Louis Gorard Wheeler
3. Harry Edward Wheeler | 2. Lori Wheeler
1. Orliana Alice Proddfoot | 1M: Dolores Fronhert | 3. Hilary Eilene Wheeler
10. Mary Frances T.V. | (1866- ) | + | 4. Tad Kenyon Wheeler
(1847-1931) | 2. Ethel May Proddfoot | 2M: Dorothy Beason | 5. Rod Hilton Wheeler
1M: Gileon Proddfoot | (1869- ) | 4. Janet La Rue Wheeler | 1. Herman George Cratty Jr.
+ (1847-1872) | 3. William Albert Proddfoot | M: Herman George Cratty | 2. Kelly Cratty
+ | (1871- ) | 3. Sally Gail Cratty
+ | 1. Mary Ann Willet | 4. Jill Cratty
+ | (1875- )
+ | 2. Robert Martin Willet
+ | (1877- )
2M: Issac Willet | 3. Homer Lee Willet
(1856-1931) | (1878- )
4. Edith Emoline Willet
11. Emmaline Gawthrop | (1880- )
(1848- )
1M: Wilson G. Reger | 1. Waldo Reger
+ (1845-1875) | (1868- )
+ | 1. Rosa J. Wood
+ | (1880- )
+ | 2. French A. Wood
2M: Joshua Wood | (1881- )
+ (1825- ) | 3. Herbert E. Wood
+ | (1883- )
3M: J.J. Jenkins | 1. Mary
1. Richard Hambleton | 2. Rosella
Gawthrop | 3. Ashford Melville Gawthrop
M: unknown | (1878- ) | 1. Eslie Gerald Gawthrop
M: Docia Phillips | (1908-1975)
2. Hulda Gawthrop | 4. Howard Gawthrop
3. Lurina Gawthrop | (1880- )
(five other children, all died young)
2. Hiet Gawthrop | 4. Phebe Catharine Gawthrop | 1. Elizabeth Kinsey
(1807- ) | M: John R. Kinsey | 2. Charles Lee Kinsey
M: Mary Pool | 5. Sarah Matilda Gawthrop | 3. Mary L. Kinsey
(1805- ) | M: Wm.Montgomery | 1. Ida Lee Dadisman
Dadisman
6.George Gawthrop | 2. James W. Dadisman
(1743-1795) | 1. Joseph M. Shinn
M:Jane Allen | 3. Evan Gawthrop | 1. Elizabeth Gawthrop | M: Ellen Short | 1. Fred Shinn
(1810- ) | (1826-1910)
M: Abel W. Shinn | 2. Annetta Shinn | 1. Gertrude Morgan
(1828-1888) | M: D.P.Morgan | 2. Charles Morgan
2. Henry Haines Gawthrop | 3. John Allen Shinn | 3. Beulah Morgan
4. John Gawthrop | (1828- ) | 4. Dora Shinn | 4. Harold Morgan
(1803-1881) | 3. Sarah Gawthrop | 5. Ashby Shinn
M: Josinah Corbin | (1831- ) | 6. Edger Shinn | 1. Blanch Shinn
( -1869) | 4. Thomas Franklin Gawthrop | M: unknown | 2. Mary Shinn
(1834- ) | 3. Paul Shinn
(child 2, 3, & 4 above | 7. Ella May Shinn | 1. Carrol Lowe
died of Scarlet Fever) | M: Charles Lowe | 2. Mable Lowe
1. Lidy Graig | 1. Katharine Dudley
5. Salina Gawthrop | M: Edward Dudley
(1837-1907) | 2. Edward Dudley Jr.
M: John L. Craig
6. Edith Hellen Mary Gawthrop | 2. Charles Craig | 1. Naomi Craig
(1839-1916) | M: Byrd Chamberlia | 2. Ruth Graig
M: B.H. Cook | 3. Charles Craig Jr.
7. Olina Arena Gawthrop | 1. Walter Willis | 1. Robert Willis
(1844-1924) | M: Bertha Orr
M: J.H. Willis | 2. Carsen Willis | 2. Virginia Willis
M: Hazel Sandusky
1. John Lowe Gawthrop | 1. Claude Garnett Gawthrop Jr. | 1. Rapp Wilson Gawthrop
(1877-1921) | (1908- ) | (1947-
M: Flora Harvey | M: Lillian Cook | 2. Dana Ray Gawthrop
2. Claude G. Gawthrop | (1951-
8. Asa Garnett | (1879-1951) | 2. Carol Burr Gawthrop

(1853-1932)

- 3. Dana Holland Gawthrop (1881-1954) M: Florida Corpering (1882-1971) LD: Clarksburg, WV
  - (1922- )
  - 1. Robert Earl Gawthrop (1902-1970) 1M: Margaret Dills 2M: Margaret Walker
  - 2. Paul Holland Gawthrop (1903-1958) M: Lillian Poling (1902-
    - 1. Barbara D. Gawthrop (1929- M: Herbert Hinkle (1925-
      - 1. Cynthia Hinkle (1953- M: D. Thornbury
      - 2. Laura Hinkle (1954- M: Ed Chenault
    - 2. Paul H. Gawthrop Jr. (1930- M: Lucille M. Hebb (1932-
      - 1. Shin Gawthrop (1960-
      - 2. David Gawthrop (1963- M: Mary Elizabeth Noblit
- 4. Perry Cleveland Gawthrop (1884-1968) M: Nocal Lake (1899-1974)
  - 1. Edward L. Gawthrop (1922- ) 1M: Betty Hawkins 2M: Martha Kyle Sayres
- 5. Robert Murray Gawthrop (1886-1983) M: Pearl Mason ( -1978)
- 6. Ray Bright Gawthrop (1888-1976) M: Lena Linn ( -1981)
  - 1. Asa David Gawthrop (1923- ) M: Betty Yocco LD: Bridgeport, WV
    - 1. Karen Lynn Gawthrop BTH: 14 April 1949
    - 2. Asa Ray Gawthrop BTH: 13 July 1954
  - 2. Ruth Gawthrop M: Leon Davis
    - 1. Jay Bee Davis (1958-
    - 2. John Neil Davis (1959-

- 6. Thomas Gawthrop (1806-1876) M: Elizabeth Wiseman (1811- )
  - 1. John Allen Gawthrop (1832-1919) M: Martha E. Knight (1839-1913)
    - 1. James C. Gawthrop (1856-1913) M: Margaret Thompson (1859- )
      - 1. Carr Gawthrop (1883-1967) M: Della Mae Loughery (1942-
        - 1. Ezra Roy Gawthrop (1904- M: Wilma Helmick
          - 1. Thomas Carr Gawthrop (1938-1966) M: Elnora Rose Clark
            - 1. Deborah Elaine Gawthrop (1964-
          - 2. Patty M. (1939- M: Blaine Crutis Campbell
            - 1. Belinda Kay Campbell twin (1963-
            - 2. Blaine C. Campbell II twin (1963-
          - 3. Abraham C. Gawthrop (1943- M: Nancy (Huet) McNeere
            - 1. James Gawthrop# (1959-
            - 2. Philip Gawthrop# (1961-
            - 3. Timothy Gawthrop (1970- [# children adopted]
          - 4. Joyce Della (1945- M: Eugene Wright
            - 1. Terri Wright (1972-
        - 2. Wilford Gawthrop (1906-1978) M: Mual Davisson (1910-
          - 1. Darrell W. Gawthrop (****- M: Jean Clevenger
            - 1. David Gawthrop (****- M: Genine Hickman
        - 3. Wilbur E. Gawthrop (1910-1980) M: Mary V. Merrifield (1922-
          - 1. Richard Carr Gawthrop (1948- M: Linda Ann Miller
            - 1. Richard Carr Gawthrop II (1983-
            - 2. Kevin Clark Gawthrop (1987-
        - 4. Robert Gawthrop (1917- M: Edith Bailey
          - 1. David Gawthrop (****- M: unknown
            - 1. Dawneda Pierce Gawthrop
            - 2. Leslie Gross Gawthrop
          - 2. Steven Gawthrop (****- M: unknown
            - 1. Matthew Gawthrop
            - 2. Rita Gawthrop
            - 3. Tracy Gawthrop
          - 3. Douglass Gawthrop (****- M: unknown
            - 1. Brain Gawthrop
          - 4. Rebecca Gawthrop (****-
      - 2. Ralph A. Gawthrop (1886- ) M: Zelma M. Robinson (1890-1980)
        - 1. Virginia Dare (1914-1991)
        - 2. Vevia Wyla Gawthrop (1916-
        - 3. Wilson Robinson Gawthrop (1924- M: Ida P. Summerlin
          - 1. Wilson R. Gawthrop Jr. (1951-
          - 2. Cheryl Norman Gawthrop (1954-
          - 3. Vance Allen Gawthrop (1958-
          - 4. Paula Robin Gawthrop (1963-
      - 3. Bertha Gawthrop (1887- ) M: Richard L. Markall
        - 1. Phyllis Markall (1912-
        - 2. Lucile Markall (****-
        - 3. Wayne Markall (1914-
      - 4. Ray Gawthrop (1889-1970) M: Maud Means
        - 1. Hellen Ruth Gawthrop (1914-
      - 5. Nellie Gawthrop (1897- )
    - 2. Burrell Lee Gawthrop (1862- ) M: Nannet Heflin
      - 1. Susan Elen Gawthrop M: L.D.Jackson
      - 2. Anna Lee Gawthrop
      - 3. William Gawthrop (1898-1902)
    - 3. Charles Seeber Gawthrop (1865- )
      - 1. Charles W. Gawthrop

- M: Edna E. Yates — (1914-

- 2. James Henry Gawthrop (1834-1890)
  M: Virginia Rector
  - 1. Cora E. Gawthrop (1865- )
  - 2. Lula Gawthrop (1873-1930\39)
  - 3. John Thomas Gawthrop (1881- )
    M: unknown
    - 1. Frank Edward Gawthrop (1906-
    - 2. Paul Ray Gawthrop (1909-
    - 3. John Earl Gawthrop (1914-
    - 4. Margaret Virginia Gawthrop (1917-1981)

- 6. Allen B. Gawthrop (1808-1887)
  M: Elizabeth H. Corder (1812-1888)
  - 1. Evan Marshal Gawthrop (1838-1922)
    M: Nancy Hustead (1854-1934)
    - 1. Allen Delbert Gawthrop (1870-1953)
      M: Fannie Holt (1875-1963)
      - 1. Garland G. Gawthrop (1896-1983)
        M: Susie Hustead (1903- )
        - 1. Eva Marie Gawthrop (1921-
          M: Arthur Currey
          - 1. Karen Marie Currey (1944-
            M: James Wase (1968-
            - 1. Shawn Wase (1971-
        - 2. Alice Jean Gawthrop (1929-
          M: Warren McVicker
          - 1. David McVicker (1955-
          - 2. Nancy Ann McVicker (1958-
        - 3. Hazel Joan Gawthrop (1932-
          M: Charles N. Patterson (1930-
          DIVO: 17 March 1977
          - 1. Charles Allen Patterson (1953-
          - 2. Pamela Ray Patterson (1954-
          - 3. Brenda Lea Patterson
        - 4. Robert Lee Gawthrop (1934-
          M: Camilla Tucker (1935-
          - 1. Randall Lee Gawthrop (1963-
            M: Rebcca Costilow
          - 2. Rodney Allen Gawthrop (1969-
            M: Carla D. Westerman
        - 5. Patricia Sue Gawthrop (1949-
          M: Dale Boyle (1940-
          - 1. Chad Chistopher Boyle (1972-
      - 2. Cecil M. Gawthrop (1898-1975)
        1M: Nora McElfresh (1900-1935)
        - 1. Carl H. Gawthrop (1923-
          M: Geraldine Spragg
          - 1. David Carl Gawthrop (1953-
          - 2. Denise Gawthrop (1955-
            M: Martin Shaw
            - 1. Allison Beth Shaw (1982- )
            - 2. Aaron Michael Shaw (1984- )
          - 3. Paul Richard Gawthrop (1958-
            M: Sue Ellen Simons
            - 1. Erica Leigh Gawthrop (1984- )
            - 2. Megan Elizabeth Gawthrop (1991- )
          - 4. Linda Gawthrop (1959-
        - 2. Clyde Lee Gawthrop (1925-1926)
        - 3. Mary Lou Gawthrop (1935-1935)

        2M: Bertha Simpson (1919-
        - 1. Bonnie June Gawthrop (1937-
          M: Frances Plymale (1935-
          - 1. Terry Lee Plymale (1959-
          - 2. Mark Allen Plymale (1963-
          - 3. Debra Kay Plymale (1969-
    - 2. George Wesley Gawthrop (1873-1952)
      M: May Newlan (1877-1941)
      - 1. Deway Ray Gawthrop (1898-1964) unmarried
      - 2. Evan M. Gawthrop (1901-1976) unmarried
      - 3. George Ottis Gawthrop (1905-1985)
        M: Alta Lillian Lawler (1908-
        - 1. Carylon Cathelean Gawthrop (1935-
          M: Clarence N. Leggett
          - 1. Shayne M. Leggett (1957-
          - 2. Craig N. Leggett (1963-
          - 3. Kimberly Lynne Leggett (1964-
        - 2. Cleota June Gawthrop (1938-
        - 3. George Otis Gawthrop Jr. (1943-
      - 4. Ada J. Gawthrop (1908-
        M: John W. Peters (1905-
        - 1. John J. Peters (1928-
          M: Virginia Cobb (@ Detroit)
        - 2. James F. Peters (1934-
          M: Ida MacDriver (@ Detroit)
        - 3. George R. Peters (1936-
          M: Linda Louise Manear (GraftonWV)
      - 5. Paul Newlan Gawthrop (1913-1964)
        M: Juanita Mea Weaver (1914-1976)
        - 1. Paul N. Gawthrop Jr. (1938-1984)
        - 2. George L. Gawthrop (1939-
        - 3. Sharon Gawthrop
  - 2. Joshua E. Gawthrop (1841-1918)

- 3. Laura Gawthrop (1877-1964)
  M: Asby Steel Law (1869-1935)
  - (1900-1961)
    1M: Hilda K. Freymeyar
    +
    2M: Sally Duff
    - 1. Frank Steel Law (1933-
      M: Tanya L. Von Bergen
      - (1958-
      - 2. Doretta Ann Law (1959-
      - 3. Bryan Steal Law (1960-
  - 2. Rosale Marie Law (1901-
    M: Raymond Otis Pettigrew
    - 1. Jean Marie Pettigrew (1939-
    - 2. Sally Louise Pettigrew

- 3. Perry Gawthrop (1843-1919)
  M: Eliya Woodyard (1844-1888)
  - 1. Clarence Gawthrop (1875-1913)
  - 2. Bertha Gawthrop (1875-1957)
    M: D.P. Logan
    - 1.twin: James Logan (1914-
    - 2.twin: Charles W. Logan (1914-
- 4. Thomas Gawthrop (1847-1927)

- 7. Enos D. Gawthrop (1810-1843)
  M: Ruth Wiseman
  - 1. Mary Jane Gawthrop (1833- )
    M: John Shriyer
  - 2. Charles F. Gawthrop (1836-1859)
  - 3. Elizabeth Gawthrop (1838- )
    M: Willis Herren
  - 4. James William Gawthrop (1843- )
    M: Mary Reger (1844-1870)
    - 1. Ola Gawthrop (1868-1869)
- 8. Sarah Gawthrop (1812-1881)
- 9. Mary Gawthrop (1815-1902)
  M: Wilson Boyle Brown (1818-1898)
  - 1. James Boyle Brown (1841-1907)
  - 2. Virginia Jane Brown
  - 3. Christopher Columbus Brown
  - 4. Jonathan Wilson Brown
  - 5. Elizabeth Ann Brown
  - 6. George Washington Brown
  - 7. Mary Emma Brown
  - 8. Charles Wesley Brown
- 10. Elizabeth Gawthrop (1813- )
  M: John Shroyer
  - 1. Jackson Shroyer
  - 2. Elizabeth Shroyer
  - 3. Louise M. Shroyer
  - 4. C. Shroyer
  - 5. Irving Shroyer
  - 6. Minarva Shroyer
  - 7. John W. Shroyer
- 11. Margaret Gawthrop
- 12. Isabella Gawthrop

- 3. Isabella Gawthrop (1778- )
  M: Daniel Wade
  - 1. Daniel Wade
  - 2. William Wade
  - 3. James Wade
  - 4. Robert Wade
- 4. James Gawthrop Jr. (1781- )
- 5. Hannah Gawthrop
  M: Jacob Jenkins
  - 1. Jonathan Jenkins
  - 2. John Jenkins
    M: Frances Smith
  - 3. Rachel Jenkins
    M: Nathan Bean
  - 4. Israel Jenkins
  - 5. Ruth Jenkins
    M: William Harlan
  - 6. Mary Jenkins
    M: Jonathan Bailey
  - 7. Ann Jenkins
  - 8. Asa Jenkins
    M: Amelia Haworth
  - 9. Edith Jenkins
    M: Isaac S. Morris
    - 1. Mariana Morris
      M: George A. Brooks
    - 2. Nellie Morris
    - 3. John W. Morris
      M: Anna Strumm
  - 10. Hannah Jenkins
    M: Lindley Wright
- twins: 6 & 7
- 6. Edith Gawthrop (1783- )
  M: Mr. Taylor
- 7. Rachel Gawthrop (1783- )
  M: Mr. Davis
- 8. Ruth Gawthrop (1791- )

## Appendix D

### George Gawthrop's Family

This appendix contains the George Gawthrop Family Chart (these pages are numbered so that they could be put together in a foldout type chart). The 6th Generation on this chart shows Ann, Thomas, Ruth, Hugh, James, and George Gawthrop, the children of Thomas Gawthrop and Isabel Crosfield. The 7th Generation shows only George Gawthrop and Jane Allen's children. Those children are: Thomas, Hannah, Isabella, James, George, Jane, William, Allen, and Elizabeth.

The 8th Generation shows 5 families: **1)** Thomas Gawthrop and Elizabeth Thompson's children: Sarah, Ann, Daniel, Jane, Allen, Lydia, Elizabeth, and James T. **2)** Hannah Gawthrop and Smithin Shortledge's children: George, Phebe, Jane, Annie, Joel, William, Evan, and Smthin **3)** James Gawthrop and Hannah Marshall's children: Mary, Jane, George, Rachel, Hannah, and James **4)** George Gawthrop and Amy Chambers' children: Ruth, Joseph C., Thomas, Elizabeth, George W., Evan, William, and Jessie **5)** William Gawthrop and Mary Griffith's children: Rachel M., Jane, and Thomas T.

The 9th, 10th, 11th, 12th, 13th, and 14th Generations show numerious families. Appendix – D \ pages D – 2 through D – 6 can be attached together making up a large pull-out chart. These pages make up the entire George Gawthrop Family as I know it to be.

6th Generation | 7th Generation | 8th Generation | 9th Generation | 10th Generation | 11th Generation | 12th Generation | 13th Generation | 14th Generation

Thomas Gawthrop (1708-1780) M: Isabel Crosfield

- 1. Ann Gawthrop (1736- )
- 2. Thomas Gawthrop (1737- )
- 3. Ruth Gawthrop (1739-1813)
- 4. Hugh Gawthrop (1741-1773)
- 5. James Gawthrop (1742-1806) M: Patience Allen
  - 1. Thomas Gawthrop (1774-1851) M: Elizabeth Thompson (1779-1864)
    - 1. Sarah Gawthrop (1801-1887) M: Joseph Seal (1788-1842)
      - 1. Thomas G. Seal (1824- ) M: Hannah Walker
        - 1. Edith Seal M: H. Thompson
        - 2. Eliza Seal
        - 3. Joseph Seal
        - 4. Mary T. Seal
        - 5. Sallie Seal
      - 2. Rachel Seal M: Joel Swayne
        - 1. George A. Swayne
        - 2. William S. Swayne
        - 3. Joseph Swayne
      - 3. William Seal M: Jane Hall
        - 1. Sallie G. Seal
        - 2. Thomas H. Seal
      - 4. Eliza Seal M: Eli Yarnall
      - 5. Sarah Ann Seal M: Thomas Bullock
        - 1. Sallie Bullock
        - 2. T. Ellsworth Bullock
      - 6. Phebe Seal M: Jackson Bailey
        - 1. Edgar R. Bailey
        - 2. Elizabeth R. Bailey
        - 3. Joseph S. Bailey
      - 7. Mary Jane Seal M: Joshua McCullough
        - 1. Robert McCullough
        - 2. Ann McCullough
        - 3. M. Ann McCullough
      - 8. Joel A. Seal M: Emilie Thompson
      - 9. Joseph Gilpin Seal M: Sarah Hall
    - 2. Ann Gawthrop (1803-1857)
    - 3. Daniel Gawthrop (1805-1838) M: Elizabeth Mitchell (1810-1838)
      - 1. Sarah M. Gawthrop (1831- ) M: William Henry Way (1829-1910)
        - 1. J. Allen Way
        - 2. Elizabeth (Lizie) Way
        - 3. Charles Way
        - 4. Amy A. Way
      - 2. Lydia Ann Gawthrop
      - 3. Amy Gawthrop M: Alexander Turner
      - 4. Emmor D. Gawthrop (1837-1920) M: Phebe Thompson
    - 4. Jane Gawthrop (1807-1837) M: Hibbard Moore (1806- )
      - 1. Gilpin Moore M: Ludisa Carswell
        - 1. Trusedale Moore
        - 2. Charles Moore
        - 3. Adda Moore
    - 5. Allen Gawthrop (1810-1885) M: Mary Ann Newlin (1811-1882)
      - 1. Joseph Newlin Gawthrop (1835-1916) M: Esther Good (1837-1884)
        - 1. Edith Newlin Gawthrop
        - 2. Annie Gawthrop
        - 3. Mary Gawthrop
        - 4. Emma Gawthrop M: J. Russel Hayes
        - 5. Frederic Herman Gawthrop (1874- ) M: Mary Amelia Hayes ( - )
          - 1. Helen Gawthrop (1900- )
          - 2. Rachel Hayes Gawthrop (1910- )
        - 6. Henry Albana Gawthrop (1877-1939)
        - 7. Joseph Newlin Gawthrop Jr. (1881-1934) M: Rebecca A.
      - 2. Emma Gawthrop M: Evans Pennington
        - 1. Henry Pennington
        - 2. Frank Pennington
        - 3. Harvey Pennington
      - 3. Alfred Gawthrop (1839- ) M: Hannah J. Stroud
        - 1. William Jones Gawthrop (1867- ) M: unknown
          - 1. Donald Gawthrop living someplace in Florida
        - 2. Charles L. Gawthrop (1868-1924) M: Mabel Jackson
          - 1. Lucy Ross
          - 2. Mary Cary Kent
          - 3. Hannah
        - 3. Elizabeth S. Gawthrop (1870- )
- 6. George Gawthrop (1743-1795) M: Jane Allen (1753-1821)

- 6. Lydia Gawthrop (1813-1842)
- 7. Elizabeth Gawthrop (1815-1819)
- 8. James T. Gawthrop (1819-1889)
  M: Priscilla Peirce (1823-1860)
    - 1. Lucy, died young (CIRCA 1856-1862)
    - 2. Ella, died young (CIRCA 1858-1859)

- 4. Henry Gawthrop (1841-1920)
  M: Mary L. Thompson
- 5. Allen Gawthrop Jr. (1843-1919)
- 6. Edith Newlin Gawthrop

- M: Frederick Genung ( - )
    - ( - )
- 5. Alfred H. Gawthrop (1881-1937)
  M: Arabela Fauntleroy McGill (1884- )
    - 1. Elizabeth Randolph Gawthrop (Didi) (1916 -
      1M: Henry M. Canby (Hank) + (1910-
      +
      2M: Henry T. Bush - (1911-
        - 1. Elizabeth F. Canby (Lisa) (1940 -
          1M: Thomas L. Pulling + (1939-
          2M: Robert Sample (1936-
            - 1. Elizabeth F. Pulling (Wendy) (1963 -
            - 2. Edward L. Pulling (Teddy) (1966 -
        - 2. Marjorie Buch Canby (1942 -
          M: Hubert E. Pepin (1940-
            - 1. Henry C. Pepin (1968 -
            - 2. Isabella C. Pepin (1970 -
        - 3. Sheila R. Canby (1949 -
          M: John C. Voss (1948-
            - 1. Tobias V.H. Voss (1985 -
    - 2. Alfred H. Gawthrop Jr. (1919-
    - 3. Samuel McGill Gawthrop (1916-
      M: Helen Lloyd Kitchel (1922-
        - 1. Samuel McGill Gawthrop Jr. (1943-
          M: Jaquilyn Smyth (1943-
            - 1. Elizabeth Renwich Gawthrop (1968-
            - 2. Samuel McGill Gawthrop III (1971-
        - 2. Ann Randolph Gawthrop (1946-
          M: Harold M. Sawyer Jr.
            - 1. Ann Randolph Sawyer
            - 2. Amy Greenwood Sawyer
            - 3. Harold Murray Sawyer III
        - 3. Lloyd Kitchel Gawthrop (1948-
        - 4. Charles Stroud Gawthrop (1950-
          M: Carol Ann Decker (1971-
            - 1. Charles Stroud Gawthrop Jr. (1978-
            - 2. Gail Marie Gawthrop (1981-
        - 5. Emily Weeks Gawthrop (1952-
          M: George Elton Walls
            - 1. James McGill Walls (1979-
            - 2. Emily Christina Walls (1981-
        - 6. James Newlin Gawthrop (1957-
          M: Ann Darickson Benzel (1959-
            - 1. James Newlin Gawthrop Jr. (1986-
            - 2. Brian Winslow Gawthrop (1988-

2. Hannah Gawthrop (1776- )
M: Smithin Shortledge (1772-1822)

- 1. George Shortledge
  M: Martha Hutton
    - 1. William Shortledge
      M: R.G. Caimont
        - 1. James W. Shortledge
        - 2. Martha E. Shortledge
        - 3. Ann W. Shortledge
        - 4. George Shortledge
        - 5. Jane M. Shortledge
    - 2. Joseph Shortledge
      M: Carrie R. Gause
        - 1. Marrien Shortledge
        - 2. Charles D. Shortledge
    - 3. Anna Shortledge
      M: William Walker
        - 1. Edith W. Walker
        - 2. Joseph E. Walker
        - 3. Phebe H. Walker
        - 4. John W. Walker
        - 5. Julieu Walker
        - 6. William S. Walker
    - 4. Lydia Shortledge
      M: Augustus C. Norris
        - 1. Pierce Norris
        - 2. Caroline Norris
        - 3. Hershel Norris
    - 5. Smithin Shortledge
      M: Jane Johnson
    - 6. Evan G. Shortledge
      M: L.A. Douglas
- 2. Phebe Shortledge
  M: Jacob Shortledge
  (no records of children)
- 3. Jane Shortledge
  M: Isaac Tussey
    - 1. Hannah E. Tussey
      M: Fenelon Darlington
        - 1. Lucey Darlington
        - 2. Jennie Darlington
        - 3. Whitier Darlington
        - 4. Annie Darlington
        - 5. Emlin Darlington
    - 2. Catherine Tussey
      M: Courtland Michener
        - 1. Laura R. Michener
        - 2. Isaac W. Michener
        - 3. Jesse L. Michener
        - 4. Morris Michener
    - 3. Sarah Tussey
    - 4. William Tussey
      M: Martha Martin
    - 5. Phebe Tussey
- 4. Annie Shortledge
- 5. Joel Shortledge
  M: Sarah Ann Boyer
    - 1. Harriet E. Shortledge
      M: E. Miller
        - 1. Annie Miller
        - 2. Howard Miller
    - 2. Mary Shortledge
    - 3. Joel Shortledge
    - 4. Isabel Shortledge
      M: Joseph Shortledge
    - 5. John Shortledge
    - 6. Sallie Shortledge
- 6. William Shortledge
- 7. Evan Shortledge
  M: S. Holland
    - 1. Smithin Shortledge

- 3. Isabella Gawthrop (1779-1847)
  - 8. Smithin Shortledge
- 4. James Gawthrop (1781-1858) M: Hannah Marshall (1784-1862)
  - 1. Mary Gawthrop (1809- ) M: Caleb J. Hoopes (1792-1865)
    - 1. Abner Hoopes M: R.A. White
    - 2. James G. Hoopes M: M.H. Boyer
      - 1. Emma R. Hoopes
      - 2. Edgar P. Hoopes
    - 3. Edith Hoopes M: E.E. John
      - 1. Ella A. John
      - 2. Caleb J. John
    - 4. Hannah G. Hoopes
    - 5. Sarah J. Hoopes
  - 2. Jane Gawthrop (1812- ) M:Joshua A. Moore offspring-John A. Moore -George G. Moore
  - 3. George Gawthrop (1815-1877) M: Mary Ann Woodward (1828-1897)
    - 1. Thomas C. Gawthrop (1847- ) M:Emma R. Pratt (1850- )
      - 1. Freddie Gawthrop (1876-1876)
      - 2. Joseph Oscar Gawthrop (1897-1972) 1M: Anna Gibson 2M: Betty Charles
        - 1. Marie Elizabeth Gawthrop M: Mr. Scott
    - 2. Howard James Gawthrop (1850-1923) M: unknown
      - 1. Robert Smith Gawthrop ( -1944) M: Emily Hoskins
        - 1. Robert Smith Gawthrop Jr. ( - ) M: Elizabeth (Betsy) Campbell
          - 1. Robert Smith Gawthrop III ( - )
          - 2. Elizabeth Gawthrop ( - ) M: John Riely
            - 1. Christopher Riely
            - 2. Andrew Riely
          - 3. Emily Gawthrop ( - ) M: Richard Klarberg
            - 1. Collis Klarberg
            - 2. Margaret
        - 2. Thomas C. Gawthrop ( - ) M:Mary Scarlett Halsted
          - 1. adopted child
          - 2. daughter
    - 3. William Allan Gawthrop (1858-1902) M: Frances A. Tanguey
      - 1. William Ralph Gawthrop (1898-1943) M: Heller Wilson
        - 1. William Ralph Gawthrop Jr. (1925-1945) (died in WWII)
      - 2. Herbert H. Gawthrop (1892-1981) M: Edith Snow (1906-1987)
        - 1. Jane E. Gawthrop
        - 2. Ruth E. Gawthrop
        - 3. Frances Gawthrop
  - 4. Rachel Gawthrop (1817- ) M: Thomas W. Parker (1814-1869)
    - 1. Hannah Mary Parker
    - 2. James G. Parker
    - 3. Sarah H. Parker
    - 4. James G. Parker M: Sarah E. Hopkins
  - 5. Hannah Gawthrop (1821-1849)
  - 6. James Gawthrop (1825-1869) M: Sarah C. Ridgway (1826-1883)
    - 1. Joseph Ridgway Gawthrop (1850- ) 1M: Hattie Mason + 2M: Ida E. DeVoist
      - 1. Lillian Maud Gawthrop
      - 2. Elsie Gawthrop M: George Scarlett
        - son, Scarlett
        - Mary Scarlett 1M: MR. Halsted 2M: Thomas C. Gawthrop
      - 3. Roselle Gawthrop
      - 4. Ridgway Gawthrop (1879-1967)
    - 2. Hannah Mary Gawthrop
    - 3. Harry James Gawthrop ( - ) M: Alice Worrall
      - 1. James Heward Gawthrop (1883-1976) M: Grace Reynolds (1893-1987)
        - 1. James Howard Gawthrop Jr. (1928- ) unmarried
      - 2. Charles Frederick Gawthrop (1886-1967) unmarried
      - 3. Norman W. Gawthrop (1898-1979) unmarried
      - 4. Sara Ridgway Gawthrop (1891-1974) unmarried
    - 4. Charles G. Gawthrop (1864- ) M: Louise Hickman
      - 1. Harold J. Gawthrop (1893-1966) M: Ruth Craighead
        - 1. Nancy Gawthrop
        - 2. Barbara Gawthrop (no dates)
      - 2. Mary H. Gawthrop M: William Shoemaker
      - 3. James Gawthrop (1897-1900)
  - 1. Ruth Gawthrop (1813- ) M:Issac Moore (1810- )
    - 1. Joseph G. Moore M: W. Townsend
    - 2. Lindley Moore
    - 3. Hannah Moore
    - 4. Thomas G. Moore
    - 5. Elizabeth Moore
    - 6. Channing Moore
    - 7. Dawwin Moore
  - 2. Joseph C. Gawthrop (1815-1892)
  - 3. & 4. Twins, died young
  - 5. Thomas Gawthrop (1818-1894) 1M:Lydia Conard
    - 1. Jesse Gawthrop (1842-1842)
    - 2. Lydia C. Gawthrop

- +
- +
- 2M: Susanna Conard (1816-1900)
  - M: George Baker
  - 2. Jane Susanna Gawthrop
    - M: Elwood Conard
  - 3. Mary Elizabeth
    - M: Harvey John
  - twins, 4. & 5., died
  - 4. George Gawthrop (1857-1857)
  - 5. Ruth Emma Gawthrop

- 5. George Gawthrop (1764-1865)
  - M: Amy Chambers (1787-1851)
    - 6. Elizabeth Gawthrop (1820-1897)
      - M: William Hughes (1819-1894)
    - 7. George W. Gawthrop (1822-1892)
      - M: Louise Way (1825-1876)
        - 1. William Way Gawthrop (1850-1932)
          - 1M: Hannah M. Gawthrop (1851-1885)
          - 2M: Kaye Isabel May (1856-1946)
            - 1. Hellen Gawthrop
              - M: Frank Gillingham
            - 2. Donald May Gawthrop (1896-1969)
              - 1M: Mariam L. Hubbell + (1895-1960)
              - 2M: Rachel Jopson (1898-1973)
                - 1. William H. Gawthrop (1921- )
                  - M: Nancy C. Webster
                    - 1. William Hubbell Gawthrop Jr. (1949-
                      - M: Deborah Kachelreiss
                        - 1. Courtney (1978-
                    - 2. Richard W. Gawthrop (1962-
                - 2. John Hubbell Gawthrop (1927- )
                  - 1M: Ann Pattison
                    - 1. John Hubbell Gawthrop Jr. (1955-
                      - M: Cynthia L. Showers
                        - 1. Sarah Ann (1978-
                        - 2. Rebecca L. (1981-
                  - 2M: Mildred Mort (1929- )
        - 2. Horace Henry Gawthrop (1861-1953)
          - M: Phebe H. Way (1863-1948)
            - 1. Horace Henry Gawthrop Jr. (1884-1884)
            - 2. Edgar H. Gawthrop (1885-1886)
            - 3. George Gawthrop (1886-1965)
              - M: Margaret Painter VanDeusen (1890-1981)
                - 1. Mary Gawthrop
                - 2. Margaret Gawthrop (1918- )
                  - M: John C. Fagan
                - 3. George Gawthrop (1922- )
                  - M: A. Katzman
                    - 2. Douglas P. Gawthrop (1958-
                      - M: Leslie L. Lang
                        - 1. Douglas Robert (1980-
                        - 2. Laura Pattison (1982-
                        - 3. Lisa Michele (1984-
                    - 1. Janice Gawthrop
                    - 2. Johanna Gawthrop
            - 4. Louise Gawthrop (1890-1931)
              - M: John Raymond Boyle
                - 1. Dorothy Louise Boyle (1914-
                  - 1M: Dr. H. W. Haines
                    - 1. Linda Louise Haines (1943-
                  - 2M: Francis J. Hipple
            - 5. Dorothy Gawthrop (1895-1896)
    - 8. Even Gawthrop (1824-1824)
    - 9. William Gawthrop (1825-1882)
      - M: Sarah Brown (1835-1916)
        - 1. Evan Brown Gawthrop (1861-1925)
          - M: Bertha M. Conard (1862-1915)
            - 1. Edna Mary Gawthrop (1884- )
              - M: Ernest B. Thomas ( -1950)
                - 1. Georgiana
                - 2. Betty Thomas
                  - M: Gilbert Wilson
                    - 1. Thomas Wilson (1957-
                    - 2. Gregory Wilson (1959-
            - 2. William Herman Gawthrop (1885-1885)
            - 1st set of twins, 3 & 4
            - 3. Everard Conard Gawthrop (1886-1955)
              - M: Ethel Regina Stahl (1881-1974)
                - 1. Herman Everard Gawthrop (1909-1918)
                - 2. Arthur Neil Gawthrop (1910-1982)
                  - M: Josephine F. Smith (1914-
                    - 1. Neil Thomas Gawthrop (1933-1933)
                    - 2. Edward Andrew Gawthrop (1937- )
                      - 1M: Patricia Kenney + ( -
                        - 1. Tracey Loraine Nimmerichter (1962- )
                          - M: Christopher K. Burgess (Lieutenant U.S.N.)
                        - 1. Theresa Leigh Gawthrop
                          - 1M: Lewis Schmitt Jr.
                            - 1. Marsha Jean Michelle (1980-
                          - 2M: Brent Shoehart
                            - 1. Britiny (1989-
                        - 2. Randell Leigh Gawthrop (1962- )
                          - M: Kay Showers
                            - 1. Ashely Marie (1989-
                            - 2. Kyle Edward (1992-
                        - 3. Neil Edward Gawthrop (1967- )
                          - M: Barbara Johnson
                            - 1. Megan Alexandra (1989-
                            - twins
                            - 2. Ryan Louis (1992-
                            - 3. Rachel Lauren (1992-
                        - 4. Gary Andrew Gawthrop (1969-
                      - 2M: Marsha Wood + (1943-1965)
                      - 3M: MaryBeth Beuchert (1950- (no children by Edward, she has two dau.: Mary Christine & Marie Constance)
                    - 3. John Michael Gawthrop (1939-1939)
                    - 4. Susan Diane Gawthrop (1941-
                      - M: Henry E. Watson (1938-
                        - 1. Diane Elizabeth (1970-
                        - 2. Keith Edward Watson (1973-
                    - 5. Jean Florence Gawthrop (1946-
                      - M: John Shichman (1949-
                        - 1. Jessica Lynn Shickman (1975-
                        - 2. Samantha Jean Shickman (1978-
                    - 6. Philip Evan Gawthrop (1949-
                      - 1M: Kay Elaine Sipe
                      - 2M: Cathy Teddy Lubis
                      - 3M: Brenda F. Thomas (1949-
                        - 1. Mitchell Bennett Gawthrop (1985-
                        - 2. Andrew Thomas Gawthrop (1990-
                    - 7. Wendy Lynn Gawthrop
            - 4. Lucile Gawthrop (1886-1958)
              - M: Joseph Walton Mott ( -1956)
                - 1. Lucile Mott ( -1983)
                - 2. Barbara Mott
                  - 1M: George Ford (5 children)
                  - 2M: William Patten
                - 3. Joanna Mott
                  - M: Mr. Kilpack
            - 2nd set of twins, 5 & 6
        - 2. Ernest Gawthrop (1866- )
          - M: Bessie, "a Pittsburgh lady"
        - 3. Mary Gawthrop (1888- )
        - 4. Joanna B. Gawthrop (1873- )
    - 10. Jessie Gawthrop (1828-1828)
- 6. Jane Gawthrop (1785-1859)
  - M: Daniel Thompson (1782-1837)
- 7. William Gawthrop
  - 1. Rachel M. Gawthrop (1819-1882)
    - M: James Huey (1804-1862)

(1798-1856)
M: Mary Griffish
(1790- )

2. Jane Gawthrop
(1822- )
M:Thomas J. Lovegrove
(1819- )

3. Thomas T. Gawthrop
(1824- )
M:Mary T. Trenchard

8. Allen Gawthrop
(1792- )

9. Elizabeth Gawthrop
(1796-1860)
M:Nicholas W. Taylor
(1794-1826)

5. Laurence Brown Gawthrop
(1889-1947)
M:Mary M. Bushorg
(1894-1976)

1. Richard Edwin Gawthrop
(1916-1974)
M: Adelaide B. Lamb
(1920-

(1957-1958)

1. Martha Bouvier Gawthrop
(1945-

2. Richard Gawthrop
(1951-

2. Raymond Gawthrop
(1926-
M: Patricia Smith
(1931-

1. Beth Virginia Gawthrop
(1956-
M: Brian Bucher
(1956-

1. Brian Henry Bucher
(1987-

2. Brett Thomas Bucher
(1988-

2. Laurence Charles Gawthrop
(1958-
M: Ida Louise Siciliano
(1956-

1. Angela Lauren Gawthrop
(1988-

2. Jessica Gawthrop
(1990-

3. Douglas Raymond Gawthrop
(1960-

6. Raymond Conard Gawthrop
(1889-1923)
M: Pearl .(no last)

1. Linda Gawthrop
(1922-

7. Leslie William Gawthrop
(1893-1897)

## About The Author

My name is Philip Evan Gawthrop. I was born on 28 March 1949 at Riverdale Hospital, Prince George County, MD. My parents are Arthur Neil Gawthrop (1910-1982) and Josephine Florence Smith (b:1914). I was raised (from age 7) in Hillsmere Shores just outside the Annapolis, Maryland city limits. I live now in Crofton Maryland. I have one brother, Edward Andrew (b: 11 Feb. 1937), and two sisters, Susan Diane (b: 15 March 1941) and Jean Florence (b: 5 April 1946). I have a medium complexion, light brown hair, hazel eyes, 6 feet 4 inches, 285 lbs.

I attended Annapolis High School (graduated '68) and then went on to college at Ohio Institute of Technology (graduated with Bachelor of Electronic Engineering Technology in 72). I played sports in high school and college and continued throughout much of my life.

My fully-time job is an Electronic Engineer and a Radio Frequency Spectrum Manager for the U.S. Department of Commerce, National Telecommunications and Information Administration (NTIA). Currently, I am a Civil Servant, GS-855-13. I have several unique part-time jobs; I umpire slow-pitch softball and have been doing it for better than 20 years. Currently (94/95), I referee girls high school varsity and junior varsity basketball for Anne Arundel County School System as well as youth basketball for Anne Arundel County.

I married Brenda Faye Thomas on 25 Jan. 1985. We have two children; Mitchell Bennett (b: 10 Sept. 1985) and Andrew Thomas (b: 25 May 1990).

www.ingramcontent.com/pod-product-compliance
Lightning Source LLC
Chambersburg PA
CBHW061725270326
41928CB00011B/2110